Routledge Revivals

Outlines of Social Philosophy

Social philosophy can be considered the study of what unifies mankind and the study of values and ideals and what their meaning and worth is to human existence. Originally published in 1918, Mackenzie's study provides a basic outline of what he believes is the origin of social philosophy whilst placing a focus on social order; dividing his work into the foundations of social order, national order and world order. This title will be of interest to students of Philosophy, Sociology and Anthropology.

Outlines of Social Philosophy

J.S. Mackenzie

First published in 1918
by George Allen & Unwin Ltd

This edition first published in 2016 by Routledge
2 Park Square, Milton Park, Abingdon, Oxon, OX14 4RN
and by Routledge
711 Third Avenue, New York, NY 10017

Routledge is an imprint of the Taylor & Francis Group, an informa business

© 1918 J.S. Mackenzie

All rights reserved. No part of this book may be reprinted or reproduced or utilised in any form or by any electronic, mechanical, or other means, now known or hereafter invented, including photocopying and recording, or in any information storage or retrieval system, without permission in writing from the publishers.

Publisher's Note
The publisher has gone to great lengths to ensure the quality of this reprint but points out that some imperfections in the original copies may be apparent.

Disclaimer
The publisher has made every effort to trace copyright holders and welcomes correspondence from those they have been unable to contact.

A Library of Congress record exists under LC control number: 18023064

ISBN 13: 978-1-138-63875-4 (hbk)
ISBN 13: 978-1-315-63759-4 (ebk)
ISBN 13: 978-1-138-63876-1 (pbk)

OUTLINES OF SOCIAL PHILOSOPHY

BY

J. S. MACKENZIE,

LITT.D. (CAMBRIDGE), HON. LL.D. (GLASGOW); EMERITUS PROFESSOR OF LOGIC
AND PHILOSOPHY IN UNIVERSITY COLLEGE, CARDIFF; FORMERLY
FELLOW OF TRINITY COLLEGE, CAMBRIDGE

LONDON: GEORGE ALLEN & UNWIN LTD.
RUSKIN HOUSE   40 MUSEUM STREET, W.C. 1
NEW YORK: THE MACMILLAN COMPANY

TO MY FRIEND

CHARLES EDWYN VAUGHAN

A SMALL TOKEN OF A VERY GREAT

GRATITUDE AND ADMIRATION

PREFACE

THIS book has grown out of a short course of lectures that I was called upon to deliver at the London School of Economics and Political Science in the session 1916-17. I have adhered to the general plan of the lectures, but have expanded their substance; and the book may now be regarded as taking the place of the *Introduction* that was written about thirty years ago, and that has now been out of print for a long time. Its scope and plan are, however, considerably different from those of the earlier work. My object has been to provide a suitable textbook for students of the subject. It is now studied in this country by a considerable number of people, differing very widely in age and previous preparation, and also in the special aims that they have in view; and it would hardly be possible to write anything that would be quite suitable for them all. I have tried to expound the leading principles in a way that might be expected to be intelligible and interesting to beginners, and at the same time to supply some material that might be useful to more advanced students, and to indicate directions in which further light could be sought on the subjects that come up for discussion. It appears to be the practice, in several places in which courses of this kind are given, to use Plato's *Republic* as a general basis for study. I believe this to be a good practice; and I have, accordingly, given frequent references to that work throughout, and have also added some Notes upon it in an Appendix. Those who have not been studying the *Republic* may ignore these Notes. Beginners may be recommended also, on a first reading, to omit the Introduction and the Note at the end of Book II, Chapter IV.

In dealing with a subject of this kind, it seems natural and proper to refer a good deal to the problems that confront us in our own time and country; and the unusual importance that has been given to some of them by the events of the last few years has made this specially desirable. I have tried, however, to avoid statements of a partisan character. I am well aware that all the subjects to which reference has to be made are capable of being looked at from many different sides, and that the problems that are involved in them cannot be solved by a stroke of the pen. My chief aim throughout has been to stimulate thought and suggest lines of study, rather than to supply information or to seek to impose my own opinions upon the reader. My general views are based largely on the teaching of such writers as T. H. Green and Dr. Bosanquet. If my book should help to induce some readers to study the ethical and political works of these and other writers, it will have served its main purpose.

May, 1918.

CONTENTS

	PAGE
PREFACE	7
INTRODUCTION	13

1. The Scope of Social Philosophy—2. Its Relations to Other Subjects.—3. Its Method.—4. Its Early Beginnings.—5. Its Later Developments.—6. Its Central Problem.

BOOK I

THE FOUNDATIONS OF SOCIAL ORDER

CHAPTER I

HUMAN NATURE	29

1. Man's Place in the Cosmos.—2. Definition of Man.—3. Three Main Aspects of Human Life.—4. The Social Nature of Man.—5. Some Historical References.

CHAPTER II

COMMUNITY	44

1. The Natural Basis of Community.—2. The Conventional Element in Community.—3. The Conception of a Social Contract.—4. The Conception of Organic Unity.—5. Corporate Action.—6. The Conception of a General Will.—7. The Conception of a Common Good.—8. Spiritual Unity.—9. Social Differentiation.

CHAPTER III

MODES OF ASSOCIATION	61

1. Society and Societies.—2. Social Institutions.—3. The Place of Language.—4. Formative Institutions.—5. Economic Institutions.—6. Barbaric Institutions.—7. Governmental Institutions.—8. Cultural Institutions.—9. Interactions of Institutions.—10. The Meaning of Civilization.—11. Plan of the following Chapters.

BOOK II

NATIONAL ORDER

CHAPTER I

THE FAMILY 77

1. The Natural Basis of the Family.—2. The Conventional Aspect of the Family.—3. The Child as Centre.—4. Eugenics.—5. Marriage.—6. Educational Functions of the Family.—7. Economic Functions of the Family.—8. Weaknesses of the Family.

CHAPTER II

EDUCATIONAL INSTITUTIONS 94

1. The General Significance of Education.—2. The Functions of the School.—3. Technical Education.—4. Higher Education.—5. Supplementary Education.—6. Education and Leisure.—7. The State and Education.

CHAPTER III

INDUSTRIAL INSTITUTIONS 109

1. The Significance of Labour.—2. Division of Labour.—3. Co-operation.—4. Land and Capital, in Relation to Labour.—5. Property.—6. Wealth and Poverty.—7. Competition.—8. Individualism and Socialism.—9. Work and Leisure.

CHAPTER IV

THE STATE 124

1. What is a State?—(1) Society; (2) Community; (3) People; (4) Country; (5) Race; (6) Nationality; (7) Nation; (8) Government; (9) State; (10) Sovereign State.—2. The Natural Basis of the State.—3. The State as Force.—4. The State as Law-giver.—5. The State and the Family.—6. The State as Educator.—7. The State and Morality.—8. Forms of Government.—9. Local Government.—10. The Evolution of the State.

Note on Theories of the State: 1. The State as Personal.—2. The State as Superpersonal.—3. The State as Power.—4. The State as Mechanism.—5. The State as a Mode of Social Unity.

CHAPTER V

JUSTICE 154

1. General Conception of Justice.—2. Distributive Justice.—3. Corrective Justice.—4. Justice in Exchange.—5. Reward and Punishment.—6. Equity.—7. Natural Rights.—8. Rights and Obligations.

CHAPTER VI

SOCIAL IDEALS 170

1. The General Significance of Ideals.—2. The Aristocratic Ideal.—3. The Democratic Ideal.—4. Fraternity.—5. Equality.—6. Liberty.—7. Personal Development.—8. Efficiency.—9. General Summary on Social Ideals.

BOOK III

WORLD ORDER

CHAPTER I

INTERNATIONAL RELATIONS 189

1. General Statement.—2. International Morality.—3. International Law.—4. International Trade.—5. War and Peace.—6. Progress in International Relations.

CHAPTER II

THE PLACE OF RELIGION 209

1. The Meaning of Religion.—2. Chief Aspects of Religion.—3. Religious Institutions.—4. Religion in Education.—5. Religion and Social Service.—6. The State and Religion.—7. Religious Toleration.—8. International Religion.—9. Defective Religions: (1) Superstition; (2) Idolatry; (3) Dogmatism; (4) Sectarianism; (5) Fanaticism; (6) Hypocrisy; (7) Individualism; (8) Mysticism; (9) Conventionalism; (10) Irreligion—10. Progress in Religion.

CHAPTER III

THE PLACE OF CULTURE 227

1. The Meaning of Culture.—2. Culture and Pedantry.—3. The Place of Science.—4. The Place of Art.—5. The Place of

Literature.—6. The Place of Philosophy.—7. The Place of Individual Experience.—8. The Social Significance of Culture.—9. Culture as the End of Human Life.

CONCLUSION

GENERAL RESULTS 241

1. Summary.—2. Practical Value of Social Philosophy.—3. Main Lines of Progress: (1) Conquest of Nature; (2) Social Control; (3) Self-Control.—4. Chief Dangers: (1) The Dominance of Vegetative Needs; (2) The Insistence of Animal Impulses; (3) The Mastery of Mechanism; (4) Anarchism; (5) Conservatism. —5. Chief Grounds for Hope.

APPENDIX

A. SOME NOTES ON PLATO'S "REPUBLIC" 259

1. Introductory.— 2. Argument of Book I.— 3. Argument of Books II–IV.—4. Argument of Books IV–VII.—5. Argument of Books VIII. and IX.—6. Argument of Book X.

B. A NOTE ON SOCRATES AND PLATO 275

INDEX 277

INTRODUCTION

1. *The Scope of Social Philosophy.*—Although it is only in comparatively recent times that social philosophy has been recognized as a distinct subject of study, it has already acquired a pretty definite meaning. It is to be distinguished from what is commonly understood by sociology; or, if the latter is interpreted in a wide sense, social philosophy is to be taken as a definite part of it. Sociology, besides being open to some linguistic objection, is a somewhat vague term, and may be regarded as covering a very comprehensive field. It includes an inquiry into the origins of human communities, the study of their various forms, laws, customs, institutions, languages, beliefs, ways of thinking, feeling, and acting. In short, it may be said to take all knowledge about human life for its province. It has to deal with such diverse problems as those of economics, politics, religion, eugenics, education, morality, etc. Hence it is a subject that can hardly be adequately dealt with by a single person or in a single book. It has to be split up into several departments; just as biology has to be divided into botany and zoology, and into the various subdivisions of anatomy, physiology, the study of animal instincts and habits, and so forth. Social philosophy has a much more restricted province. It differs from the special branches of sociology—or from the *other* branches of sociology—in the way in which philosophy in general is distinguished from the particular sciences.[1]

[1] This distinction is well brought out in *A Philosophy of Social Progress*, by Professor E. J. Urwick. Although a good deal has been written in this country on various special branches of sociology,

A science means a body of particular facts or of general truths, or of both facts and truths, together with some organized methods of investigation relating to some limited circle of objects, with the view of understanding and interpreting the facts and truths within that circle. Human life, which is always in some degree social, provides such a circle of objects, in the study of which various methods may be adopted and a number of interesting and important facts and truths may be ascertained. Sociology is concerned with all these, except in so far as the more purely individual aspects of human life can be distinguished from those that are definitely social. If anthropology were taken to mean the general study of humanity, it might be divided into the two main branches of idiotology and sociology (or politology), each of which would comprise a considerable number of separate sciences. Philosophy, on the other hand, as distinguished from science, is an effort to view particular objects in relation to the whole within which they are included. In its largest aim, it seeks to interpret the particular facts and truths in the world of our experience as forming parts or aspects of a single universe or cosmos. Social philosophy, in particular, concentrates its attention on the social unity of mankind, and seeks to interpret the significance of the special aspects of human life with reference to that unity. It thus means mainly the effort to study values, ends, ideals—not primarily what exists or has existed or may be expected to exist, but rather the meaning and worth of these modes of existence. This, of course, must not be taken to imply that it can afford to ignore what is ascertained by the particular social

there has not been much attempt in recent times to deal with the whole subject systematically; but there has been an extensive literature of this kind in America. The writings of Lester F. Ward are very comprehensive; and for more summary treatment the *Principles of Sociology*, by Professor F. H. Giddings (which contains an excellent bibliography), and the more recent work by Professor A. W. Small on *General Sociology* may be recommended. The smaller book by Professors Small and Vincent (*An Introduction to the Study of Society*) is probably the most suitable for beginners.

sciences. It is not safe in philosophy to ignore anything. But it is not the special province of social philosophy to discover facts—it has to accept its facts from other sciences —but rather to try to interpret them. How this is to be done, we may be better able to see as we proceed. As a general statement, this must for the present suffice.[1]

2. *Its Relations to other Subjects.*—Having thus indicated the general place of social philosophy in relation to those sciences that are grouped under sociology, we may now notice some special subjects with which its connection is very intimate. The chief of these would seem to be general biology, psychology, the theory of education, ethics, politics, law, economics, history, and the philosophy of religion. Its relations to each of these may be very briefly noted.

Human beings are evidently forms of life, and a good deal of light may be thrown upon their nature by the study of life in general. In particular, the illuminating conception of evolution may be expected to help us in this inquiry, as it has done in other vital studies. Whatever may be thought of the value of Herbert Spencer's work in other respects, he must always have considerable credit for the emphasis that he laid on this conception, and the definiteness with which he applied it, in the

[1] There is some difference of opinion among recent writers on sociology as to whether social philosophy is properly to be included within its scope. Comte, who may be regarded as the founder of the science, attempted to set forth a general philosophy of society; and the same may be said of Herbert Spencer. But in both cases it may be doubted whether their general conceptions of philosophy were such as to furnish an adequate foundation. The general account of the method of sociology (*Les Règles de la Méthode sociologique*) that is given by Professor Durkheim, who is certainly one of its leading exponents, would seem to exclude social philosophy. Professor Small, on the other hand, is inclined to give it a place (*General Sociology*, p. 83). In view of the very large domain that is covered by sociology, I am disposed to think that, in any comprehensive treatment of it, the leading principles of social philosophy might be introduced at the beginning and its general conclusions at the end.

interpretation of human life. No doubt he had been anticipated to a large extent by Aristotle, Hegel, Comte, and some others; and in many respects their interpretations—especially those of the first two—are more profound; but the connection with general biology was perhaps most definitely made by Spencer.

What is specially characteristic of human life, however, is the presence of mind, both in its lower and in its higher phases; and the science that deals with mind will have to be appealed to in the course of our treatment. The appetites, the instincts and the emotions cannot be ignored in considering the growth and activities of human societies. These aspects of human nature are commonly studied by psychologists in their more purely individual manifestations; but social psychology is now recognized as an important branch of study.[1] What has been called crowd psychology is a special aspect of it;[2] and the study of language may be regarded as another.[3] The control and modification of the more purely animal elements in human nature has to be specially considered in dealing with human society.

The theory of education is important for our purpose, in so far as it traces the processes by which the individual, partly by natural growth and partly by external guidance, is developed into a responsible member of a community, fulfilling definite functions in its life.

The science of ethics deals with the ends that are aimed at in this life, and is thus still more intimately connected with social philosophy than any of the foregoing. Social philosophy might, indeed, be said to be a part of ethics or ethics might be said to be a part of it. On the whole, however, it is convenient to distinguish the two subjects. The one is concerned primarily with the conduct of individuals; though of course we have always to bear in mind

---

[1] Dr. McDougal's book on *Social Psychology* is a good introduction. See also Professor Wallas's *Human Nature in Politics*.

[2] See Le Bon's works on this subject.

[3] The two bulky volumes of Wundt's *Völkerpsychologie* are entirely concerned with language.

that they are individuals living within a community. The other is primarily concerned with communities; though again we must always remember that these communities are composed of individuals, and that the ultimate ends pursued by the individuals and by the communities are essentially the same. But there is enough material relating to the two sides to form separate studies. The relations between them are somewhat similar to those between individual and social psychology.

Politics, or the theory of the State, is an important aspect of the study of society. All societies of any considerable degree of development have some form of government; and the problems connected with this are so complex and difficult, and involve such momentous issues, that they demand treatment in a separate science. Only the most general considerations relating to them can be included in social philosophy.

The question of justice is one of the most fundamental of those with which social philosophy has to deal; and this is closely connected with law. But here again it is only the most general considerations that fall properly within the scope of our subject.

Industry and commerce form so large a part of the activities of human societies that their place is necessarily considered with some care in any philosophy of society; but in this case also many of the problems are of so complex a character that they have to be regarded as belonging to a separate science—that of economics. The questions relating to this subject are to a considerable extent capable of being stated in terms of quantity, and lend themselves readily to mathematical treatment. Hence the study of them has a greater appearance of exactness than any other special study of social problems. Partly for this reason it has been more fully developed as a science than any other department of sociology; and its immediate bearings on the practical activities of the great mass of human beings has given it an unusual degree of popular interest. Both its exactness, however, and the direct value of its practical applications are in some danger of being exaggerated. Its exactness depends, in general, on somewhat questionable assumptions; and its practical applications often require to be modified by considerations of a different kind. Some of the questions that fall within its scope will have to be noticed briefly in the course of our treatment.

All these aspects of social life change and develop from age to age, and have their characteristics determined and modified by many circumstances of time and place. History, which is occupied with the record of such circumstances and changes, throws light on many important aspects of social life; and, on the other hand, a general philosophy of society should help us to interpret what without it is apt to seem arbitrary and chaotic in the panorama of history.[1] But obviously the details of historical development lie outside our province.

Those beliefs, ideals, and aspirations that are described as religious have so large a place in human history, and embody so much of what is most characteristic of humanity, that some interpretation of them also is called for in social philosophy; though some of their aspects belong rather to ethics and metaphysics, and some are best regarded as constituting a separate subject of study.

It is evident from all this that social philosophy touches on a great variety of topics, and that it has no lack either of material or of interest.

3. *Its Method.*—It is not easy to lay down at the outset, especially in a subject that is still in the making, any definite statement with regard to the method that is most suitable for its development. We can hardly begin with axioms or postulates; and, as it is not an empirical

[1] Hegel's *Philosophy of History* may be specially referred to. Dr. Beattie Crozier's *History of Civilization* has considerable value. B. Kidd's book on *The Principles of Western Civilization* contains a few good points, and Houston Chamberlain's work (*The Foundations of the Nineteenth Century*) is not to be altogether ignored; though the views set forth in both these treatises have to be taken with some caution. Professor P. Barth has written an interesting book on sociology, regarded from the point of view of the philosophy of history (*Philosophie der Geschichte als Soziologie*).

study, we can hardly begin with a collection of facts. It might be possible, as we have seen, to treat it as a continuation of ethics; but it seems desirable, on the whole, to try to give it an independent start. As we are concerned with a particular aspect of human life, it may be simplest to begin with an inquiry into the general characteristics of that life, and then to proceed to ascertain how these general characteristics give rise to the special features of social unity. We may then find it possible to discuss these special features in a connected order. If this is possible, the method of treatment will grow naturally out of the subject-matter. A short reference to the history of the subject may, however, be useful at this point, and may help to justify the general method of entering on its study that I am now suggesting.

4. *Its Early Beginnings.*—The beginnings of almost all scientific and philosophic studies are to be found in the work of the early Greek thinkers. There were vague speculations before their time, some of them of very considerable interest; but it is doubtful whether there is anything that could be regarded as having scientific value. Even among the early Greeks, the precise significance of the conceptions with which they dealt is often difficult to discover. It seems clear, however, that they singled out general aspects of the world around them: elementary distinctions, such as those between fire, air, water, and the solid material to which they gave the general name of earth; or again, between attractive and repulsive tendencies, between permanence and change, between unity and multiplicity, between matter and form, and so forth.[1] The general fact of life was one of the first things that attracted their attention, and of course human life more than any other. They tried to connect it with other facts in the world around them. Heraclitus, for instance, connected it with the general tendency to a movement upwards and downwards which he seemed

[1] A good general account of all this can be got from Professor Burnet's *Early Greek Philosophy*.

to see throughout the whole of nature—e.g. in the rise of vapour and the fall of rain, in day and night, in summer and winter, as well as in waking and sleep, life and death, growth and decay, virtue and vice, progress and deterioration. Such methods of approach brought some of the early Greek thinkers pretty close to the modern conception of evolution, and to its application to human life. But at a very early stage they seem to have begun to be impressed by the comparative irregularity of human life, more particularly in its social aspects. They had acquired a fairly definite conception of the forces of nature as being essentially uniform in their operation. Fire, they saw, has a definite way of burning, which is the same in Greece as it is in Persia. The same may be said, on the whole, of the growth of plants, the instincts of animals, the movements of the heavenly bodies, and other natural processes. Hence they were led to regard it as a characteristic of everything natural, that it is invariable. Human life alone, especially in its social aspects, seemed to be a notable exception. The comparative freedom of choice that man possesses tends to appear at first as purely arbitrary. It needs a more profound insight to see in it the manifestation of a higher law. Even in modern times we are apt sometimes to contrast the lawlessness of human action with the regularity of natural events, such as the motions of the heavenly bodies.

> They cannot halt or go astray,
> But our immortal spirits may.

It was chiefly among that group of remarkable public teachers that grew up in Greece about the middle of the fifth century B.C., commonly referred to as the Sophists, that this antithesis between what is natural and what is relatively arbitrary and conventional was brought into prominence. They were travelling teachers, and they were specially impressed by the very different customs, laws, and forms of constitution that they found in different places. These, they tended to say, not

INTRODUCTION

having the uniformity of natural objects, must be regarded as merely conventional. They depend on human agreements or contracts, or on the arbitrary choice of particular rulers, and have no real foundation in the nature of things. Thus the distinction between what exists by nature (φύσει) and what exists only by human law or convention (νόμῳ) was definitely introduced and sharply emphasized.[1]

Now, it was specially with reference to this antithesis that the first great treatise on social philosophy was written—the first and still, in many respects, the most profound and interesting. Plato's *Republic* is, in the main, a discussion of the question whether human law can properly be regarded as having any real foundation in the nature of things. It begins with an inquiry into the meaning of Justice or Righteousness (δικαιοσύνη) and leads on from this to the question whether the social order, in which justice seems to be embodied, is natural or artificial. The Platonic Socrates contends that it is essentially natural. He seeks to show this by tracing the origin of social unity as growing out of a particular fact in the nature of man—the fact, namely, that he is not self-sufficient, and is consequently led to co-operate with others. On this basis, an attempt is made to sketch the form of human organization in which this need for co-operation would be most perfectly supplied. We are thus led to the consideration of an ideally constituted State, and incidentally to an account of the kind of education that is necessary for the maintenance of such a State. We may have occasion to refer to several points in connection with this as we proceed. The absorbing interest of Plato's *Republic* depends on the deep insight, the comprehensive outlook, and the almost prophetic vision, by which the treatment of the fundamental problem is connected with all the main interests of human life. But it is only with the fundamental problem that we need concern ourselves at present.[2]

[1] See, on this, Burnet's *Greek Philosophy* (Thales to Plato), chap. vii. Reference may be made also to his *Early Greek Philosophy*, pp. 12, 13. [2] See the Notes on Plato's *Republic* in the Appendix.

The kind of State that Plato had chiefly in mind was the kind with which he was most familiar—the small City State, which reached its most perfect development in Greece. A State of this type differed in many important respects from what we commonly think of as States in modern times. In particular, it was characterized by an intense and intimate unity which would not, in quite the same mode and degree, be possible in an extensive Empire or even in a comparatively small modern nation. The study of a modern State, as such, would generally have to be distinguished from the study of the other aspects of the social life of its citizens; whereas in a small City State there seemed to be hardly any distinction between the political life of the State and the other aspects of community within the social group. Hence social philosophy was for Plato almost the same thing as politics, and hardly distinguishable from ethics and the theory of education. Nevertheless, the general foundations of the study were by him well and truly laid; and it is probably still correct to say that there is no writer from whom so good an introduction to it can be had as from him.

5. *Its Later Developments*.—We need not linger long over the subsequent course of the development of social philosophy, which is too complex to be summarily treated, except in its barest outlines.

Aristotle made a more definite distinction between ethics and politics than is to be found in the work of Plato; though he still regarded the former as being essentially a part of the latter. The one deals with the citizen, the other with the city. But the distinction became, through Aristotle's method of treatment, rather more marked than he was at first prepared to allow. He was led to recognize —as indeed, Plato also was—that a man is more than the citizen of a particular State; and that the claims of citizenship have sometimes to be subordinated to those of the larger life. According to our modern way of regarding the subjects, some parts of Aristotle's *Ethics*—

especially his treatment of justice and certain aspects of his treatment of friendship—would seem to belong more properly to social philosophy than to ethics. They appear to form the connecting link between ethics and politics.[1]

After the time of Aristotle, the decay and final overthrow of the Greek City States led to a still more definite separation between ethics and politics. The great Empires —whether of Macedonia or of Rome—could hardly be regarded as complete embodiments of the moral aspirations of their citizens; as, with just a little idealization, the small City States might. Hence the Stoics and Epicureans did not so naturally think, as Plato and Aristotle did, of the life of an individual as being necessarily bound up with that of an organized State. The Stoics tended to think of the best type of man, not merely as a " good European," but as a citizen of the world, rather than of any special community. He belonged essentially to the world-community (πολιτεία τοῦ κόσμου). The Epicureans were even less favourable to the political life. They were interested in societies of friends—bearing, in fact, a considerable resemblance to what is known in modern times as the Society of Friends—rather than in organized States.[2]

It was partly through the influence of these later bodies of thinkers—though partly also through the revival of earlier modes of thought—that the study of politics became more definitely separated off from that of ethics, and that social philosophy gradually came to be recognized as a study somewhat distinct from both. The elaboration of the system of Roman Law, largely carried out on the basis of Stoical conceptions[3]—especially on what came to be described as the Law of Nature—gave greater definiteness to the idea of the State as such, and,

[1] Mr. Ernest Barker's book on *The Political Thought of Plato and Aristotle* may be referred to for further particulars.

[2] W. Wallace's *Epicureanism* is a little book of singular charm, and may be consulted with great advantage.

[3] Maine's *Ancient Law*, chap. iii, may be referred to on this subject.

more particularly, to that of the State as law-giver. This aspect became dominant in political thought through the work of such diverse writers as Machiavelli, Grotius, Spinoza, Locke, and Rousseau; though the last two, in particular, tended to restore the educational aspect of social life, which had been so prominent with Plato, to something of its old pre-eminence.

Some other circumstances that have tended to bring out the distinction between the study of social philosophy and that of politics and law may be very briefly noticed. The difficulties in the way of reconciling the rival claims of the Church and the State in the Middle Ages accustomed men's minds to the idea of two distinct authorities in life—the one more purely political and legal, the other religious and moral. The Reformation tended to make the latter authority more purely moral, and gave increased emphasis to the contrast between the spiritual basis of community and the more material power of the State. The struggle for religious freedom, the increasing prominence of industrial problems (due in part to the development of the special sciences and arts) and the greater facilities for intercourse between different countries, all contributed to give a certain importance to social questions other than those that are purely political or legal. Economic questions, in particular, began to absorb a great deal of attention. Then the French Revolution, with its ideals of Liberty, Equality, and Fraternity, did much to "rend and deracinate the unity and married calm of States," and to suggest some larger unity of humanity. It was under the influence of this conception of a larger unity that Comte laid the foundations of his sociology. His study of social problems was combined with the effort to introduce a new religion of humanity.[1] Spencer, in a somewhat similar manner, was inspired by the idea of Liberty, and was strongly opposed to the dominance of

[1] Partly for this reason his work has not attracted quite as much attention in this country as it deserves. It has been much more influential in France. But a good account of it can be got from E. Caird's *Social Philosophy and Religion of Comte*.

the State. Thus it has gradually come about that the study of society has a much wider meaning than the study of the structure and activities of the State, and that it has become divided up into a number of separate studies. But it is only in quite recent times that social philosophy has become definitely recognized as one of these; though of course writers on sociology, as well as on law and politics, have always had some philosophical basis for their methods of treatment.[1]

6. *Its Central Problem.*—The sketch that has now been given of the origin and growth of social philosophy may enable us to understand more clearly both the scope of the study and the central problem round which it turns. That problem is still, on the whole, the one that was raised at its first beginning—viz. in what sense, and to what extent, can human society be properly described as natural? If it is purely arbitrary or conventional, its study can be little more than an attempt to trace the external, variable, and, in a sense, accidental circumstances by which its forms have been, from time to time, determined. If, on the other hand, it is in its essence natural, we have to try to explain in what sense it is natural, and what are the particular forms to which its fundamental nature gives rise. This, as we have noted, was what Plato and Aristotle sought to do, in opposition to the teaching of some of the Sophists. They contended, in effect, that what is natural is not necessarily invariable, and that the special features of human nature give rise to special kinds of order which, though not uniform, are not without law and reason. In fact, they even urged that the rational

---

[1] Mill described his *Principles of Political Economy* as " including some of their applications to social philosophy " ; and the same might be said of some other works of a primarily economic character, such as the recent books by Mr. Hobson (*Work and Wealth*) and Professor Pigou (*Wealth and Welfare*). Dr. Marshall has also kept the wider bearings of economic questions pretty steadily in view. But when social philosophy is approached from the purely economic side, its outlook is necessarily somewhat narrowed.

nature of man supplies a more definite principle of order than any that is found elsewhere, and that it is the lower forms of existence, rather than the higher, that may be characterized as relatively lawless and chaotic, containing, as they do, a certain element of contingency.[1] The Stoics also used the expression " Laws of Nature " primarily with reference to the principles of order that are furnished by reason and that can be embodied in the structure of a human society ; and it became the task of the physical sciences to show that there are laws of nature in the material universe as well as in the life of man. The tables were thus, to some extent, turned. Nevertheless, the old antithesis has tended, in some degree, to persist ; and it has, from time to time, been emphasized afresh—especially in connection with the idea of a social contract. Hobbes, for instance, contrasted the state of nature with the social order that is introduced by contract. The statement with which Rousseau opened his *Contrat social*, that " man is born free, and yet is everywhere in chains," gave an even wider currency to the same antithesis ; though Rousseau himself did much to remove it, or at least to soften it, by explaining that the contract on which human society is founded is itself based on the essential nature of man. The significance of this will come out more fully in the sequel. In the meantime, the persistence of the problem that is thus suggested gives us a ground for commencing our study with a consideration of the sense in which the unity and order of human society may be said to rest on nature—i.e. on the special nature of man. Accordingly, we proceed in the following chapter to attempt to discover what are the most fundamental aspects of human nature.

[1] For some discussion of this, I may refer to my *Elements of Constructive Philosophy*, Book III, chap. ii.

BOOK I

THE FOUNDATIONS OF SOCIAL ORDER

CHAPTER I

HUMAN NATURE

1. *Man's Place in the Cosmos.*—The large and difficult problems connected with the interpretation of our universe as a Cosmos cannot be here discussed. It is enough for our present purpose to note that the investigations of modern science and philosophical reflection upon their results have led us to think of the universe in which we live, mysterious though in many of its features it remains, as an orderly system in which there is a more or less continuous process of development.

So far as our own planet is concerned, human life appears to represent the highest stage that has so far been reached in this process; though it is not all at the same level, and even in its best types is pretty obviously capable of further improvement. Though man is the " paragon of animals," and has become something of a little god in the world that he inhabits, he still remains one of the products of that world, racy of the soil, and very evidently of the earth earthy. He is sometimes " in doubt to deem himself a god or beast," and has to recognize, on the whole, that he is a little of both. His thoughts may wander through eternity, but his bodily existence is very narrowly circumscribed. No account of human nature can be satisfactory—and this applies to its social aspects as well as to any other—which does not do justice both to its lowly origin and to its lofty aspirations. It will be well, from the very outset, to try to realize as clearly as possible both these aspects of our complex nature. To bring this out, we may proceed to consider how man may best be defined.

2. Definition of Man.

Various definitions have been attempted, from the most humorous "a featherless biped" to the most serious "a rational animal," but none of them is wholly satisfactory. Bagehot said that he is "a soul masquerading as an animal," but this somewhat underrates the intimacy of his connection with animal life. If we call him "a laughing animal" we may be confronted with the goose and the hyena and with the gravity of some savages and some sages. If, with Franklin and Carlyle, we describe him as "a tool-using animal," we have to acknowledge that some human beings are almost innocent of their use, though perhaps no adult is completely so; and that some of the lower animals, such as elephants, appear occasionally to use them.[1] If we point to the use of language, it may be urged that there are many other animals that communicate with one another by expressive vocal signs, and that some of the lower races of mankind do not rise very conspicuously above that level. It seems clear, however, that the possession of reason is man's most distinctive mark, by which all other characteristic features may be explained. It is the use of reason that enables him to develop vague animal cries into an articulate language, the manipulation of external objects into elaborate tools and machinery, the appreciation of particular sounds, colours, and forms into various types of imitative and expressive art, anger into the use of aggressive weapons, fear into elaborate defences, scorn into satire and humour, sympathy into charity, surprise into awe, submission into reverence, dominance

---

[1] See Professor Lloyd Morgan's *Animal Life and Intelligence*, p. 370. It may be well to note here that, when man is described as a tool-using animal, tools have to be understood in a very wide sense, including machinery, books, institutions, the use of the lower animals, etc. It would be less misleading to say that he is a capital-using animal. Other animals labour, and have stores and various kinds of property; but it is, on the whole, true that man is the only capitalist, and that every advance in human life is dependent on the use of capital. In a wide sense of the word, every human being is a capitalist. See below, Chapter VII, § 4.

into law and government, mutual aid into a co-operative commonwealth.

But all this is not accomplished at once; nor is it even from the outset anticipated and understood. Man, it would seem, cannot without some qualification be characterized as a rational animal, but rather as an animal with the potentiality of reason, and capable by its gradual cultivation of transforming the activities and the circumstances of his life.

But to say this is hardly enough. It is clear that, even with the potentiality of reason, man's life would not have become what it is, unless he had been endowed with a particular bodily structure. Without an elaborate muscular and bony framework, he would not have been able to "erect His stature and upright with front serene Govern the rest." Without well-developed eyes and other sense-organs, he could not have observed objects with sufficient accuracy to adapt them to his purposes. Without mobile hands,[1] he could hardly have constructed and used the variety of tools and other machinery with which we are familiar—which, indeed, at least in their primitive forms, may be regarded as little more than an extension of his bodily organs.[2] Without a complex vocal apparatus, he could not have elaborated and employed the languages that are current among us; without delicate ears, he could not have apprehended them; without the use of fingers, he could not have made them into an enduring record; without a sensitive nervous system, he could hardly have attained to the production and appreciation of the higher forms of art. Even for the use of reason itself, a brain would appear to be an essential condition. Hence we have to recognize that

---

[1] Anaxagoras seems to have attributed the superiority of man entirely to his possession of hands; but, if so, the apes might be expected to rank even higher. See Burnet's *Early Greek Philosophy*, p. 297. The differentiation of hands and feet must be recognized as an important advance.

[2] Samuel Butler, among others, brought this out in *Erewhon* (chap. xxv).

man is not only a rational animal but an animal of a particular type, with a peculiar and complicated structure, by which his thoughts, feelings and actions are largely determined. If we had been in the form of horses, like Swift's "houyhnhnms," instead of in that of the higher apes, our rational life would have been very different from what it is—if, indeed, it could ever have been developed at all. If reason had been developed in ants or bees, it would at least have been a reason that would have led to very different results from those with which we are acquainted in the life of humanity. And we cannot hope to have a thorough understanding of human life without taking a full account of all the peculiarities of human structure. It would, however, carry us too far, and would not be necessary for our present purpose, to inquire into all these peculiarities. They must be left to writers on anatomy, physiology, psychology, natural history, and anthropology. We must assume that the main features are sufficiently familiar to us, and must content ourselves with some reference to those aspects that are of fundamental importance.

3. *Three Main Aspects of Human Life.*—Recognizing that man is an animal of a particular type, with a variety of special bodily aptitudes and tendencies, we have next to ask what are the general characteristics of the life of animals. But here our account must be of a very summary character. It seems clear that in some respects animal life resembles the life of plants, but in other respects it is markedly different. From some points of view it might be thought to be inferior. Animals in general lack something of the repose, the harmony and beauty that are so attractive in some forms of plant life. But what is lower in the scale has generally some points of superiority. Even inanimate objects may excel plants in those respects to which we have referred. Flowers have not the repose and sublimity of the everlasting hills ; and the lower animals have been contrasted by Walt Whitman with the perturbed existence of mankind:

"They do not sweat and whine about their condition; They do not lie awake in the dark and weep for their sins; Not one is respectable or unhappy." In general, where there is greater activity there is less peace. Even in human life, there is a sense in which it is in our infancy that heaven lies about us; and the peasant has perhaps generally a less perturbed existence than the philosopher or the politician.

But, on the whole, the life of animals is evidently higher and more complex than that of plants; just as human life is higher and more complex than that of other animals. The difference, as is usual in natural objects, is not always very sharply marked; but, in general, it is at least obvious that animals, besides growing like a tree, and reproducing their species as plants do, have some capability of motion from place to place, some degree of sensitiveness to surrounding objects, some instinctive tendencies to action; and that the higher animals, with which man is most nearly akin, have complex emotions and large powers of adjustment to the conditions of their lives. Hence, although there are many grades of animal life and many varieties of plants, we may say broadly that an animal is a plant with the addition of certain more or less conscious capabilities of apprehending, feeling, and acting. And, if we are right in saying this, we may say that a human being is essentially a plant, with highly complex animal characteristics superadded, crowned with the potentiality of thought and with all that thought implies. No doubt it implies, among other things, a certain weakening of some of the more purely animal powers and tendencies; so that to speak of addition may be slightly misleading.

We are thus led to think of the life of man as having three main aspects—a vegetative aspect, an animal aspect, and an aspect that is more peculiarly his own. The glory of human life depends on this complexity; but it is also the source of our difficulties and sometimes of our degradation. We are to some extent rooted like plants, at the mercy of winds and seasons. Like animals, we are apt to be swayed by our appetites, our instincts, and our emotions. The potentiality of reason gives us a controlling power, but one that is only gradually developed, and that seldom gains a complete mastery over the lower elements in our being. The complexity of our nature gives us the possibility of a comprehensive insight and sympathy, such as pure intelligences might be supposed to lack; but it also gives us the possibility of imparting a larger power to our animal appetites and impulses, and of perverting them to unnatural uses.[1] Though reason may be said to be a light from heaven, it may easily, when it is still imperfectly developed, be a light that leads astray. It may be used, as Mephistopheles declared, only to make man more beastly than any beast. The great problem of human nature is that of finding the proper balance for its complex constitution.

We have now to notice how the social aspect of human life is affected by this complexity in its general structure.

4. *The Social Nature of Man.*—In considering how far it can be maintained that man is essentially social, we have to take account of all the main factors in his constitution. It seems clear that the purely vegetative side of his nature does not of itself afford much basis for social unity. Plants are not in any definite sense gregarious, though of course they are not absolutely isolated individuals. Even a rock or a mountain is seldom that. It is connected in a complex and often extremely interesting way with the general processes of the earth's development, and has often subtle influences on the lives of plants, animals, and human beings. All plants are at least reproductive, and tend to grow together in groups; and the fertilization of many plants involves the co-operation of more than a single specimen. Similar facts in the life of animals may fairly be regarded as belonging primarily to the vegetative side of their nature, and in most animals they lead to more or less definite forms of association. The generation of most animals involves at least sexual

[1] This is well emphasized in Green's *Prolegomena to Ethics*, § 126.

differentiation and sexual intercourse. Their young are generally in some degree helpless, and need the care of one or both of the parents for a considerable period. The dangers to which they are exposed often necessitate their protection by a group to which they are attached. In many cases also food has to be stored up at certain times in the year for use at other times; and sometimes this can only be done effectively by co-operative action. Hence most of the more highly developed species of animals are naturally gregarious; and this may rightly be said to be dependent primarily on the vegetative side of their nature, though it is only made possible by their powers of apprehension and movement and by the development of their instincts and emotions.

Now, it is clear that human association may often be explained in a similar fashion. Societies, as Aristotle said,[1] are first formed for the sake of life; though it is rather for the sake of good life that they are subsequently maintained. The care of the young, the preservation of food and drink, the provision of adequate shelter and protection, would suffice to account for the existence of human societies, even if there were no other circumstances to account for them; and for this reason alone it might at least be maintained that it is not natural for a man to be alone, and that some form of social unity is implied in his essential structure. The naturalness of such association is not really affected by the fact that its forms may be found to vary at different times and places. The kind of food that is procurable is different in different places, and its storage is more important in some places than in others. The dangers that have to be guarded against are also a variable element—sometimes heat, sometimes cold, sometimes drought, sometimes floods, sometimes wild beasts or other men. Even animals are capable, to some slight extent, of adapting themselves to variable environments; so that the modes of behaviour within a single species, though always natural, are not always quite uniform.

[1] *Politics*, Book III, chap. vi.

But, besides this explanation of social life on purely vegetative grounds, there are several facts more definitely connected with animal nature that make some form of association natural. Some animals prey upon others. This is an element in their nature as animals; and it tends to lead to associations for defence, and sometimes for attack. There is also, to some extent, a struggle for existence among animals of the same species; and, though this may be said to be a disruptive force, the instincts connected with it tend in some degree to lead to association. Dogs delight to bark and bite, and even birds in their little nests do not always agree; but they have to come together to quarrel as well as to co-operate; and it does not seem altogether fanciful to say that the fighting instinct is sometimes a bond of union. It is, on the whole, indifference that keeps individuals apart. Strife, as well as love, brings them together. Heraclitus censured Homer for the aspiration "Would that strife might perish from among Gods and men!" He held that the cessation of strife would mean the cessation of life. Without accepting this contention, we may at least say that strife is sometimes a factor in the formation of animal associations. They sometimes keep together, not that they may help one another, but that they may not be outdone by one another. Of course, neither of these aims may be consciously present: they may only work in the form of blind impulses. Those who hold aloof from one another do not co-operate, but they also do not compete. Conversely we may regard both co-operation and competition, both love and strife, as connected with impulses that help to give rise to social unity among animals.

These forces are evidently operative in human life as well. Mutual aid and rivalry lead to the formation of tribes and peoples, or help to strengthen their bonds of union. Sometimes they are supporting one another, sometimes they are contending against each other; but, in either case, they have a keen interest in each other's doings. And thus we may urge that human beings would be naturally social, even if the distinctive attributes of humanity were not superimposed upon those of plants and animals.

But the characteristics of man as man give a new significance to these associative tendencies. Reason is essentially a unifying power. The accumulation of knowledge requires more co-operation than the accumulation of food. It has to be preserved from generation to generation, and not merely from year to year. The preparation of the young to think, and to apply thought in the guidance of their conduct, requires a longer and more intimate association than their preparation to walk or fly. The use of tools and machinery introduces both more mutual aid and more complex forms of rivalry than the use of teeth and claws. The use of language binds man to man and generation to generation in a way of which no animals are capable, and at the same time introduces a deeper cleavage and a more intense opposition between different races and peoples—an opposition that often gives rise to more complex modes of union. And, whatever may be the correct theory with regard to the inheritance of acquired characteristics in animals,[1] it is clear at least that the most distinctively human acquisitions are only inherited through some form of association.

From such considerations it becomes very obvious that the diversities that we find in human societies are not a sufficient ground for denying that some form of association is natural to man. Rather it is apparent that almost all the characteristic aspects of human nature have some

---

[1] This is a question that appears to be still unsettled, and the discussion of it must be left to biologists. Lamarck believed that such characteristics are inherited; and his view was, in the main, accepted by Spencer. Darwin threw doubt upon it, and Weismann turned the doubt into an emphatic negative. It seems safe at least to believe that qualities acquired in the lifetime of an individual are not readily transmitted to his offspring. Hence education is the chief means by which valuable acquisitions are preserved in the race. This was one of the main contentions of Benjamin Kidd in his *Social Evolution*, and it has been further emphasized in his book on *The Science of Power*.

tendency to differentiate, to introduce distinctions and oppositions, as well as to integrate; and that both tendencies are in some degree associative, but naturally give rise to forms of association that are diverse and subject to change.

In the light of all this, we are now prepared to consider more definitely the general characteristics of those modes of community that may be truly said to be natural to man.

5. *Some Historical References.*—It may be well at this point to notice some of the chief ways in which the analysis of human nature has been applied as a foundation for social studies. Plato and Aristotle are the chief writers who call for notice in this connection. Accordingly, we may refer briefly to their views, and then notice some of the tendencies of later thought.

(*a*) The threefold division that is given in Plato's *Republic* corresponds, to a considerable extent, to that which is here adopted; and he makes it the basis for his recognition of three distinct classes in the ideal state.[1] The three elements, according to his account, are the appetitive, the spirited or passionate, and the rational; and the three corresponding classes are the industrial, the military, and the governing—the last two being, in many respects, regarded as a single class. Many objections may be made to this scheme; but the following would seem to be the most important. (1) As the three fundamental elements are found in all human beings, they do not provide a real basis for distinct classes in the community. (2) The appetitive aspect is too sharply contrasted with the other two. (3) The emotional or spirited aspect is not adequately represented by military activity. (4) The work of the ruler can hardly be properly described as purely rational. On each of these objections a few words may be useful.

(1) All human beings—at least all classes of human

[1] This is worked out chiefly in Books III and IV. See the Notes in the Appendix bearing upon these Books.

beings—have necessarily some concern with the purely organic needs, the maintenance of life, growth, and the reproduction of the species. These are partly subserved by the appetites, but partly also by various modes of sensibility which are not commonly classed as appetites—experiences of heat and cold, pain, and other forms of bodily discomfort. And all human beings have some degree of reason to guide them in the satisfaction of their appetites and in the removal or mitigation of their discomforts. All are, moreover, more or less aware that these are by no means the only needs which as human beings they experience. Hence, though different persons may be mainly employed in providing for the satisfaction of different needs, it can hardly be said to be natural that any class should be occupied exclusively with one aspect of life. This defect becomes pretty apparent in the course of Plato's own treatment. He seeks to emphasize the unity of his ideal State; yet it seems clear that the sharp division of classes would effectually prevent the development of that like-mindedness which is essential to the unity of a people. The lower classes would not understand the higher; and the higher, however well educated and well intentioned, could have but little genuine sympathy with the lower.

(2) This defect is specially apparent in the separation that is made between the industrial class, concerned with the satisfaction of the appetites, and the other two classes that are supposed to be more definitely guided by reason. It is only for the latter that any definite education is provided; and yet the industrial class is not only expected to be willingly subject to the others, but even to be capable of giving such an artistic finish to its work as to provide a beautiful environment for the whole. Probably Plato meant to imply that the rulers would provide the kind of education that is needed for this; but it is surely evident that such an education would be essentially similar to that of the higher classes, and would make the division that is postulated between them largely unmeaning. This difficulty, along with

several others, was well brought out by Aristotle;[1] and it has become more obvious in modern times, in which the technical methods of industry involve the application of mathematical and other sciences, requiring the same kind of preparation as that which is presupposed in the conduct of war.

(3) That the military life should be regarded as the natural form in which the spirited or passionate element in human nature receives expression is also pretty obviously wrong.

Plato himself represents war as arising from a diseased state of society; and yet his ideal community is organized largely with a view to it. Surely the passionate side of man's nature shows itself in love as well as in strife, in the impulses of play, in the spirit of adventure, in poetry and all the higher arts. Plato, though himself a poet and a dramatist, could hardly find a place for the poetic art, except in early education, and for the dramatic art not at all. Yet it would seem that Keats, for instance, was finding expression for the spirited side of his nature in his later poetry, as well as in his earlier fightings. In modern times, the military art has become almost as purely mechanical and scientific as the industrial arts, and is carried on, in the main, by the same type of people.

(4) The rulers of a state must certainly have reason, and no doubt they need to apply it in a more comprehensive way than captains of industry, but hardly than the higher artists or men of science. Plato required that his kings should be philosophers. It is undoubtedly desirable that they should have some philosophic cultivation, but the general principle of division of labour seems to make it natural that there should be some difference between the students of pure and of applied science, and between those who are mainly wise in theory and those who are mainly wise in practice. This also was convincingly emphasized by Aristotle, to whom we may now turn.

(*b*) Aristotle recognized more definitely the three aspects

[1] See his *Politics*, Book II, chaps. ii-v.

of life to which we have referred. The vegetative aspect he treated as irrational, the animal as subject to reason; and he distinguished between reason as guiding and controlling the animal impulses and reason as pursuing its own peculiar ends.[1]

This is not quite satisfactory, and it tends to introduce some degree of confusion into his treatment of the moral virtues.

They have to be regarded as partly concerned with a certain moderation in the supply of our organic needs, and partly with the control of our animal impulses; and yet it would seem that it is only with the latter that the reason is properly concerned. But the discussion of this must be left to ethics. In social philosophy or politics, he avoids the sharp distinction of classes, and so tends to advocate a more genuine unity of the whole people than Plato was able to provide for (at least if the *Republic* is to be taken as correctly representing the Platonic teaching) On the other hand, his distinction between the two types of reason[2] leads him to make a sharper separation between the theoretical and the practical life than is to be found in the work of Plato. Sometimes he speaks as if the life of the philosopher and man of science were wholly different in kind from that of the statesman and citizen.[3] This is partly modified by the recognition that the latter is the necessary foundation for the former. "There is no leisure for slaves." We have first to secure the necessities of life, and even of good life, before we can have the supreme happiness of knowledge and contemplation.[4]

---

[1] See his *Nicomachean Ethics*, Book I, chap. xiii.

[2] Theoretical reason (σοφία) and practical reason (φρόνησις). No doubt it is possible to press this distinction too far. Reason is essentially the same, whether it is applied to theoretical or to practical problems; and a thoroughly wise man understands how to apply it to both. But it remains true that some are mainly skilled in ordering their thoughts in a reasonable way, and others mainly in ordering their feelings or actions.

[3] *Ethics*, Book X, chaps. vii and viii. See also his *Politics*, Book IV.

[4] *Politics*, Book IV, chap. xv.

But he hardly seems to recognize sufficiently that knowledge and contemplation are themselves instruments for the realization of a better life for men in general. How far this is a fair criticism, however, we cannot here discuss. What we are really concerned with is not what either Plato or Aristotle said, but rather what they ought to have said and at least partly did say. If they said it wholly, or meant to say it, that is of course all to the good. At any rate, they went a considerable way in what appears to be the right direction.

(c) In modern times the theories of Plato and Aristotle have had a considerable influence. They have been partly counteracted, however, by the sharper opposition that was made by the Stoics between the life of pure reason and the less rational elements in human nature. The Cartesians, on the whole, supported this antithesis; and the opposition between the secular and the sacred aspects of life, though somewhat different, and emphasized by different people, has given some encouragement to a similar dualism. On the other hand, recent psychology has tended to emphasize the unity of conscious life in a way that has sometimes tended to make the different aspects of man's life appear of little importance. Hence there has been, on the whole, some lack of clearness in co-ordinating the different aspects of human life; and sometimes one and sometimes another has been rather unduly stressed. In recent times, the economic side of life has been very prominent. The science of economics has been more fully dealt with than any other science dealing with society; and it has been apt to be regarded as having a more central position than it deserves. Carlyle and Ruskin did good service in protesting against this, and affirming the claims of morality and art. But perhaps they a little overdid their protestations. On the other hand, the friends of culture have sometimes had a rather undue contempt—a little supported by Greek ideas—for the industrial and commercial aspects of life; and the friends of morality and religion have sometimes had but little sympathy either with the industrial life or with the claims of art and culture. It is chiefly the renewed study of Greek philosophy, and especially of the writings of Plato and Aristotle, that has helped us to recover a more balanced view of the different elements in human nature.

This survey is necessarily a very imperfect sketch ; but it may perhaps enable us to see more clearly what we are to aim at in the treatment that follows.

CHAPTER II

COMMUNITY

1. *The Natural Basis of Community.*—It is apparent from what has now been stated that society rests upon a natural basis. All the most fundamental facts of human nature give rise to some form of social unity. As beings with needs (which may be called vegetative) for food, drink, shelter from heat and cold, from storm and flood, from disease, from the attacks of wild beasts, and as beings predisposed to the perpetuation of their species, we find the necessity for co-operation as an essential adjunct to individual effort. Our more distinctively animal impulses also, our tendencies to love and strife, and the various instincts and emotions that circle round these central dispositions, lead us inevitably into close relations to one another. Still more imperatively are we urged to associate by the more purely human attributes that grow out of our developing reason. In face of such considerations, it can hardly be denied that at least some form of social unity is as natural to man as some form of eating and drinking. As Bishop Butler said:[1] "There is such a natural principle of attraction in man towards man, that having trod the same tract of land, having breathed the same climate, barely having been born in the same artificial district or division, becomes the occasion of contracting acquaintance and familiarities many years after ; for anything may serve the purpose. Thus relations merely nominal are sought and invented, not by governors, but by the lowest of the people ; which are found sufficient to hold mankind together in little fraternities and co-

[1] *Sermons on Human Nature*, I.

partnerships; weak ties indeed, and what may afford fund enough for ridicule, if they are absurdly considered as the real principles of that union; but they are in truth merely the occasions, as anything may be of anything, upon which our nature carries us on according to its own previous bent and bias; which occasions therefore would be nothing at all were there not this prior disposition and bias of nature."

2. *The Conventional Element in Community.*—Nevertheless it is not to be denied, as indeed Butler has indicated in the passage just quoted, that the actual forms of association that we discover among mankind may be properly described as conventional, like the use of forks or glasses. It is one of the implications of our rational nature that we have the faculty of choice, the power of adaptation, and the tendency to devise machinery. Our modes of association are not instinctive, as the gregarious dispositions of the lower animals are. We select our friends and our enemies on various grounds, sometimes well considered, sometimes arbitrary, sometimes almost instinctive. Our manners and customs are partly based on reflection, partly on habits that have grown out of inherited impulses, partly on a gradual and almost unconscious adaptation to our surroundings, partly on the dominating influence of strong personalities, partly on traditions whose origin can hardly be traced, and often, in particular peoples or groups, by the definite compulsion of others. Our laws and forms of government have, for the most part, been established through a slow process of development in which conscious choice has played a considerable part, but in which that choice, in the minds of those who have been mainly responsible for it, has been largely guided and often thwarted by the force of circumstances, by the numbing power of tradition, by apathy, by the desire for compromise, and by many influences that we cannot clearly explain, but can only vaguely characterize as accidental. But if the forms that thus emerge are to be described as conventional, we may at least add that

the establishment of such conventions is also natural to man. It is as natural for man to have particular laws and customs and modes of government as it is for birds to have particular forms of nests ; and it is natural that the former should be more variable than the latter. The results of instinct are, in their main aspects, uniform ; those of choice are endlessly diverse. What is partly based on instinct, partly on choice, partly on the pressure of changing conditions, may be expected to display both uniformity and diversity in the most complex interrelation ; and this is, on the whole, what we are compelled to acknowledge in dealing with human societies.

The recognition that human association is natural and vital has led to its characterization as an organic unity. The recognition that it involves accident and choice has led to the conception of a social contract. Some reflection on these two modes of conceiving it may help us to arrive at a clearer understanding of its essential nature. It may be best to begin with the conception of a contract.

3. *The Conception of a Social Contract.*—This conception was already suggested, but only to be set aside, in the Second Book of Plato's *Republic.* In more modern times it has had a long and chequered history, on which we can only briefly touch. It was put in its most brutal and perhaps also its most logical form by Hobbes.[1] According to him, the natural state of humanity is one of a war of all against all, in which man is to man a wolf— *homo homini lupus.* Life in this state, however, is " solitary poor, nasty, brutish and short." The approximate equality of human beings prevents any one from gaining permanently that dominance over others at which each one naturally aims ; and hence all become eventually disposed to call a truce to the universal war and establish some mode of pacific understanding. This they do by entering into a contract with one another, in accordance with which they abandon their more violent claims

[1] The main points in the theory of Hobbes can be got sufficiently well from Croom Robertson's *Hobbes,* pp. 138–55.

and set up a government for the maintenance of order to which they are then bound by the terms of the contract to offer their allegiance. By the establishment of such an authority, man becomes to man a god—*homo homini deus*.

Other writers, largely by reflection on the work of Hobbes, have conceived of the original contract in somewhat different ways. Spinoza and Locke refused to recognize the absolute surrender to authority which Hobbes maintained; and Rousseau represented the contract, not as a deed that is accomplished once for all, but rather as an understanding that has to be constantly renewed by the operation of the general will. This is a conception that we shall have to consider shortly. In the meantime, it may suffice to state that it has gradually come to be recognized that the conception of a state of nature in which human beings were without any social bonds is a pure fiction, and not a very enlightening fiction. What has finally destroyed it, is the recognition of the close relationship between human life and animal life, in which the rude beginnings of civic association are already apparent. The modern doctrine of evolution has made it impossible to ignore this connection. No doubt, even before any such doctrine had been clearly conceived, the analogy of animal life was to some extent recognized. Shakespeare, for instance, described bees as

> Creatures that by a rule in nature teach
> The act of order [1] to a peopled kingdom.
> They have a king, and officers of sorts:
> Where some, like magistrates, correct at home;
> Others, like merchants, venture trade abroad;
> Others, like soldiers, armèd in their stings,
> Make boot upon the summer's velvet buds,
> Which pillage they with merry march bring home
> To the tent-royal of their emperor;
> Who, busied in his majesty, surveys
> The singing masons building roofs of gold;

---

[1] "Act of order" means, of course, "orderly action."

> The civil citizens kneading up the honey;
> The poor mechanic porters crowding in
> Their heavy burdens at his narrow gate;
> The sad-eyed justice, with his surly hum,
> Delivering o'er to executors pale
> The lazy yawning drone.

This is, of course, somewhat fanciful,[1] but contains at least enough truth to make it seem strange that human life, even in the state of nature, should be supposed to be more chaotic than the life of brutes. No doubt it may be urged that the reflective power in man, and the large claims which it enables him to make, tends to break up the natural unity of society; and that a more complicated unity has to be devised, based upon definite contracts. But this is very different from the conception of an original contract prior to the existence of any form of social unity. That conception may be said to have been overthrown by Rousseau, though not very clearly.[2] Perhaps the death-blow was most definitely given by the famous declaration of Burke: "Society is indeed a contract. Subordinate contracts for objects of mere occasional interest may be dissolved at pleasure—but the State ought not to be considered as nothing better than a partnership agreement in a trade of pepper and coffee, calico or tobacco, or some other such low concern, to be taken up for a little temporary interest, and to be dissolved by the fancy of the parties. It is to be looked on with other reverence; because it is not a partnership in things subservient only to the gross animal existence of a temporary and perishable nature. It is a partnership in all science; a partnership in all art; a partnership in every virtue, and in all perfection. As the ends of such a partnership cannot

---

[1] Probably the account in Maeterlinck's book on the bee is also somewhat fanciful. Fabre, who is more reliable, gives some delightful illustrations of rudimentary modes of social life in his book on *Social Life in the Insect World*.

[2] The best account of Rousseau's view is to be found in Professor C. E. Vaughan's Introduction to his *Political Writings*.

be obtained in many generations, it becomes a partnership not only between those who are living, but between those who are dead and those who are to be born. Each contract of each particular state is but a clause in the great primæval contract of eternal society, linking the lower and the higher natures, connecting the visible and invisible world, according to a fixed compact sanctioned by an inviolable oath which holds all physical and all moral natures each in their appointed place. This law is not subject to the will of those who by an obligation above them, and infinitely superior, are bound to submit their will to that law." [1] No doubt this passage is too vague and rhetorical for scientific purposes ; and it does not sufficiently distinguish between the general unity of society and the more special kind of unity that is involved in the life of a state. But it helps at least to bring out the absurdity of the conception of an original contract, and serves to introduce the very different conception of a natural, vital, or organic unity.

4. *The Conception of Organic Unity.*—The view that a human society may be compared to a living organism is one that occurred very early to reflective minds. It forms the basis of a good deal of the discussion in Plato's *Republic*. It is vividly set forth in the parable of the belly and the members, said to have been employed by Menenius Agrippa.[2] It is implied in some of the utterances of Christ and of St. Paul; and it has been effectively used by many modern writers. But its most elaborate statement is to be found in the sociological works of Herbert Spencer [3] and Schäffle.[4] These writers have developed the analogy between a human society and a living body with a wealth of

[1] *Reflections on the French Revolution*. Burke's views are admirably expounded and criticized in Professor MacCunn's book on *The Political Philosophy of Burke*.

[2] See Shakespeare's *Coriolanus*.

[3] *Principles of Sociology*, vol. i.

[4] *Bau und Leben des sozialen Körpers*—an important work, but one that on the whole seems to me, in more than one sense of the word, monstrous.

detail that is almost overwhelming. But such an analogy is perhaps fully as misleading as it is enlightening. What is valuable in the conception may be stated very briefly.

A society is a living thing, in the sense that it is not a mere mechanical device, as the conception of a contract tends to suggest, but rather a natural growth. But if this is over-emphasized, as it often is by those who make use of the idea of organic unity, it is apt to lead us to ignore the element of choice that is also involved in a human society. A natural organism cannot add a cubit to its stature, nor can it make any radical change in the disposition of its parts. A society may transform itself out of all knowledge, may dissolve itself and be born again. If it grows, it does not necessarily decay. It may renew its youth like the eagle, or rather like the fabled phœnix. If it is an organism, it is at least an organism of organisms, each one of which has a life of its own. Its relations to others also are not merely external, but may interpenetrate its own being. It is indeed alive, but it is alive with thought. It " distinguishes, chooses, and judges," and shapes its future by reflection on its past and criticism of its present. This twofold aspect of human society, as at once a natural growth and a reflective structure, is partly brought out by the conception of a General Will to which reference has already been made, and which we may now briefly consider. But first it will be well to notice what is to be understood by corporate action.

5. *Corporate Action.*—Any organized mode of social unity is frequently forming decisions and carrying out actions in its corporate capacity. Hence, by a sort of legal fiction, corporations are often described and treated as persons. Even states have been so described.[1] They decide and act as a united whole, just as persons do. Indeed, even herds of animals are capable of such united action. The particular way in which such action is determined varies greatly with the particular type of social unity. The decision may be taken by a particular

[1] See the Note at the end of Chapter IV of Book II (p. 146).

ruler or leader; and, in forming it, he may or may not take account of the needs and wishes of his subordinates. Or the decision may be arrived at, after discussion, by a small governing body, which may or may not represent the opinions of the whole society. Or, again, the whole society may have definite means of making the wishes of its members effectively heard. Moreover, the decisions arrived at, whether they are made by one, by a limited number, or by the collective pressure of the whole, may or may not be directed towards the good of the whole. All decisions have reference to some real or imagined good; but the kind of good that is aimed at, consciously or unconsciously, may vary greatly. An army is an organized body, having a certain individuality of its own; but the decisions of a Commander or of a General Staff are not necessarily made with a view to the good of the army, but rather with reference to the ends that the army subserves; and the same may be true of the decisions of other societies or corporations. Even the decisions arrived at by a state are not necessarily directed exclusively to the good of that state, still less of its individual members. They may be directed towards some more general end, such as the protection of other nations or the support of some form of religion. But it is generally true that the actions of any organized society have some reference, direct or indirect, conscious or unconscious, to the real or supposed good of that society.

Thus we have to recognize that, in corporate action, there may or may not be the presence of what may be characterized as a General Will, and that there may or may not be a definite direction of that will towards a Common Good. But we are at least now in a position to consider more precisely what is to be understood by a General Will and by a Common Good.

6. *The Conception of a General Will.*—This conception was introduced by Rousseau,[1] as an explanation of that

[1] He was to some extent anticipated by Spinoza's conception of a Common Will and a Common Good. For an account of this,

persistent rather than original contract by which he conceived that the social unity is sustained; and it has been subsequently used, though not always in quite the same sense, by several writers. The contention is that a body of people, as well as a single individual, may be rightly said to exercise volition; and that it is upon such volition that the united action of a society depends. Rousseau appears to have held that this volition is most definitely expressed by the majority of votes in an assembly brought together for the purpose of deciding some important question. It is not easy to reconcile this with the distinction which he sought to maintain between the general will and the will of all. Mere voting is the action of a collection of individuals, rather than of a united whole, and the decision thus expressed would seem to be only the will of the largest number in that collection. It might be called a joint will, but hardly a general will. Dr. Bosanquet [1] and others have not accepted this interpretation; but have contended that there is a "real will" of a people, though it cannot be quite so simply ascertained. It is arrived at rather by discussion than by voting. Such an interpretation seems to be more satisfactory; but a consideration of the general nature of volition may enable us to see more clearly in what sense it may rightly be maintained that there is a general will of a people.

The will of an individual on any particular occasion is a decision arrived at by deliberation. In any case of real choice there are several alternative courses of action (one of which may sometimes be that of taking *no* action) upon which a decision has to be formed. Usually there are some considerations in favour of each of the alternative

---

see Dr. R. A. Duff's book on *Spinoza's Political and Ethical Philosophy*, especially pp. 130–1 and 316–17. The whole subject is very fully and carefully dealt with in Professor Vaughan's Introduction to his edition of *The Political Writings of Rousseau*. The Essay on Rousseau in E. Caird's *Literary Essays* is, I think, still worth referring to as a general summary of his attitude.

[1] See his *Philosophical Theory of the State*, especially chap. v.

courses, and their relative importance has to be more or less definitely determined.[1] In the case of a purely individual decision, the point of view of that individual is the sole determinant. He decides on the basis of his own valuation of the relative advantages and disadvantages. But in many cases—probably in much the largest number—the point of view of others has some influence on the result. Some examples may help to make this clear.

When Macbeth and Lady Macbeth are deliberating about the murder of Duncan, it is by Macbeth himself that the deed is to be done; and it is on him that the ultimate decision depends. But, according to Shakespeare's representation (which does not appear to have any historical basis), his own deliberation would have led him to abandon the enterprise. Lady Macbeth also, it would appear, would have shrunk from the act if the ultimate decision had rested with her. She was, however, sufficiently determined in its favour to be able to remove the doubts and scruples of her husband, and the deed was eventually done. Here it may be said that the volition was a co-operative one, in the sense that the decision of the agent was partly determined by the point of view of another working along with his own. This is hardly a case of a general will; nor can it be properly described as a joint will; but it may be said to be a case of a co-operative one.

Take again the instance of a family deciding to go somewhere for a holiday. Each member of the family, we may suppose, wishes to go; but their conceptions of a holiday are not quite identical. One wants boating, one wants mountaineering, one wants cycling, one wants sketching, one wants to " loafe and invite his soul." How are they to decide? Obviously there are many possibilities. They may go off separately at their own

---

[1] On the general nature of volition, reference should be made to Professor Stout's *Manual of Psychology*, Book IV, chap. x. My own view is given more fully in my *Manual of Ethics*, Book I, chap. i.

sweet will, each one arriving at a separate decision. The head of the family may determine the matter, and the views of the others may count for nothing. That would be the will of one. They may find some place that would be suitable for the fulfilment of all their wishes, and they may unanimously decide on that. This would be a case of the joint will of all. The views of the minority may be overruled by the majority. This also would be a joint will, but only of some. They may talk the matter over and arrive at some compromise which would be more or less satisfactory, and perhaps also more or less unsatisfactory, to them all. This would be a co-operative will. Or, on talking it over, they may come to the conclusion that the requirements of one member—who perhaps is ill—are more important than those of the others; and the others may agree to waive their claims. I think this last is the case that might be most truly characterized as a general will. It is not a mere compromise between different points of view, but rather a decision arrived at by abandoning the individual standpoint and surveying the situation as a whole. If this is the right interpretation of what is meant by a general will, it would seem to involve two things: (1) the concurrence of a number of persons in a single decision; (2) the fact that the decision is taken with reference to the good of the whole group, and not merely by a balancing of individual wishes. Both these conditions seem to me to be important.

Another illustration, of a somewhat different kind, may perhaps help us. In mediæval Europe few actions were more popular than Crusades. Almost every one in Christendom who thought about public activities at all was desirous of expelling the infidels from the sacred soil. This desire, of course, was not by itself a decision. But many rulers, with the aid of their counsellors, and sometimes in consultation with other rulers, decided, from time to time, to undertake expeditions with the object of satisfying this desire. Such rulers might be said, in a sense, to be carrying out a general will; in the sense, namely, that the decision which they formed was supported by the wishes of the whole, or at least of the " compact majority," of their peoples. The people joined in with right good will. In this phrase, however, will does not properly mean a decision, but rather the sentiment by which a decision is supported. The term is constantly used in this sense, especially in such phrases as " good will " and " ill will," or in such phrases as that of the apothecary in *Romeo and Juliet*—" My poverty but not my will consents." In technical language it is a *wish* rather than a *will*—perhaps hardly even so much as a wish, only a vague desire or sentiment. But, in the present instance, as in the previous one, the essential point is that the decision is one in which a number concur, and that it is in harmony with, if not directly affected by, the points of view of others than those on whom the decision depends. It involves, in the words of Green,[1] " a sense of possessing common interests, a desire for common objects on the part of the people." In this sense, it seems clear that we may rightly speak of a general will, and that the actions of large bodies of peoples can seldom be either wise or effective without such a will. Indeed, without some degree of it, they could hardly act as a body at all.

If this is what is meant, however, it is important to remember that the actual decision is carried out by particular individuals, though they take some account of the desires of others. A statesman, for instance, may have to form an important decision ; but, before actually forming it, he may not only consult his colleagues and friends, but also read the newspapers and try to ascertain what the majority of people would be likely to think about it. Some of those who use the expression do not appear to have very definitely before their minds the distinction between the actual decision and the opinions and sentiments by which it is supported ; and, without a clear apprehension of this, the phrase is apt to be misleading. Rousseau, for instance, maintained that the

[1] *Principles of Political Obligation*, § 84.

general will cannot err; and this appears to be what is meant by the common saying *Vox populi vox dei*—if, indeed, it has any meaning. It seems obvious, however, that the decisions of the majority may err; and almost equally obvious that a decision arrived at by taking account of the wishes of all concerned may be a mistaken one. The utmost that can be well maintained is that such a decision is, in general, much less likely to be wrong than one that is arrived at in any other way. Yet it might sometimes be the case that a decision arrived at by a single wise and well-informed individual—a Pericles or a Cavour—would be a better decision than one that was weakened by taking account of the opinions and wishes of those who were less wise or less well informed. Dr. Bosanquet does not claim any such infallibility for the general will, as he conceives it. Yet, in his account of it as the "real will," he appears to assume too readily that the will to which he refers is not only general but directed to the true good of the community. I see no ground for believing that this is necessarily the case. But reference to this leads us to notice the closely connected conception of a Common Good, which is, I think, not always clearly distinguished from that of a General Will,[1] and which seems to me to be a much safer and more fruitful conception.

7. *The Conception of a Common Good.*—A generation or two ago, the expression "the greatest happiness of the greatest number" was widely current as a summary statement of the end that ought to be kept in view in all public action, and more indirectly in private action as well. It is now generally recognized that the phrase, though sometimes useful, is theoretically inexact and apt to be practically misleading. The shorter and simpler phrase "the common good" is less liable to be misinterpreted, though it also is not entirely free from ambi-

[1] For some further discussion bearing on the subject of the General Will, see Prof. MacIver's *Community*, Appendix A, and Prof. Hobhouse's *Social Evolution and Political Theory*, chap. iv.

guity.[1] In one of the illustrations in the last section—
that relating to the action of a family—it is pretty clear
that the conception of a common good is applicable. A
holiday may be supposed to be not only desired but
desirable. It may be beneficial to all the members of a
family, or to one or more who specially need it. It may
not actually produce the benefit that is anticipated; but
at least we may suppose that it is willed with a view
to this. Even if the direct benefit is specially intended
for one, it is yet a common good, in the sense at least
that it is something that is chosen by all as desirable.
How far the instigators of the Crusades adopted a similar
attitude may be more open to question. Historical instances cannot be as easily interpreted as those that are
specially devised to illustrate a particular point. The
Crusaders may have been impelled by a sense of obligation,
by the spirit of adventure, or by the passion of hate, rather
than by any definite anticipation of benefit; or the forces
that moved them may have been of a highly complex
character. In general, however, it seems safe to say
that most of the public actions of a civilized society are
undertaken with the object of securing something that is
thought of as good; and, on reflection, we should seldom
feel justified in approving of the action unless we thought
that the good to be secured by it was, in some sense and to
some extent, a common good.

Obviously, some good things may be described as
common in a pretty complete sense. " The highest good,"
according to Spinoza, " is common to all, and all may
equally enjoy it." It is, for instance, generally good for
a whole people to be free from subjection to another people.
A fine poem or painting or a wise discourse may be a good
that all, or at least very many, may appropriate and
appreciate. Some other good things—especially those
that are destroyed in the using—cannot be so readily

[1] T. H. Green probably did more than any one else to clear
up the conception of a Common Good. See his *Prolegomena to
Ethics*, Book III, chap. iii, and *Principles of Political Obligation*,
§§ 117–36.

shared. Yet even a plentiful provision of food or a good supply of water, though consumed in separate portions, may fairly be described as a common good, in so far as all participate. It would seem that the general will, as characterized in the previous section, is best conceived as aiming at some such good; but, owing to the ambiguity of that phrase, it is probably best to avoid it.

To prevent a possible misunderstanding, it may be well to notice here that the conception of a common good has no necessary connection with what is meant by Communism. The emphasis on a common good is certainly opposed to an individualistic conception of human life. But when individualism is contrasted with communism, socialism, or collectivism, these terms are generally understood to refer to the common ownership of property or the collective control of industry. This we shall have to notice again, when we are dealing with industrial institutions. In the meantime, the term communalism might be used with advantage, as opposed to individualism in the more general sense. A good that is essentially common may be produced, owned, and used by separate individuals. The health of a community, for instance, is a common good; yet each one has his own separate health, and may separately care for it. But we shall be in a better position to consider this later.

8. *Spiritual Unity.*—In the light of these considerations we may now see more clearly what is the general nature of the unity that is properly to be ascribed to a human society. It is perhaps best characterized as spiritual unity. It is a kind of unity of which only spiritual beings —i.e. persons—would seem to be capable. Such beings are more or less clearly conscious of themselves as persons pursuing some good, and conscious of those with whom they are associated as other persons pursuing the same or a similar good. Only beings who think can regard themselves and others in this way. Bees or beavers may, as a matter of fact, be led by their instincts to a

good that is common; but they do not know it; and they cannot choose it, except in the sense that they are impelled towards it. To some extent this may sometimes —perhaps even often—be the case with human beings also; but, as their instincts are not as simple and constant as those of animals, such blind impulses in men are often apt to be a source of disunion, rather than of unity. At any rate, they do not lead to the kind of unity that is most characteristic and most fruitful in human life. A well-ordered society is, in general, based upon a pretty clear consciousness of things to be pursued that are, in some degree, for the benefit of all; and it is at least safe to affirm that the more fully this is the case the more complete is the unity of the whole. Further than this we need not at present go.

9. *Social Differentiation.*—It is evident that a unity of this kind is a unity of things that are in many respects diverse. Not only does it consist of a number of individuals whose goods—and, still more, whose conceptions of their true good—are not quite identical; but, in a complex society, it will usually consist of a number of distinct groups, within which separate decisions are taken, having reference to distinguishable ends, however true it may be that all these ends are included within a more comprehensive end that is for the benefit of all. If such a society is to be called an organism at all, it is at least important to remember, as we have already noted, that it is an organism of organisms; and that each of these minor organisms is also an organism containing others within it. Hence the simple conception of organic unity is inadequate to describe it. It is a spiritual whole, containing within itself lesser wholes, some of which may also be called spiritual, others organic, and others mainly mechanical, but all in some degree co-operating, in a well-ordered society, for the general good.[1]

[1] On the philosophical interpretation of the social unity, some interesting remarks will be found in Dr. McTaggart's *Studies in*

It is now time, however, that we should try to see more definitely what are the most conspicuous parts into which such a society tends to be differentiated and what are their respective functions.

Hegelian Cosmology, chap. vii. My own view on the whole subject is given more fully in my *Elements of Constructive Philosophy*, Book II, chaps. vii–xi.

CHAPTER III

MODES OF ASSOCIATION

1. *Society and Societies.*—We have now seen what are the natural and the conventional aspects in the structure of a community. In a wide sense, the whole human race forms such a community; but parts of the human race are to a large extent cut off from one another by local separation, by differences in language, religion, education, modes of life, and other circumstances that prevent that degree of like-mindedness which is necessary for genuine human intercourse.[1] Even those who live somewhat closely together, and have a good many bonds with one another, have often but little direct intercourse; and such relations as they have may be a kind that divides quite as much as it unites. Even fathers and sons,[2] brothers and sisters, husbands and wives, often appear to be somewhat repellent atoms. Yet there are few human beings who have not intimate relations with some others, though the circle with which they are associated may be of a very limited kind. Some are almost confined to their family, some to their business, some to their church; some live mainly in the world of books, some mainly in that of art, some mainly in that of politics,

---

[1] On the importance of the recognition of "likeness of kind" as a basis for association, reference may be made to Professor Gidding's *Principles of Sociology*, pp. 104–8. I think, however, he attaches undue importance to likeness of *kind*, as distinguished from likeness of *mind*.

[2] For illustration of this, Tourgénieff's *Fathers and Sons*, Strindberg's *Son of a Servant*, and Mr. E. Gosse's *Father and Son* may be referred to.

some mainly in that of sport or amusement. Human society is thus split up into a number of more or less separate societies, each having a certain unity of its own, though some are much less closely bound together than others. Families and nations would seem on the whole to be the two forms of association in which there is the most intimate bond of union, by which all the main aspects of life are affected; but these, like other forms of association, vary very much in their degree of intimacy and permanence. This depends partly on the degree in which they are supported by definite institutions, such as marriage and government. Besides these two fundamental forms, by which hardly any one can fail to be in some degree affected, there are special combinations for the purposes of education, industry, commerce, play, the pursuit of science, art, and literature, the support of morality and religion, the intercourse of friendship, the establishment of international relations either in the way of co-operation or of rivalry, and a variety of other objects. In dealing with these in a somewhat summary fashion, it will be well to bear in mind the fundamental aspects of human life to which we have already referred. Associations may be based primarily, as in industry and commerce, on the supply of men's vegetative needs; or, as in play, on the satisfaction of animal impulses; or, as in science, art, and religion, on aims that are distinctively human; or, as in the Family and the State, on all the aspects of our composite nature. A brief reference to the chief of these may help to bring this out; but first it may be well to give some account of the significance of institutions.

2. *Social Institutions.*—This term may be used in a wider or in a narrower sense. In the wider sense, any mode of association may be described as an institution. The Family, the State, language, education, religion may all be called institutions, inasmuch as they are structures that are formed to a large extent by human choice; but, so far as they are natural growths, rather than voluntary

creations, the term is not very suitably applied to them. In a narrower sense, it may be confined to the particular instruments or devices by which modes of association are formed and maintained, and by which their special functions are fulfilled.[1] In this sense it might be held that marriage, or some particular form of marriage, is an institution, but that the Family is not; that the State is not an institution, but that the House of Commons is; that language is not an institution, but that a printing establishment is; that education is not an institution, but that a technical college is; that religion is not an institution, but that a State Church is; and so forth. It does not seem possible, however, to draw any sharp distinction between the wider and the narrower senses; and the question as to the most correct usage is largely a verbal one. So far as it is not simply verbal, it would seem to be a question of the degree in which some definite human choice is involved, and of the degree in which that choice is expressed in a more or less permanent form. On the whole, it might be well to distinguish between a particular mode of association, the institutions that give it definiteness and permanence, and the instruments by which these institutions are supported and through which they act. But, while the distinction between a mode of association and its instruments can generally be clearly drawn, an institution—which lies somewhat between the two—is apt to partake of the nature of both. A school is an institution, but it may also be regarded as an instance of a special mode of association. The House of Commons is an institution, but it might also be described as an instrument of the general institution of government. Language is an instrument; but it is an instrument that is formed by such a process of almost unconscious growth, and is so intimately bound up with all modes of human association, that it might almost be characterized as an institution, or even as one of the fundamental modes of association. At any rate, in view of its essential place in

[1] This is emphasized in Professor MacIver's book on *Community*, Book II, chap. iv.

all human intercourse, it will perhaps be best to begin our account of the chief modes of association by some reference to the special function of language.

3. *The Place of Language.*—Language means primarily modes of speech addressed to the ear. Most forms of language, however, appeal both to the eye and to the ear; and some forms, such as hieroglyphics or the language of deaf-mutes, appeal almost exclusively to the former. The blind, again, are usually to some extent dependent upon touch. Ordinary writing and printing are, of course, addressed primarily to the eye, but generally suggest the audible word as well.[1] In a wide sense, language may be taken to include all modes in which definite meanings are conveyed by one or more human beings to others. It is probably best, at least for our present purpose, not to take account of the somewhat vaguer suggestions that are made by or to animals or by inanimate objects, or (as some believe) by other spiritual beings. It is only with human life that we are here directly concerned. Among the modes in which meanings are conveyed, we may mention expressive gestures, exclamations, mathematical symbols, musical notes and their arrangement, paintings and sculptures, flags, ceremonies, processions, presents, and sometimes even modes of eating and drinking. As illustrations of the last, and of some of the others as well, reference might be made to the Communion service and to such songs as "Drink to me only with thine eyes" or "Auld Lang Syne," or to the poems of Omar Khayyám.

Now, it is clear that no human association could well be conceived without the use of language in this extended sense—hardly even without language in the narrower sense. It is for the psychologist to consider all the functions that are fulfilled by language in the development of the human consciousness,[2] and for the logician to dis-

---

[1] It is a recognized weakness of the English language that sometimes the one does not very directly suggest the other.

[2] See Stout's *Manual of Psychology*, Book IV, chap. v.

cuss the implications of the meanings that are conveyed.[1] What it is important to notice here is, in general, its subtler influences on human society, and more particularly the fact that it may serve as an instrument of division, as well as of unity. The story of the Tower of Babel gives vivid expression to the latter point; and it must be confessed that human efforts to reach the skies—or, in other words, to realize their social ideals—are probably more hampered by differences of language (at least in the more extended sense of the term) than by any other single cause. This applies not only to the larger differences that exist between different nations in their words, in the structure of their sentences, and in their expressive and symbolic usages; but also to the smaller differences of dialect within nations, and to the still more minute differences in pronunciation, in the use of particular phrases or gestures or other modes of expression, by which different classes in the same community are apt to be distinguished. In our own country the use of the letter *h* is one of the most conspicuous instances. Other illustrations, with some comic exaggeration, and with much emphasis on their social significance, are supplied by Mr. Shaw's *Pygmalion*; and no doubt others will readily occur to the reader. All dialects contain expressive words and phrases that convey a wealth of meaning to those who are familiar with them, and thus create a somewhat exclusive circle; and the same applies to many forms of slang. On the more positive side, as showing the value of a common language, the important part that was long played in Europe by the use of Latin—and that is still played to some extent by the use of French or English—as a general means of international communication, may serve to enforce the considerations that have to be borne in mind. Those who differ in their modes of expression, or in the suggestions that particular expressions convey to them, are almost necessarily distinct also in their modes of thought and feeling. They are not like-minded; and, without this kind of community, there

[1] See Welton's *Manual of Logic*, vol. i, chap. i.

cannot be much intimacy in social intercourse or any very deep realization of a common good.[1]

Looking at language in this somewhat wide way, we may certainly maintain that it is quite the most fundamental of all social institutions, so far as it is right to describe it as an institution at all.

4. *Formative Institutions.*—We may next notice those institutions whose primary aim is the building up of social unity, rather than the maintenance of any special form of such unity. These may be characterized broadly as educational, though in some cases the educational aim may not be quite definitely recognized. The Family, for instance, may he held to be mainly educational in its purpose, though of course it serves other ends that are not definitely of this character. Certainly it exists largely for the nurture of young children and their preparation for entry upon the life of a larger community. Schools and colleges, of course, are more obviously and more consciously designed for the continuation of this work; and it is more clearly right to describe these as institutions. We shall have to consider the significance of these shortly in some detail; and it is hardly necessary to dwell upon them at present.

5. *Economic Institutions.*—There are other institutions that serve, not so much for the formation of human life, as for its preservation. These are primarily concerned with the supply of what we have described as the vegetative needs. Human beings are very obviously in need of food, drink, air, sunlight, sleep, exercise, warmth, shelter, etc., though their needs in these respects vary very much in different places and circumstances, and to some extent also with differences of bodily structure and habits of life. The instruments and facilities for the supply of such needs are the main grounds for the various forms

---

[1] It is this, to a very large extent, that makes it difficult to have any recognized body of international law and morality. See below, Book III, Chapter I.

of industry and commerce; though, of course, industry and commerce are also concerned with the satisfaction of other wants—such as those for books, pictures, munitions of war, materials for sport, conveniences for travel, musical instruments, etc. But the conditions on which the demand and supply of such goods depend are so different from those by which the others are determined, that it is probably best not to regard them as essentially economic goods at all. For the present, at least, we may regard economic institutions as those that are designed primarily for the satisfaction of vegetative wants. The great majority of the institutions that are connected with industry and commerce are concerned mainly with these —e.g. methods of land tenure, factories, markets, exchanges, co-operative societies, trade unions, harbours, shipbuilding yards, etc.; though problems that are not purely economic are nearly always mixed up with the primary functions that such institutions fulfil.

6. *Barbaric Institutions.*—I use this term, for lack of a better, to characterize those institutions that are primarily concerned with the satisfaction of animal impulses. It is not necessarily to be understood in a derogatory sense, but, in employing it, I have a reminiscence of Gray's expression, in his address to Eton College, " There are our young barbarians all at play," and of Matthew Arnold's statement [1] that the upper class in England consists of barbarians. It would be difficult to point to many institutions that minister to nothing but animal propensities. But, if we take movement as the essential need of animal life, and love and strife as its most fundamental impulses, it is not difficult to see that many modes of association are designed primarily to satisfy them. When we see the young barbarians at play, we see them behaving very much as young animals may behave; except that

[1] *Culture and Anarchy*, III. As a further illustration of what I mean, I may instance the Boy Scout movement as having largely the character of a barbaric institution. See also Professor Veblen's *Theory of the Leisure Class*, especially pp. 378–9.

they generally make of their play some definite institution with recognized rules and instruments. Of course, these may sometimes serve an educational function, as all human things may; but the primary need that finds expression in them is not educational; and they appear to lose some of their zest and significance if an educational end is too consciously combined with them. Nor can they be regarded simply as gymnastic exercises, though this purpose is also contained in them. The animal impulses of love and strife, however, seem to enter largely into them; as they do still more noticeably in primitive forms of dance. Most games are in some degree competitive, and imply both friendly co-operation and rivalry. In early forms of art also the commemoration of love and strife, appealing to these natural impulses, seems to be very prominent; and even in the most developed forms of art it seems fair to say that these impulses occupy a larger place than purely artistic demands would justify.

Other ways in which love and strife give rise to modes of association are not hard to discover. The family has certainly one of its roots in love; and it tends also to give rise to some other institutions that are more or less opposed to the life of the family. It leads also to convivial gatherings, the main object of which is seldom the satisfaction of vegetative needs or the promotion of intellectual or artistic aims; though these may often be combined with the more primitive impulse to be with others and enjoy them as boon companions. With this an element of strife is frequently combined, as in games of chance and skill, wit combats, and other forms of competition, and sometimes even in actual quarrelling and fighting. How far the combative impulse is involved in competitive games is, no doubt, often difficult to determine. Even in fencing and boxing, the need for physical exercise and the more purely human interest in the skilful adaptation of means to ends may sometimes be sufficient motives; and sometimes the end in such activities is definitely educational. But it can hardly be doubted that the combative impulse generally contributes something to the joy that is found in competitive games and even in talking for victory, like Dr. Johnson. But the combative impulse directs itself more readily and strongly to those who are outside the particular group to which an individual belongs. This would seem to be the primitive foundation on which war rests, though competition for the satisfaction of vegetative needs or of some of the higher wants of human nature readily associates itself with the more purely barbaric " delight of battle." But even in highly developed communities it is pretty obvious that this impulse is not wholly submerged. Civilized people like to think that with their elaborate military organizations they are fighting for freedom, for culture, for religion, or for the protection of others; but it can hardly be doubted that in many minds there is a latent, sometimes a quite avowed sympathy with the saying of Nietzsche—interpreted in its crudest sense—that " a good war sanctifies any cause."

7. *Governmental Institutions.*—The various modes of association that have now been referred to would obviously result in a somewhat chaotic condition of society if they were not to some extent controlled and co-ordinated. Man, as a thinking being, no less than a being with vegetative needs and animal impulses, is naturally led to some attempt at such co-ordination and control. Hence, in all societies but the most primitive—if even they can be wholly excepted—we find some recognized form of government. It may only take the form of the recognition of a tribal chief or a council of elders; but conflicts with surrounding societies, as well as the difficulties of internal discipline, soon lead to the establishment of a more elaborate system, in which primitive customs are consolidated into laws; and thus the State becomes an institution, to which all other institutions are in some degree subordinated. Rights are gradually defined, and their corresponding obligations enforced; and the conception of justice acquires a certain prominence. As this mode

of subordination almost necessarily implies some exercise of force, the military element naturally becomes more or less dominant in such an organization. Indeed, as Plato noted, it is largely the demand for military action that makes strong central government necessary. But the further consideration of all this must be reserved for a later chapter.

8. *Cultural Institutions.*—As the more distinctively human aspects of life become prominent, those that are connected only with the vegetative or animal nature begin to be treated rather as means than as ends; and the supremé end is gradually recognized as consisting in the cultivation of the power of reason, and of all that goes with that. This recognition leads to new modes of association. Institutions are formed not merely for the instruction and training of the young, but for the advancement of knowledge and the development of intellect and character. The simple play impulse is transformed into the desire for expression in various forms of art; and these gradually take on a deeper significance as expressing, not merely the impulses of the animal nature, but the subtler and more reflective emotions and sentiments, and, ultimately, a thoughtful outlook on life and an attempt at its interpretation. A rational basis is sought for law; and its external power of coercion gives place by degrees to the recognition of moral obligations. The view of life as a whole embodies itself in religious creeds, in which the conception of the perfecting both of the individual personality and of the social order becomes more and more a dominating motive. All these growing aspects of what is characteristically human both introduce modifications into the other institutions of social life and give birth to new institutions devoted more particularly to the promotion of these higher ends. Scientific societies are founded, artistic groups formed, and churches grow up for the promotion of morality and the cultivation of religion. The deepening sense of the essential unity of human life and of the value of the ends

that it implies, tends, moreover, to break down the antagonism between different societies, and leads gradually to the establishment of well-defined international relations, and of a number of institutions for the furtherance of their intercourse with one another.

9. *Interactions of Institutions.*—The complex system of institutions that thus arises involves some degree of conflict, which is not always easy to overcome. Man, as we have already urged, is hardly a rational animal, but rather an animal that is becoming rational; and the higher potentialities of his nature do not easily or at once gain control over the lower. Sometimes the conflict between the higher and the lower leads to the attempt to crush out the lower altogether. The ascetic sage becomes a notable type in many societies. In other cases, a division tends to be drawn between the more secular and the more sacred aspects of life. An attempt is made to render to Cæsar the things that are Cæsar's and to God the things that are God's; and this is apt to be done somewhat crudely. It is urged that "business is business" and that it is quite distinct from morality, or that, in international relations, might is the only right. But attempts of this kind to separate the main interests of life are soon found to be unsatisfactory. The unity of life asserts itself against its differences, and leads to a gradual readjustment of all the aspects of our nature to its fundamental ends. But this takes time, and a considerable element of conflict and chaos is almost inseparable from the process of adjustment. Hence we must not look for any easy solution of the problems of human life.

10. *The Meaning of Civilization.*—The process by which this adjustment of the various elements of human nature is brought about, and the results to which it gradually leads, are generally expressed by the term Civilization. The Germans use the term Kultur to indicate the particular form that is taken by civilization at a particular place

and time.[1] The term Civilization, like the term Citizenship, indicates that it is chiefly in cities that the process has been observed in its most intense form. It is usually in cities that the different aspects of human life are brought into the most intimate contact with one another, and that the need for their adjustment is most strongly felt. The independent City State in Greece shows this in the highest degree; but in a less degree it is apparent in most modern cities as well. The difficulties that the process involves are apt to give rise to many incidental evils. City life is liable to be less healthy than the less strongly unified life of the country. The vegetative and animal sides often suffer; and their suffering reacts prejudicially on the moral and religious life, sometimes also on the artistic, and to a less degree on the purely intellectual. Hence there is sometimes a strong reaction against it, and an effort to return to modes of life that are apparently simpler and freer. The life of the comparative savage is sometimes held up as a pattern for the more highly civilized. This tendency is on the whole represented in the earlier writings of Rousseau, for instance; and, in more recent times, Mr. Edward Carpenter has written an interesting book on *Civilization: its Cause and Cure*. But both Rousseau and Mr. Carpenter were, after all, led to the conclusion that the only cure for the evils of civilization is to be found in *more* civilization—a hair of the dog that bit us. It is to be hoped that both the difficulties and the methods by which they are to be met will become more apparent as we proceed.

11. *Plan of the following Chapters.*—It is evident that any attempt to deal at all fully with the various aspects of social life to which reference has now been made would involve a very elaborate study. It must suffice, in such an outline as this, to touch upon what appear to be the

[1] The significance of the German use of this term has been very well brought out by Professor Burnet in his book on *Higher Education and the War*, chap. i. See also Sir Charles Waldstein's *Patriotism, National and International*, pp. 21-6.

most important considerations. It seems best to begin with that mode of unity which is on the whole the simplest and the most obviously natural—that of the Family, growing as it does out of some of the most elementary of our needs, yet in certain ways ministering to almost all, and readily capable of being brought into the service of the highest. From the Family there is an easy transition to education, and from that to the industrial forms of life. The State will then have to be considered with some care, and this will lead on to the conception of justice and to various ideals of social organization. The consideration of international relations and of the place of religion and culture may be reserved for the closing Book. The modes of unity implied in these may be regarded as relating essentially to humanity as a whole, rather than to any limited mode of association.

BOOK II
NATIONAL ORDER

CHAPTER I

THE FAMILY

1. *The Natural Basis of the Family.*—That the family is natural to man [1] is almost sufficiently apparent from the fact that it is natural to most of the more highly developed animals. It is obvious that the care of the young becomes increasingly important in the higher types of animal life, because they tend more and more to be helpless at birth, and are more and more in need of care for their proper development. It does not fall within our province here to discuss by what processes, whether by natural selection or otherwise, the instincts of the parents become adapted to cope with these necessities. It is enough for our purpose to recognize that they are met, in general, by some form of family unity. The initial stages in the care that is required—except in such abnormal cases as that of young cuckoos—falls normally upon the parents; sometimes only upon the mother, and mainly upon her in most cases, but usually in some degree upon the father as well. This may be taken as constituting the natural basis of the family; and the question with regard to its most satisfactory form must always turn largely upon the consideration of the best way in which this primary end can be achieved. The monogamic family would seem, on the face of it, to be the best adapted for this purpose, being the only one in which both parents can normally devote themselves whole-heartedly, and with

[1] On the whole subject of the family unity, Mrs. Bosanquet's treatment in her book on *The Family* seems to me both the most comprehensive and the most delightful.

cordial co-operation, to the necessary task. It is to be confessed, however, that, if we look for the natural basis of the family in the lower world, it would seem to be chiefly in certain species of birds that this form of family life is seen in its greatest perfection; and, as these are not very closely akin to human beings in other respects, it might be urged—and it has sometimes been urged— that there is no obvious reason for thinking that it is the most natural form for us. But in reality some birds are closely akin to human beings in what is the most essential point—the need of special care and preparation for the young.[1] Flying is the natural mission of many birds, as thinking is of men; and the young are, in general, quite unfitted for either of these functions. In both cases also the mother is liable to be partially incapacitated for a considerable period by her attention to the young, and requires the help of the father. Hence, apart from any special consideration of what is peculiar to human life, we may certainly maintain that the monogamic family is *prima facie* a natural form of association.

2. *The Conventional Aspect of the Family.*—If it is true that the family has so obvious a basis in the nature of things, why, it may be asked, has it ever been supposed to be merely conventional? To this there may be many answers, some of which may become more apparent as we proceed. But one of them may be stated at once. What is very obvious on reflection is not always obvious to the unreflective. To the superficial eye the child is by no means the most important member of a family. In fact, there may not happen to be a child in it at all. The word "family" itself throws some light on what I think we may call a superficial way of regarding its essential

---

[1] It is probable that the extent to which even the lower animals are prepared for the conduct of life by their inherited instincts, without parental care, has tended to be a good deal exaggerated. There is some interesting material bearing upon this in Benjamin Kidd's posthumous work on *The Science of Power*, pp. 276-289. See also Lloyd Morgan's *Habit and Instinct*, especially pp. 181-2.

nature. The Roman *famulus* was a domestic slave (the English word *slavy* is a reminiscence of that position); and the *familia* meant primarily a collection of slaves attached to a household.[1] Then the family came to mean, not merely the slaves, but all the persons included within the regular household; all regarded, more or less, as the property of the head of the family—the head being, not the child, but the father. This conception of the family appears also, to some extent, in the Ten Commandments: "Thou shalt not covet thy neighbour's house, thou shalt not covet thy neighbour's wife, nor his manservant, nor his maidservant, nor his ox, nor his ass, nor any thing that is thy neighbour's." It is significant that the children are not mentioned here. Did the framer of this commandment feel ashamed to include them among the possessions of one's neighbour? Or did he only suppose that they were not things that any one would be likely to covet? It is noteworthy also that, while there is a commandment to honour father and mother, there is none to care for children. Possibly it may have been thought that Nature herself might be trusted to teach this.

Now, it is no doubt true that we have ceased to think of a man's family as his slaves, and have at least partially ceased to think of it as his property; but it can hardly be denied that the common way of regarding it is still a good deal influenced by these older ways of thinking. If the family is the property of the father, why should it be treated differently from any other property? If he may have many oxen and many children, why not also many wives? If he may sell his ox and buy another, why not also exchange his wife? Or, if we have gone so far as to recognize a certain equality on the part of the woman, we may still ask, Why may they not both agree to dissolve the union, whenever they please, or whenever one of them pleases? Looking at it in this way, we do not see any natural constraint in this mode of association.

[1] *Domus* appears to be the nearest equivalent in Latin for what we understand by a family.

Marriage appears to be only an artificial contract, not in any sense a sacrament. It is chiefly in this way that the family comes to be thought of as only conventional, and not very firmly rooted in nature. Having stood the pyramid on its point, we expect to see it topple over.

Now, it is not to be denied that there is some natural basis even for this way of regarding the family. We shall have to take some account of it later. But, in the meantime, we may perhaps be allowed to assume that the other way of regarding it calls attention to a more fundamental feature.

3. *The Child as Centre.*—Taking the child as the natural basis of the family, we have to regard his preparation for life as the primary function of that mode of association. If we may treat the family as a little state, the child is its legitimate sovereign;[1] but he rules through his ministers. His wishes are not necessarily always carried out—especially when there are a number of children in the family; but it would seem that the normal function of the family is primarily to secure what is best, or the best available, for the nurture of the children, with a view to their preparation as citizens of a larger community. The other functions involved in the life of the family are naturally to be regarded as subordinate to this fundamental conception. It is not, however, altogether easy to determine the precise manner or degree of subordination that naturally belongs to them. They vary very greatly in different circumstances. Yet a few general remarks may be useful at this point.

However firmly we may hold to the view that the care of children is the natural or logical basis of the family, we have yet to remember that what is logically first is seldom first in the order of time, and may not always even be first in the order of importance. A family is founded in time by the marriage of two persons of opposite

---

[1] In the sense in which we speak of the " sovereign people," who rule through their representatives—not in the sense in which we speak of an autocrat as sovereign.

sexes. Such an association does not necessarily result in children; and, even when it does, the union is generally prolonged beyond the period during which the care of children is essential. Hence it is not unnatural to regard love between persons of opposite sexes, rather than the care of children, as the fundamental basis of the family. This is, indeed, a natural basis; and we see it in animal life, as well as in that of human beings. But it appears, on reflection, that it is normally subordinate to the other basis. There may be intense love between individuals of the same sex or between brothers and sisters; and this may give rise to associations of a very delightful and valuable kind, but not to families. It is the possibility of children to be cared for that differentiates marriage from other associations that are based on personal affection; and it is obvious also that marriage is not always based on this. Hence, although love between adults may sometimes be the basis of a finer and more valuable form of union than that which is based on the care of children, it cannot be regarded as the essential foundation of the family.

Again, it has to be recognized that the long period of growth in human life puts a heavy burden upon the mother, especially when the family is a large one and her own resources slender. It is natural that this burden should be made more supportable by the help of the father, as we see in many instances of animal behaviour; and this support is usually in some degree important even beyond the period during which the care of children lasts. It is natural also in human life—though for this there would seem to be less foundation in the purely animal world—that, when the children come to maturity, they should make some recompense for the care that has been bestowed upon them. Sometimes—perhaps most notably in Japan (which has been described as the paradise of children)—this aspect of the family is even more strongly emphasized (partly no doubt, because it is less obviously natural) than that of care for the young. Even in animals some appearance of gratitude for benefits received is often observed. It at least forms a natural basis for friendship; and, as the aged are often in special need of help, it seems most appropriate that they should receive it from those whom they have brought into being. But it is not, in the same degree, necessary that they should require such aid. They may have made sufficient provision for their old age; or the community that they have served may make it for them. At any rate, it seems important not to allow this consideration to obscure the fact that the fundamental basis of the family is care for the young.

It must not, of course, be inferred that the recognition of this makes marriage meaningless in the absence of children. To this we must return shortly.

4. *Eugenics.*—In view of the natural basis of the family, we are immediately led to recognize how important it is that the child should be well born; and this is a subject to which a great deal of attention has been given in recent years.[1] Plato also emphasized it rather strongly—perhaps almost brutally. Certainly the natural sovereign must, if possible, be every inch a king. Among the lower animals, the young that are unfitted for the conditions of life are apt to die early, in spite of parental care; whereas medical skill and careful nursing may preserve many human lives that would not otherwise have come to maturity. It is sometimes urged that such preservation tends to bring about the deterioration of the race; and it appears to have been partly for this reason that the ancient practice of the exposure of infants was adopted. But it is not so easy to determine what are the qualities that fit one for human life as it is in the case of the lower animals. Some of the men to whom mankind is most deeply indebted would probably have been put to death in early childhood if the practice of exposure had been in force. Moreover, as such individuals seldom have families, it is probable that the race does not really suffer by their preservation.

[1] Galton was the first who brought it into prominence; but it is now pretty generally recognized as an important branch of study. See Hobhouse's *Social Evolution and Political Theory*, chap. iii.

What modern students of eugenics are chiefly inclined to urge is rather that some precautions should be taken to prevent unsuitable marriages. This also is not a matter on which it would be easy to arrive at any sound decision except in cases of conspicuous disease. There is perhaps more to be said for giving special encouragement to marriages that may be expected to yield good results. It is doubtful whether the science of eugenics is yet sufficiently advanced to supply much guidance in this direction; but there are some grounds for expecting that it will be able to give more in future; and it is evident that, with the necessary knowledge, there are many ways in which the desired encouragement could be given. But it hardly falls within our present province to do more than allude to this subject.[1]

5. *Marriage.*—On the general subject of marriage, however, some further observations may be here in place. The supreme importance of the primary basis of the family gives a sufficient ground for attaching a certain sanctity and permanence to the institution of marriage. Nature herself provides some forces that tend to give it a somewhat unique strength. Even in animal life, when there is anything at all comparable to human marriage, it would appear to be not easily dissolved. The sexes are evidently in some respects complementary to one another; and the natural attraction between them tends, on the whole, to be strengthened, rather than weakened, by habitual association. Romantic writers may have somewhat exaggerated this tendency; and, by reaction, other writers have probably unduly depreciated its force. Human nature is, no doubt, less stable than the nature of most animals is. Both men and women are liable to undergo considerable changes in their tastes and in their modes of thought and feeling; and such changes may readily lead to the desire for a dissolution

---

[1] Professor J. B. Haycraft's *Darwinism and Race Progress*, though perhaps rather one-sided, may be referred to in this connection: also the Preface to Huxley's *Evolution and Ethics*.

of the marriage bond. Indeed, there is some reason to doubt whether the type of animal to which the human race is most closely akin is one of those that are best adapted by nature for a permanent association of this kind. Hence there are grounds for thinking that it is desirable to supplement the natural tendencies in the direction of permanence by the more artificial sanctions of religion, law, and popular sentiment. There has been some disposition in recent years to urge that these sanctions have in this country at least been somewhat too sharply stressed, and to plead for greater facilities for divorce. It is noteworthy, however, that in some countries—such as Japan—where considerable facilities in this direction have long been in existence, it has been found desirable to strengthen the bond.[1] What is of primary importance is, of course, to secure adequate care for children and, only in a somewhat less degree, for mothers; and it is difficult to secure this when there is general laxity in the treatment of the marriage tie. But this is a difficult subject, which it is not possible to consider here in a detailed way.

6. *Educational Functions of the Family.*—The care of the young means primarily the preservation of life and health, through the provision of suitable food, drink, shelter, air, sunlight, and those other bodily needs that have been referred to as vegetative. But the development of the animal instincts, especially the need of movement and expression, have also to be considered; and it falls naturally within the province of the family to cultivate at least the rudimentary use of language, the control of the passions (which should, as far as possible, be self-control), and the elementary rules of social behaviour These may have to be delegated to others to some extent. In the case of the higher classes in his ideal community, Plato proposed that all these functions should be discharged by public officials. He did not suggest this in the case of the industrial class; but some in recent times

[1] See on this R. P. Porter's book on *Japan, the New World-Power*, chap. viii.

appear to be prepared to advocate this method as a general principle. But this appears to be somewhat contrary to nature. The natural affection of parents, and especially of mothers, for their offspring—an affection which they have in common with most of the lower animals—makes it true, in general, that no others are so well adapted to care for them in their early state of helplessness. It has to be admitted that in some parents the natural affection is comparatively weak, and that it is sometimes stronger in those who are not parents. It has to be admitted also that natural affection and instinct are not adequate guides for human beings in the nurture of the young. Those who have made a special study of children and their needs would, in many ways, be better fitted to deal with them; but it may at least be doubted whether this applies in general to the very earliest years of life. In dealing with questions of this kind, it seems best to begin with the consideration of what is the most satisfactory arrangement in normal cases. Those that are in any way abnormal can afterwards be dealt with on their merits. Obviously, where one or both of the parents die or are seriously ill or incapable, or are compelled to be much away from home, or when a child happens to be very different in temperament from its parents, the conditions are somewhat abnormal, and may call for abnormal treatment. But it is at least pretty safe to say that any arrangement that excluded altogether the element of parental care could only be regarded as a second-best alternative. Even when the children go to school, the family would appear to be the natural centre for some of the most important aspects of education, especially those relating to conduct and the cultivation of the affections.

There is also a larger sense in which the family is a natural centre of educational influence. The parents, as well as the children, may normally derive considerable educational benefit from it, and that in a variety of ways. We learn by teaching. The effort to convey ideas to immature minds nearly always serves to clear up the ideas of those who have to make the effort. Apart from this, there is generally a certain inspiration in any close intercourse with the young:

> A child, more than all other gifts
> That earth can offer to declining man,
> Brings hope with it and forward-looking thoughts.

Even those who cannot be described as declining often experience some expansion of soul in entering into the lives of those who are younger. It sometimes seems to be an added life to themselves; and though the vision of the new life is often overshadowed by disappointment, it can hardly fail to be something of a liberal education.

Another important educational influence is the interparental one. There are obvious differences, in general, between the sexes, in temperament, taste, and outlook on the world. In any well-assorted union, much is learned by intercourse between persons who thus differ, and who are yet bound together by natural affection and intimate association. It is no doubt partly for this reason, working somewhat unconsciously, that unions of this kind are very commonly formed between persons who are, in certain respects, markedly different. This is frequently observed even in ordinary friendship. "He was rich," Tennyson notes of Hallam, "where I was poor." The importance of this aspect of family life is one of the strong arguments in support of monogamy. In a polygamous relation, the position of women tends to become degraded, and can hardly be such as to yield that close personal tie of equal fellowship which monogamy makes possible. That the possibility is not always actualized does not invalidate the argument. It is fair, on the whole, to judge institutions by the best that they can give.

These aspects of the family, however, taken in conjunction with the problem of eugenics, previously referred to, make it apparent that the relationship we are here considering is not one to be lightly formed. Swift said that unhappy marriages were largely due to the fact that girls are often taught to make nets instead of cages. It hardly falls within our scope to consider how such dangers may best be obviated; but it may at least be urged that a judicious treatment of the problems connected with intersexual intercourse should have a prominent place in the general education of the young This is a matter to which a good deal of attention has recently been directed, and we need not dwell upon it here.[1]

7. *Economic Functions of the Family.*—The life of the family, as we have already noted, has an important economic aspect. As the care of the young, especially in its earlier stages, falls almost necessarily upon the mother, the father is normally called upon to provide for her support, as well as that of the children. Even in the case of some of the lower animals, this is to some extent true. The extent to which it is important in human life varies greatly at different times, in different countries, and among different classes of the community in the same country at the same time. In certain circumstances marriages tend to be arranged largely on financial grounds; and, even when they are not so arranged, financial considerations are seldom without some weight. Their weight might be somewhat diminished by some form of state endowment for motherhood; but it does not seem probable that this could do more than very partially remove the difficulty.

The economic needs of the family are sometimes prejudicial to its unity, and may seriously interfere with the discharge of its educational functions. In comparatively primitive conditions of life, the family may support itself by labour carried on within the home or in its immediate neighbourhood; but the growing complexity of life renders this less and less common.[2] Of course,

---

[1] I may refer to Mr. E. W. Pugh's book *The Eyes of a Child*, in which the normal attitude of the young on this subject, as well as on several others, is strikingly brought out.

[2] Mrs. Bosanquet has urged that it is more common even now than is generally supposed. See *The Family*, chap. viii.

there are great compensations for this change in the increased facilities for travelling, and in other amenities that a complex society provides. Still, it has to be reckoned among the circumstances that make it more and more apparent that the family cannot be regarded as self-sufficient. The father may be so constantly away as to be almost negligible for the special purposes of the family. That the mother should be frequently employed in outside work, not bearing on the life of the family, is probably, in general, a more remediable evil; and this is still more clearly the case with regard to the employment of young children in the discharge of economic functions at a time when their energies should be reserved for growth and education. At any rate, it is chiefly in such circumstances that the family is liable to fail as an educational centre.

Another difficulty that is largely of an economic kind may also be noted at this point. We have already referred to the fact that the *familia* meant primarily domestic slaves; and that, though the family has ceased to have any such significance, there are still some slight traces of the old way of regarding it. Hired labour, in general, unless carefully guarded, has some tendency to approximate to a servile condition. Under good conditions this is probably less true of domestic service than of most other kinds of employment; but it is rather more dependent on the conditions, and especially on the personalities of those concerned, than most others are. The somewhat close relationship that is involved in it is apt to be found irksome on both sides. Some have suggested that this might be remedied by the method of associated homes;[1] and, though it seems clear that such a method could not at present be adopted on an extensive scale, it is possible that the introduction of it in a considerable number of cases might help to give a different character to the way in which the relationship is conceived, and gradually

---

[1] Reference may be made to the writings of Miss J. H. Clapperton on this subject—especially *Scientific Meliorism*, chaps. xv and xvi, and *A Vision of the Future*, Part VI, chap. ii,

introduce freer conditions. At least, it is pretty clear that the less we retain of the old conception of the *familia*, and the more we can approximate to the conception of the family as based on love and on the nurture of children, the more are we likely to give it an opportunity of realizing its essential functions.

8. *Weaknesses of the Family.*—The various considerations that have now been referred to may enable us to realize that, though the family is deeply rooted in nature, and most of all in human nature, there are yet some circumstances that tend to weaken it and sometimes to make it ineffective and even pernicious in its influence. It may be well to try to give here a definite summing up of the chief respects in which such weakness is apparent. In general, it may be affirmed that they are connected with certain conflicts that tend to arise between the family and some other important interests in human life. The chief of these other interests would seem to be those of industry, politics, comradeship, and what may for the present be broadly characterized as culture. To each of these we may now briefly refer.

(a) The industrial aspect has been referred to in the preceding section, as disturbing the unity of the family. It is rather the converse aspect that has now to be noticed, i.e. the way in which the unity of the family may be prejudicial to industrial development; but of course these two influences are closely connected. If the family is liable to be disturbed by industrial movements, it almost inevitably follows that emphasis on the unity of the family must interfere with industrial development. It is worth noting that Plato, who was rather drastic in his general treatment of the family, does not appear to have felt any special difficulty on this score. Apparently he did not intend that the industrial class in his ideal community should have its family life interfered with. He probably assumed, in general, that children would follow the employment of their parents, or at least would not greatly diverge from these; except when they were definitely transferred at an early age to a different class. They would thus be prepared for their industrial occupations either at home or by some simple form of apprenticeship. In primitive communities, and in the less strongly industrialized regions even in highly developed countries, such a method may still be, to a large extent, practised; but the progress of industrial life makes it less and less possible. It becomes more and more true that individuals are not born into any particular kind of work, but that every career is open to all the citizens.[1] To make this workable, a suitable education, both general and special, has to be made accessible even for those whose work is to be of an industrial character. This may involve their partial withdrawal from home influences at a comparatively early age; and, if the conditions of family life make this difficult, the family may be felt to be a hindrance rather than a help. This difficulty, however, connects so closely with the next one, of which it may be regarded as a special aspect, that we may at once pass on.

(2) There is apt to be a certain conflict between the family and the state. This was the chief ground for Plato's strictures on the life of the family. He urged that those who are to be specially concerned with the defence and government of the state should be released from the limiting interests of the family. Now, in modern democracies at least, it would be generally recognized that industrial work is fully as important as military for the welfare of the state, and that every one has some concern in the proper government of the state. Hence the distinction between different classes in this respect seems no longer tenable. But it remains true that there is apt to be some conflict between the claims that the family makes upon an individual and those that are made by the state. In particular, the claims of the state to provide a suitable education for all its citizens, and to secure that they are adequately fitted to fulfil their special functions in the life of the larger community,

[1] Of course, this is still very far from being the case, as Mrs. Bosanquet has shown in the chapter already referred to.

interferes somewhat with the claims for parental control that are apt to be put forward from the point of view of the family. It is in this connection that it is particularly important to have a clear view of the essential function of the family. The difficulty is largely solved, at least in theory, when it is fully recognized that the authority of the parents is only that of councillors; that, properly speaking, the child is the sovereign of the family until he becomes the subject of the state (in which also he may eventually acquire a partial sovereignty).

(c) The claims of friendship or comradeship are also apt to be somewhat inimical to the unity of the family. The family, at its best, is somewhat like a garden, sheltered from the world; and there is often a danger that it may become rather like a hot-house. This is especially the case when the housing accommodation is inadequate; and it is one of the circumstances that give urgency to the housing problem. It is partly the desire for friendship or comradeship—a natural human need—that drives men out from the limitations of the home circle to clubs and taverns.[1] To find a proper balance between the claims of family life and those of the wider life of human brotherhood is not the least of the general difficulties of human life. It is hardly necessary to add that the particular difficulty in question is a specially delicate one when the friendships that are sought involve relations between persons of opposite sexes. The danger of licence in such cases is apt to lead to some overstressing of the limitations of the family. It would seem that difficulties of this kind could only be satisfactorily met by an ampler provision for friendly intercourse under conditions that do not introduce special dangers.

(d) Besides the claims of industry, the state, and friendly intercourse, the larger demands of religion, art, science, and those other human interests that may be described as cultural, are apt to be somewhat inimical

---

[1] Charles Lamb's short essay on the saying that "Home is home, though it is never so homely" is worth referring to in this connection.

to the family. The artist tends to become something of a "Bohemian." He finds himself hampered by the petty interests of the family, and often by its economic needs, which necessitate the production of "pot-boilers," check his free creative activities, and hinder the realization of his artistic ideals. Similarly, St. Paul and others have felt that the dedicated life of devotion to moral and religious progress was incompatible with the limitations of the family. Yet the withdrawal from it has prejudicial effects on human life as a whole, and probably in the end even on the ideals of the artist or the saint. It would at least be a misfortune for the world if its finest spirits produced no offspring. "From fairest creatures we desire increase"; and surely not least from those who are fair within. Galton, in his book on *Hereditary Genius* (pp. 344-5), has a striking passage on the harm that was done to civilization by the action of the Mediæval Church. "The Church," he says, "having first captured all the gentle natures and condemned them to celibacy, made another sweep of her huge nets, this time fishing in stirring waters, to capture those who were the most fearless, truth-seeking, and intelligent, in their modes of thought, and therefore the most suitable parents of a high civilization, and put a strong check, if not a direct stop, to their progeny. Those she reserved on these occasions, to breed the generations of the future, were the servile, the indifferent, and, again, the stupid." It is possible that Galton somewhat exaggerated the extent to which such qualities are inherited; but any one who will reflect on the valuable work that has been done in recent times by people who were the sons or daughters of clergymen may realize how much the world would have lost by their enforced celibacy. That there might have been some compensations, may of course be admitted. Even with reference to mediæval times, it may be allowed that the world has profited both by the meditations of the recluse and by the sufferings of the martyr.

Reflection on such difficulties has led some modern thinkers, as well as Plato, to seek freer modes of life, at least for certain types of individual and certain forms of activity. Mr. Russell is a noteworthy advocate of proposals of this kind.[1] But, in a free community, as distinguished from one in which there is a system of castes, it is difficult to have different laws, or even widely different customs, for different classes of people. Perhaps some general simplification of the conditions of life may provide a more satisfactory solution. But we may be better able to consider this at a later stage. In any case, as Mrs. Bosanquet says,[2] " Even if the world could carry on without the Family, it could not afford to lose the qualities which would go with it. It is a sombre world as it is, and no shade or tone of feeling that makes for depth and variety and richness can be spared from it. To reject the source of so much warmth and beauty because it sometimes fails, would be like banishing the sun from the sky because it is sometimes covered with clouds."

---

[1] See his *Principles of Social Reconstruction*, chap. vi. I am doubtful whether he has sufficiently thought out the consequences of his proposals.

[2] *The Family*, p. 245.

CHAPTER II

EDUCATIONAL INSTITUTIONS

1. *The General Significance of Education.* — Education may be understood in a wider or in a narrower sense. In the wider sense it is a process that goes on throughout life, and that is promoted by almost every experience in life. It may even be said to be the chief end of life.[1] It means, in this sense, the general process by which personality is developed, and by which persons are enabled to realize their relations to one another and to the universe in which they live. This comprehensive conception of education is well emphasized in the account that Plato gives in the *Republic* of the influences by which those who are to occupy the highest positions in the ideal community are to be shaped and developed. But it would be generally recognized by modern thinkers that it would not really be possible to devise a definite scheme of this kind even for a particular type of individuals, and still less for the community as a whole.

Understanding education in this large sense, we have to recognize that a considerable part of it—sometimes even the most important part—comes to us unconsciously. It comes from the problems of life with which we have to deal, from the influences and suggestions of nature, from intercourse with our fellow-men, often from our failures and sufferings.

In a narrower sense, it may be taken to mean any consciously directed effort to develop and cultivate our powers.

[1] This aspect of education is dealt with below, Book III, Chapter III.

Goethe, for instance, seems to have made the complete unfolding of all his capacities a main object—perhaps the main object—throughout his life. Shakespeare may have been, essentially, even more fully developed; but it would appear to have been in a more unconscious way. Professor Dewey has used [1] the expression *intentional* education to mark the distinction between that which comes to us unconsciously and that which implies a definite purpose. But even such a conscious self-cultivation as that of Goethe would not usually be described as education. The term is most commonly used for a process consciously organized by the state or the family or some other authority for the development of young people towards some end regarded as important by the authority in question—an end which may or may not involve a general cultivation of personality. It may be best for the present to regard it in this somewhat narrow sense, in which it leads to the establishment of definite social institutions, reserving its larger meaning for further consideration at a later stage.

When we understand education in this limited sense, its social significance is probably best seen by regarding it as the transition from the family to the state, or at least to some larger community of which the child is to become a member. The preparatory stages of education are normally given within the family itself, but its later stages are usually handed over to schools and colleges. Even when education is more privately conducted, it tends to be guided, to some extent, by the same aims and methods as those that are adopted in schools and colleges. Within the family, as we have urged, the child is essentially the sovereign; but the larger community seeks to prepare him to be its servant, though he may perhaps eventually become one of its masters or guides.

The detailed consideration of the aims and methods of education must be left to those—happily now a considerable number—who have made it their special study.

[1] See his book on *Democracy and Education*, pp. 22-4 and 45.

All that can be here attempted is a general survey of the functions that it fulfils in the life of an organized community.

2. *The Functions of the School.*—The primary function of the school would seem to be that of initiating the child into the life of the larger community. The natures of children probably differ almost as widely from each other as those of adults; yet there appear to be some general statements with regard to them that may properly be affirmed, and some that may properly be denied. Professor Dewey[1] and others have rightly, I think, protested against the view that the child is by nature an egoist. On the other hand, the worship of the child is sometimes carried to excess. The doctrine that heaven lies about us in our infancy must be regarded, on the whole, as a perversion of the Platonic conception of the latent potentialities that we bring with us into the world. There is a charming innocence in childhood, and a readiness to appreciate everything by which it is surrounded; but it can hardly be maintained that there is present in it any definite conception of a common good. It seems, in general, truer to think of the child as bringing with him the instincts of a more or less benevolent despot. He has to learn to be a constitutional monarch, and by degrees an equal citizen with others. Unhappily, he is often taught this rather too early and too sharply. Sometimes he is even taught to be a slave, and to surrender the birthright of his all-embracing interests. This is now generally acknowledged to be the crime of *lèse majesté*. But of course it does not follow that the child is simply to be left alone, and trusted to unfold himself like a flower. What has chiefly to be imparted to him is his heritage in the common life that he is gradually to share. For this purpose, he has to acquire the language of his people, in which the knowledge, the insight, the purposes and ideals—unhappily also the prejudices and the limitations —of the community are largely embodied. It is evident

[1] *Democracy and Education*, pp. 28 and 52.

that this heritage can only be very gradually acquired, and the order of its communication must be determined by a careful study of the development of the human mind in general, and by sympathetic insight into the needs of particular individuals. This, of course, as is now pretty universally recognized, implies a considerable limitation in the size of classes.

It seems obvious enough also that the earliest initiation of the child should be into what is simplest and best in the traditions of his community. Golden apples on vessels of silver should be first set before him. Plato emphasized this very well in his account of the use of music and poetry in early education; though, no doubt, his suggestion of an expurgated edition of the Homeric poems (perhaps never very seriously meant) is rather out of date. What is wanted is to a considerable extent supplied by the simpler kinds of poetry that Wordsworth and others have provided, by the fairy tales that are so plentiful in many modern literatures—certainly not least in our own. The old saying, "Let me make the songs of a people, and whoever will may make its laws," retains its force; at least if songs are interpreted in a sufficiently liberal sense. A fine thought or a deep experience enshrined in a beautiful story, or embodied in an immortal phrase, sinks readily into the heart, lingers long in the memory, is stored up as a joy for ever, and becomes an inspiration throughout the whole of life. Laws, on the other hand, are chiefly important as giving definiteness and permanence to the best traditions of a people, which must be engraven on their souls before they can have much efficacy on the statute-books.

Gradually, however, the child's relations to his actual surroundings have to be made more precisely apparent. The study of nature is now generally recognized as one of the most valuable, as it is certainly one of the most fascinating methods of opening up the mind. It begins as observation, but soon involves reflection; and it leads on easily to the study of human life in its more obvious features. This at once opens up some of the simpler questions of civic and moral obligation, and leads on by degrees to the consideration of the more prominent features of human history. Interest in history readily connects itself with the acquisition of some knowledge of the language of those peoples that have played specially important parts in historical evolution.

But, along with all this, it is of course of the highest importance that the child should have been learning to make use of what he studies—to do, as well as to know and appreciate. He may learn to sketch natural objects, he may invent simple stories for himself, he may take part in the acting of simple plays, he may compose descriptions, propound problems, and construct simple objects, having some regard for their beauty as well as for their utility.[1] And, of course, it goes without saying that he should be provided with the means for the necessary physical exercise and recreation in which he may at the same time be learning valuable lessons in co-operation.

As he becomes more capable of analytical thought, he will naturally begin to gain some understanding of those subjects that supply a key to the structure both of human life and of the surrounding world—such as grammar, arithmetic, geometry, and, eventually, some rudiments of logic, the simpler conceptions of morals, economics, and politics, and some insight into the religious ideas by which men have sought to interpret the universe in which they live. I suppose it is almost self-evident, however, that they should not be expected to commit themselves to any religious creed or to any form of party politics till they are mature enough to weigh the arguments on different sides. But no doubt they are likely to be forming some opinions for themselves, even before they are mature for them; and in this there may be no harm.

[1] The importance of this aspect of education has been emphasized by many recent writers. It may be enough to refer to Professor Dewey's books on *Democracy and Education* and *The School and Society*, to those by Mr. E. G. A. Holmes on *What is and What might be* and *In Defence of What might be*, to Sir Rabindranath Tagore's *Personality*, and to *The Play Way* by Mr. Caldwell Cook But many others might be mentioned.

Further, it is of great importance that, as boys and girls approach adolescence, some understanding of the difficulties and dangers connected with the relations between the sexes, and of the general problems of the life of the family, should be made accessible in a clear and definite form. Their studies of nature and of human history, and their observation of the life around them, would have formed a good preparation for this.

By such an education it may be hoped that at least those who have been well born will have been well nurtured; and that even those who have been less fortunate in their birth will have acquired some love of knowledge and wisdom, some appreciation of beauty, and some degree of the spirit of devotion to the common good. This much, I should suppose, ought to be made readily accessible to every one who is to become a citizen of a civilized community. But the detailed consideration of the order in which the different elements are to be taken, and of the methods by which they are to be treated, does not fall within our province.

3. *Technical Education.*—By such means as those that have now been somewhat sketchily indicated, the child may be supposed to have been gradually prepared for the general duties of good citizenship within the particular community to which he belongs. But the good citizen must not only be good in general, but good in some special way. Hence his general education has to be followed by some special training of a more technical kind, preparing him for the particular function for which he is found to be fitted by natural ability and circumstances. The ascertainment of this is in many cases not easy, and obviously should not be attempted at too early a stage. Hence it is important that a somewhat prolonged period of education should be provided for all, except those who are manifestly incapable of profiting by it. In the case of some of the more technical forms of work, however, a considerable part of the necessary preparation may be acquired by some form of apprenticeship, and, in the case

of girls, at home. Where any special manual dexterity is needed, it is no doubt necessary that it should be acquired early.[1] Those who have a special gift for music, for instance, usually begin to display it at a very early age; and perhaps any aptitude of this kind may be a ground for some modification in the general scheme of education. A certain elasticity is a very essential feature in any good scheme.

4. *Higher Education.*—The kinds of education that have so far been roughly sketched would appear to be, in some form or other, required for all the citizens. The forms would vary considerably according to their individual capacities and the kinds of work for which they were found to be specially fitted, and the period devoted to different stages might be longer or shorter. In general, it would probably be safe to assume that the sort of education so far in view would not be completed before the age of sixteen and would not usually extend much beyond twenty. Those who are fitted for work that requires a more elaborate preparation, such as the advancement of knowledge, artistic creation, the applications of the more complex sciences (including law and medicine) to technical problems, the vocation of teaching in its various aspects, or organizing and administrative functions, would generally want the kind of education that is provided in colleges and universities; and it is important to have a general view of the relation of this kind of education to the more elementary forms that have been already referred to.

Unfortunately, the distinctions between schools, technical institutions, colleges, and universities are not very clearly

[1] Recent experience, however, seems to point to the conclusion that those whose general intelligence has been well developed can adapt themselves to different kinds of work more readily than had been commonly supposed. It is chiefly in the higher forms of artistic work, and in those industries that are dependent on mathematical calculations, that an elaborate preparation of a specialized kind appears to be necessary. In general, the cultivation of an adaptable intelligence is the most important thing.

drawn in our country. In Germany the system is more easily intelligible; and probably the new organization of education in Japan is the most perfect that has so far been elaborated.[1] We cannot here enter into the consideration of the detailed arrangements in different countries and different parts of the same country, but can only attempt a brief indication of what appears to be the best way of drawing the most important distinctions.

What are called colleges are often, either partly or wholly, institutions for some form of technical instruction; and even what are called university colleges generally include some work that is of this character. We must here regard this as belonging properly to the type of educational work that was referred to in the preceding section; and it will be convenient to treat a university college as being primarily and essentially quite distinct from this. A university, again, is often understood in this country as being little more than an examining body. In Germany, however, it is pretty definitely understood to mean an institution in which a particular kind of education is given —a kind that is, on the whole, clearly distinguishable from that given in university colleges, and even from most of that which is given in the Universities of Oxford and Cambridge.

I conceive the main function of a university college to be that of providing a form of liberal education of a higher kind than that which is given in schools. The normal age of students in such institutions may be taken as lying between eighteen and twenty-one. Their studies are somewhat more specialized than is commonly the case in schools, but still aim rather at general cultivation than at specialized knowledge or skill. They are designed, on the whole, for those whose abilities and prospects are such as to fit them for some form of leadership in the life of the community. For this it is important that they should have a fuller grasp of the general problems of human life than is usually to be gained in schools.

[1] See R. P. Porter, *Japan, the New World-Power*, chap. ix, and for a more detailed treatment, Baron Kikuchi's *Japanese Education*.

Some general study of the main problems of philosophy and social science would seem to be naturally an almost essential part of this type of education. In Japan this appears to be pretty definitely recognized, and perhaps also in France and some other countries. In England there is some tendency to ignore this. The main features of historical development would also seem to be too important to be omitted. What other studies should be specially pursued might probably be left largely to individual taste, together with some consideration of the special work that is to be afterwards pursued.[1]

In a university, on the other hand, if we understand this term in its stricter sense, the studies are definitely specialized, and are designed to qualify the students (usually between the ages of twenty-one and twenty-five) for some specific work of the kind that has been already indicated. Its relations to a university college are, on a higher level, pretty nearly the same as those of a technical institution to a school. It seeks to make accessible all the knowledge and skill that is available in particular departments, and to prepare the way for further advance. It must be admitted that in this country there are hardly any institutions that are definitely and exclusively of this type. What we call universities generally combine, in a not very efficient manner, some work of this kind with a good deal that belongs more properly to the university college, the technical institution, or even the school.

[1] This paragraph was written before I had seen Professor Burnet's *Higher Education and the War*. He suggests (especially on p. 167) that it would be well to adopt the distinction between college and university that is commonly recognized in the United States, the former giving general culture and the latter specialized instruction and training. What he says about the importance of recognizing the colleges as distinct both from the school and the university seems to me very admirable and very timely. Some Americans are inclined to regard even Oxford and Cambridge as being colleges, in their sense of the word, rather than universities, owing to the relatively small provision that is made in them for post-graduate studies. But of course there is some exaggeration in such a view.

munities there tends to be such a gulf between those who have leisure for the cultivation of their minds and those whose opportunities for this are very restricted. Hence it becomes an important element in education to create a better understanding between these types. University Settlements have this object more particularly in view; and it is also aimed at by some more definitely religious organizations, as well as by some forms of art. But we may have a better opportunity of considering these at a later stage.[1] In the meantime, some reference to the place of leisure in education may be useful.

6. *Education and Leisure.*—It is not without significance that the terms "school" and "scholar" are derived from the Greek word for leisure. Unconscious education may often come to us in the course of the active business of life; but conscious education at least usually implies some detachment from that business. "Es bildet ein Talent sich in der Stille."[2] The young person who is receiving a definitely organized education is hardly yet a citizen. He has not yet found the place in which his service to the community is to be rendered; and it is in general true that, if he is to continue his educational development after he has found his place (unless his place happens to be an essentially educational one), he must have some leisure from the specific duties of that place. Further, as we have just noted, it is important that the education that fills his leisure time should not be exclusively concerned with the special duties of his station. Now, such a detached time, suitable for use in educational advancement, is not always readily to be obtained. Even in the early years of life there are often obstacles in the way. Hence education tends to be thought of, not as the natural prerogative of every citizen, but rather as

[1] See Book III, Chapter II.
[2] "Talent is cultivated in retirement." Goethe contrasts this with character, which is cultivated rather by active contact with the world. Of course, this antithesis must not be overstrained. Both are cultivated at once from within and from without.

the special privilege of the few who have leisure. Even Plato gave countenance to this view. Thus leisure came to be highly prized, as that by whose means the definitely human ends are to be secured, and became contrasted with the life of continuous labour which is the lot of slaves or of an inferior class, and which is hardly to be reckoned as human at all. This does not of course mean that those who labour continuously have learned nothing at all. What it does mean is that they have learned only what is immediately useful. The special distinction of the free man is that he studies what is not immediately useful. Thus there comes to be a certain antithesis between culture and utility; and the more ornamental aspects of education are regarded as more valuable than those that can be shown to be serviceable. The man who is a "gentleman and scholar" comes to be distinguished from those who are neither; and he is sometimes rather apt to pride himself on the distinction and to seek to maintain it. This is one of those cases of what Mr. Veblen has characterized as "reputable waste," of which many instances may be found wherever there is a "leisure class."[1] It is one of the difficulties of civilized life. On the one hand, it is a source of variety and beauty, and often the most valuable discoveries have been made in the pursuit of what is apparently useless. On the other hand, it is somewhat opposed to the conception of a common good, and tends to interfere seriously with the unity of social life. But the whole question of the significance of leisure and its proper use is not a purely educational one, at least in the narrower sense of the term; and we shall be in a better position to deal with it at a later stage. In the meantime it may suffice to state that it is important that all citizens should have sufficient leisure to be able

---

[1] Mr. Veblen's book on *A Leisure Class* deals very fully with this subject; but he perhaps hardly does justice to the importance of the freedom and exuberance of life that is made possible by leisure. This is specially emphasized by Sir Rabindranath Tagore in his book on *Personality*—especially in the chapter on "What is Art?"

to give some cultivation to their whole nature as human beings, and not to sink into the slavish position of being merely machines for the performance of particular services; and that, on the other hand, no one should be regarded as simply a human being without a specific obligation.[1] If this is admitted, it seems clear that the education of every one should be partly for work and partly for leisure. But the right balance between these sides is not easy to establish, and we have already noticed some of the agencies by which the difficulties that thus arise may be partially met.

7. *The State and Education.*—The cultivation of good citizenship in its various aspects is so essential to the life of a community that it can hardly be left exclusively to the efforts of private individuals. It needs a well-planned organization; and it is naturally regarded as one of the functions of the State to provide this. On the other hand, as it has to be adapted to the special needs of particular localities, and even to the aptitude of particular individuals, it seems clear that it is not desirable that its details should be under any very rigid central control. The function of the State in this connection would seem to be mainly that of providing opportunities and trying to ensure that they are effectively utilized. Provision for the preparation of suitable teachers is of course specially important for this purpose; and, when the right persons have been secured, it is, I suppose, hardly less important that they should have the fullest freedom in the exercise of their functions. One might almost as well seek to control the brush of a painter or the pen of a poet as the work of a skilled educator. Like the painter or the poet, however, he may be all the better for some occasional

---

[1] Green's statement about this (*Works*, vol. iii, pp. 475-6) has often been quoted; but perhaps it will bear quoting once more. " I confess to hoping for a time when that phrase [' the education of a gentleman '] will have lost its meaning because the sort of education which alone makes the gentleman in any true sense will be within the reach of all."

criticism; and this also can, with advantage, be provided by the State. But in this case also we may be in a better position to deal with some aspects of the work of the State, in relation to education, after we have considered the general nature and functions of the State.

But there are some signs of improvement, and I have been trying to indicate the arrangement that ought to be aimed at.[1] It is well to bear in mind that, if education is taken to mean the general development and cultivation of the faculties of an individual, it is only schools and colleges that are specially concerned with this. Technical institutions and universities aim rather at special forms of instruction and training, and at the promotion of research in particular departments. The two objects are distinct, and it is very confusing to mix them up with one another.

5. *Supplementary Education.*—We have already noted that the education that is supplied by definite institutions is only a part of the educative influences that are derived from the experiences of life. But, even without regarding education in so large a sense as this, it may be urged that a large part—perhaps even the main part—of the value of what educational institutions provide, is to be found in the suggestions and guidance that they offer for the further pursuit of particular studies. When they fail to do this, they may very well be prejudicial rather than useful. Byron's reading of Horace at school is said to have had the result that he never wanted to read Horace again; and it is probable that similar results are often experienced. On the other hand, any good education makes us want to continue, if not exactly with the same things, at least with other things for which those have prepared us. Those who have sufficient leisure and resources can do this without much difficulty; but those whose leisure and resources are small are more in need of continued guidance after their definite period of organized education is completed, and this is especially true when their education within that period has been for any reason curtailed or defective. This need is partly met by a variety of supple-

[1] Professor Burnet, in the book to which I have just referred, is mainly occupied in urging the importance of the college. I think it is equally important that we should have real universities, in which the work of research could be thoroughly carried on.

mentary agencies, such as continuation schools, University Extension lectures, the classes of the Workers' Educational Association, reading circles, and books of a simple and readily accessible type, such as those contained in the Home University Library.

There is, however, a further consideration that it is important to notice at this point. We have been regarding education as an instrument for the development of the good citizen and for fitting him to find and occupy the station for which he is best fitted and to fulfil its duties. It is possible to exaggerate the importance of this kind of preparation. Probably most modern readers would be disposed to think that it is somewhat exaggerated in Plato's *Republic*. Socrates is represented as urging against dramatic performances that they cause men to accustom themselves to play a variety of parts, whereas each one has his own special function to fulfil. It is no doubt sometimes necessary to dwell upon this. " He who would accomplish anything," as Goethe said, " must learn to limit himself." Perhaps the lively Athenians were specially in need of such a warning; and perhaps it is one that would naturally occur to such versatile geniuses as Plato and Goethe. But many are more liable to err on the side of contraction than on that of expansion. The mere need of relaxation makes it undesirable to restrict oneself too closely; and, besides this, it is important that fellow-citizens should understand one another, should be able to appreciate one another's work and sympathize with one another's difficulties. Hence some variety of studies is desirable, besides various forms of social intercourse, among which dramatic performances may well have a place. Much of what is necessary in this way comes readily enough in the way of recreation; but there are some directions in which it seems important to give it a more definite organization. It sometimes happens that there is too great a separation between different classes in a community. There would probably have been such a gulf in Plato's ideal community between the industrial class and the others; and certainly in modern com-

CHAPTER III

INDUSTRIAL INSTITUTIONS

1. *The Significance of Labour.*—Some confusion is apt to be occasioned by the use of such terms as "work" and "labour." It is customary to distinguish workers or labourers from other classes in the community—a distinction, it should be remembered, that does not at all correspond to the Platonic distinction of classes in the ideal community. The industrial class, according to Plato's conception, includes all who render any useful service to the community other than that of military duty and the work of political and educational organization. The modern distinction is rather between work that is mainly manual and other kinds of service, and it consequently has some tendency to coincide with the distinction between poor and rich; whereas, on Plato's scheme, all the rich at least, and, one may add, all the poor as well, would be in the industrial class.[1] The other classes would have neither poverty nor riches, but just what is necessary for a cultured life. According to the modern usage, artists, teachers, and even those engaged in such professions as law and medicine, or in the organizing and management of industrial operations, are not usually regarded as workers. There is of course some ground for this distinction; and indeed perhaps, in its general spirit, it is not far removed from the Greek distinction. Purely manual work is in many ways different from that which involves a considerable degree of intellectual

[1] The poorest would presumably be slaves, though Plato does not explicitly say so.

cultivation or artistic skill, and tends to make a real difference in men's general outlook on life. But the difference cannot be very sharply drawn; and it seems best to begin at least by interpreting work or labour as including all forms of exertion that are directed to the promotion of some definite social end. What is done merely or mainly for personal enjoyment is rightly regarded as play, though it may sometimes be quite as strenuous as work, and may often have some indirect social utility of a high order. Taking labour in this wide sense, we may notice several distinctions that appear to be of some importance.

(1) Some labour is directed to the supply of what we have referred to as vegetative or economic needs: other kinds of labour are directed to the supply of needs that are rather those of the animal nature or of the more purely human aspects of life. But evidently this distinction cannot be very sharply drawn. A worker in wood is supplying a purely economic need when he is helping to build a simple cottage for shelter; but he is not supplying such a need when he is making instruments to be used by an artist, in war, in a game, or when he is making a desk for a writer of fiction or of works on philosophy. Still, the distinction is one of some importance; and it is generally possible to say that a particular kind of work is mainly concerned with the supply of economic needs, or that it is mainly of a different type.

(2) Some labour is undertaken by the choice of the person who undertakes it. Other kinds are undertaken under direct compulsion (as in slavery) or under the pressure of economic necessity or of social requirements or conventions. Here again the distinction is not one that can be very sharply drawn. When an artist produces a picture from the impulse of creation or self-expression or to embody an ideal of beauty or convey some moral or religious idea, he may be said to be choosing freely his mode of work. When, on the other hand, he produces a "pot-boiler," or a work specially ordered by a patron, he may still be partly free in some details of

the execution, but he is largely determined by needs that are economic or conventional, or by the arbitrary choice of others. Similar distinctions may be drawn in many other cases. There is very little work that is quite freely chosen. Even when it is nominally free, there is in most cases some pretty definite element of constraint.

(3) Some labour is disagreeable and exhausting. Some other kinds are their own reward, by yielding enjoyment and recuperation. This might be expressed by saying that some have positive value and some have negative value But this distinction is seldom to be found simply in the nature of the work. It depends largely on the attitude of the worker. In general, what is freely chosen is pleasant, even when it is difficult ; and what is done under constraint is disagreeable, even when it is easy. Men enjoy doing many things in play which would be thought extremely irksome if done under compulsion. Much depends also on individual aptitude, on the state of health at the time, on the presence of other interests that are more attractive, and on a variety of other circumstances. Still, it is possible to say that there are some kinds of labour that are generally irksome, and that are undertaken only as means to an end, while others are to a large extent ends in themselves.

(4) Some labour is almost purely manual. Other kinds involve thought or artistic skill.

(5) Some labour, though socially useful, is not primarily undertaken for this reason, but rather for personal gratification or for some personal reward. Other labour is undertaken from a sense of duty, or at least definitely as social service. Here again it is often difficult to make a sharp distinction. Sometimes a particular kind of work is undertaken as social service, but the special form that it takes is determined by personal inclination or by the expectation of reward. Nevertheless, the distinction can be broadly drawn, and is of some importance.

Now, though these distinctions are not very sharp, they do serve to mark important differences ; and I think it may be said that, in the narrower sense of the word, labour is generally applied to those forms of human effort that are mainly or primarily (1) directed towards the satisfaction of economic needs, (2) undertaken to some extent under compulsion or pressure, (3) in some degree disagreeable and exhausting, (4) almost purely manual, or at least not involving thought or skill of a highly specialized kind. The fifth distinction that has been referred to can hardly be applied to modes of effort that are, in this restricted sense, labour.

For our present purpose, however, this restricted sense is not the one that is important. What concerns us, for the present, is effort directed towards the satisfaction of needs that are mainly economic, whether such effort is free or compulsory, manual or intellectual, disagreeable and exhausting or otherwise. Though the term "industry" is not usually confined to work of this kind, yet such work constitutes the largest and most typical part of the effort that is commonly understood by the term; and it will be convenient for our present purpose to interpret it in this sense.

2. *Division of Labour.*—Whether we take labour in a wider or in a narrower sense, it is in general true that each individual can only with advantage undertake some special kind of it; and this becomes more and more true as communities increase in size and in complexity. Sometimes, of course, the kind of work that is done by a particular individual may contain a good deal of variety within it. An actor may play many parts, though he could hardly play all parts satisfactorily. A writer may deal with many subjects, and some, such as Goethe, are almost encyclopædic in their range; but one does not look to such writers for the precise details of any subject. It is especially, however, in the satisfaction of economic needs that the division of function is most prominent. There may be some who are almost universal providers, but not universal producers. Economic needs are the most universal and the most insistent; and the satisfac-

tion of them occupies a larger place in human effort than any others. Hence the importance of a definite organization of the production and distribution of the goods that are required for their satisfaction has been more definitely felt than in any other case. It was primarily in connection with such needs that Plato was led to emphasize the importance of division of labour; and a similar emphasis has been laid upon it, with special reference to modern conditions of work, by Adam Smith [1] and by most later writers on economics.[2] Almost every kind of work requires some special kind of skill for its satisfactory performance, though it may only be the kind of skill that is involved in manual dexterity. Employment in other work would sometimes tend to destroy the skill that is needed, or at least to prevent it from being steadily and persistently applied. In any case, time is apt to be lost in passing from one occupation to another; though occasionally there is some compensation for this in the freshness and zest that is gained by a certain variety. It is also important, in dealing with the prime necessities of life, that, when anything is urgently wanted, some one should always be available to supply it. This applies most of all to medical attendance, but also to food and drink, and, in a somewhat less degree, to clothing, warmth, and shelter. Even for things that are not quite so necessary, it would be very inconvenient not to be readily able to find some one whose special business it is to supply them. Hence, on the whole, it has to be recognized that, in the purely industrial domain at least, it is essential in general that each one should have his own special kind of work to perform.[3] And, though this is not quite so apparent in other kinds of work, it is pretty clear that everything is done most thoroughly by those who are not distracted by a variety of occupation. It

[1] *Wealth of Nations*, Book I, chaps. i–iii.
[2] See Marshall's *Principles of Economics*, Book IV, chap. ix.
[3] The more general aspects of this subject were well brought out by Mr. Bradley in the chapter on " My Station and its Duties " in his *Ethical Studies*.

is probable that even the literary work of Goethe suffered from lack of concentration.

3. *Co-operation.*—It has to be recognized, further, that the various forms of work have to fit into each other. This is true, in some degree, of all forms of work; but here again it is most obviously true with reference to work of the purely economic type, on account of the universality and urgency of the needs to which it ministers. These needs constitute a connected system of requirements relating to man's bodily nature; and it is important that they should all be adequately provided for. Not only has each his proper task; but there must be a sufficiency of all essential modes of work, all co-operating towards the common end, which is the maintenance of life and health. The securing of this requires organization and directing skill; and the effort to supply these needs, though not commonly described as labour, is evidently as essential a form of work as any other. The consideration of this and of the difficult problems connected with the adjustment of demand and supply, belongs to the province of the economist; and, having due regard to the importance of division of labour, we can only thus briefly allude to these subjects.

4. *Land and Capital in Relation to Labour.*—Labour of an economic kind is not creative. It may be doubted, indeed, whether any form of human labour can properly be said to be so. Poets and artists are sometimes said to be creative; and it is no doubt true that, in their most perfect activities, what they contribute is much more important than the material with which they deal. Yet it is obvious that they do deal with certain materials, which partly help and partly obstruct them in their efforts. Though it is an exaggeration to say, as is sometimes done, that a statue pre-exists in the block of marble from which it is hewn, yet it is true that the marble lends itself more or less readily to particular modes of treatment. But with instances of this kind we are not

at present concerned. In labour of the more purely industrial type, the material with which the worker has to deal is, in general, more obvious, and undergoes less modification than it does in artistic work. Often the labour simply moves it from one place to another, as when water is conveyed from a lake to supply a town. The seed that the farmer sows is not brought to fruition by his efforts, though without his efforts it would go to waste or be inaccessible for human use. Moreover, the labour that is bestowed on particular material is hardly ever unaided. Tools or machinery or horses or other animals are employed in almost all kinds of industrial work.

There are thus two factors, besides labour, involved in the production of economic goods. These have sometimes been referred to as land and capital. The latter term meant originally the *capita*, or heads of cattle and horses, with which a farm was stocked; so that both the terms here used referred primarily to simple forms of agricultural labour. As applied to modern industry, they are very misleading. It is still true, however, that we can distinguish the raw material (though it is hardly ever quite raw) from the instruments that are used in dealing with it. The latter are themselves the results of previous labour that has been applied to particular materials. Even horses have been caught, tamed, bred, reared, tended and trained for special purposes with a great deal of human effort; and it is still more obvious that tools and machinery have been produced by the application of much labour to materials extracted from the earth. Hence what has to be said, in general, is that economic goods are the results of the application of labour to raw materials; and that the labour applied at any one time is dependent on a great deal of other labour that has been applied in the past. It is, of course, very apparent also that labour must here be understood in a wide sense, as including the efforts of thought involved in the consideration of the goods that it is necessary to provide, in inventing and constructing the necessary instruments, in organizing the methods of production, in managing their application, and in conveying the products to the places where they are required.

It is well to bear in mind that the same distinctions apply to artistic work. The poet, for instance, works on certain raw materials, such as the things seen and heard in the world around him. He is also dependent for his methods of treatment on the labours of his predecessors. This is especially apparent in the more elaborate forms of artistic work. The Greek dramatists, for instance, invented very little. They made use of material that was already shaped by long traditions, and they dealt with it by methods that had become largely conventional. Yet it remains true that what is most valuable in their productions is the particular way in which they applied these methods. Similarly, it is in general true that neither the material nor the methods of treatment that Shakespeare used were actually his own invention; and it is very obvious that the work of such writers as Virgil and Milton is dependent at almost every point on the writings of their predecessors. Their land consists partly of inherited traditions: their capital is the methods of treatment that have been elaborated by others. Thus the three factors roughly described as land, capital, and labour, may be said to be involved in all forms of production, but most simply and obviously in those modes of production that are essentially economic or industrial.

5. *Property.*—If the various factors in production are to be effectively used, it is evident that they must, in some degree, be under the control of those who use them.

The conditions of this control, however, may and do naturally vary very much in different cases. The raw material must usually be completely at the disposal of the person or persons who work upon it. A sculptor must, in general, have his block of marble, and a painter his canvas, entirely under their personal control Even a poet must have paper or its equivalent; though most of his other materials, such as the sights and sounds of nature, need only be readily accessible. The farmer, in like manner, must have some control over his land; the worker in wood or metal must be able to use these substances freely; and similarly with other workers. How far their ownership should extend is a more difficult question. The control of capital, again, is generally somewhat more complicated. As its employment seldom means that it is used up, it need not be permanently held. Horses and cattle can be transferred pretty readily from one to another. It is evidently convenient that portable tools should usually belong to the person who works with them. Fixed machinery, on the other hand, has to be controlled by some relatively stable authority, generally by those who organize or manage the works within which it is used. The chief capital of an artist, on the other hand, lies in his memories and acquired aptitudes, which cannot easily be taken from him or transferred to another. Finally, labour itself may either be freely controlled by the person who exerts it or be under the control of others. There are many possible gradations here, from complete slavery, through serfdom and hired labour, to work regulated simply by the demand of a market and, last of all, to work that is chosen quite freely by him who performs it. The first type, and even the second, have practically disappeared from the civilized world: the last type is, in any full sense, extremely rare. Most work is done either for a wage or for the sale of the product in some form or other. Even what is done for fame or honour is partly determined by the choice of others.

In general, it may be affirmed that the absolute ownership of anything is exceptional, whether it be of raw material, of capital, or of labour. The State at least usually reserves some right of control over the possessions of its citizens; and, though the State claims the ownership of the country in which it has its jurisdiction, it acknowledges the rights of individuals to control, with some restrictions, particular parts of the country and particular objects within it. Various questions connected with this will have to be considered later.[1]

6. *Wealth and Poverty.*—The degree in which individuals or nations have valuable objects under their control constitutes their wealth or poverty. Money is valued as the symbol of such control and as a recognized title to its exercise under certain definite conditions. The power of exercising such control is the chief circumstance, apart from the natural capacities of mind and body, that gives superiority to one human being over another, and that prevents the good of the members of a community from being, in the fullest sense, a common good. Hence the practical problem with regard to the extent to which such control should be entrusted to individuals is one of the most important within the range of social philosophy. Plato specially urged that it is one of the chief functions of the rulers of any organized community to secure that there is neither excessive wealth nor excessive poverty within it. But it is not easy either to determine what is excessive or to ensure its elimination; so far as we can deal with this subject at all, it must be reserved for a later stage. Some further points in connection with it may, however, be noted here.

7. *Competition.*—Economic goods can, in very many cases, only be owned by one person at a time; and, when the supply of such goods is limited, possession by one implies the deprivation of others. This is, no doubt, to some extent true also of goods that are not strictly economic, in the sense in which that term is here being used. Rare books, even if kept in a public library, may not be readily accessible to all. Even fine scenery can only be fully enjoyed by a limited number at any particular time, and some may hardly have access to it at all; but the latter difficulty is generally due in part to the pressure of economic needs. In general, however, it seems to be true that the more purely human goods can

[1] See especially Chapter V of this Book.

readily be made common; whereas the more purely economic—especially in view of the fact that they are more necessary for life and more universally in demand—are liable to be appropriated by some to the detriment of others. Hence, in dealing with such goods, there tends to be a prominent element of strife. There is, of course, rivalry with regard to other goods as well; but the most serious forms of strife that arise in connection with them are often due to differences of valuation rather than to difficulties about possession. When people quarrel, for instance, about religion, it is usually because each wants to confer his religion upon the other, rather than to appropriate that which the other holds. This applies to nations as well as to individuals. Both between nations and between individuals, strife for possession is nearly always strife for goods that are essentially economic. Such strife may take the form of actual combat or of competition. In both cases the strife may be either regulated or unregulated; but however it may be conducted, it tends seriously to interfere with the recognition of a common good. In its more elemental forms, it becomes a simple struggle for existence, and threatens to degrade human life to the level of the brutes. But, here again, the difficulties that are raised by this problem are not such as can be satisfactorily dealt with at the present point.

8. *Individualism and Socialism.*—It is chiefly the difficulties connected with the competitive aspect of industrial life that give rise to those discussions that circle round the terms "Individualism" and "Socialism." On the one hand, it is urged that competition is an essential feature of economic life; and that it is only by the interaction of individual demand and supply that economic values can be satisfactorily measured and economic goods satisfactorily distributed. On the other hand, it is contended that this method is chaotic and wasteful, that it leads to grave injustice, and hence it is desirable that some form of central control should be substituted for the method

of competition. The problems involved here are large and difficult. Some of them will have to be considered at a later point. In the meantime, there are a few general considerations that it may be useful to set forth.

(1) It is important to distinguish the purely industrial problem from considerations of a more general kind. The terms "Individualism" and "Socialism" are generally understood with reference to methods of industrial organization; but they are also sometimes applied to more general theories of society.[1] In this wider sense, Individualism means the view that a community is simply a collection of individuals, while Socialism means that there is some intrinsic bond (an organic unity or a general will or a common good) connecting the individuals of which a society is composed. In this sense, we have already urged that the organic or communistic conception is the truer one. But we have noted also that, to avoid confusion, it would be better to use some such expression as Communalism, which does not carry a definitely economic connotation, to distinguish this general view of the social unity from those more special conceptions of industrial organization to which the term "Socialism" is commonly applied. When Socialism is taken in the sense of state organization, its opposite is Anarchism (the absence of central control) rather than Individualism. But anarchists are generally communalists—that is, they recognize the essential unity of society, but conceive that it is so intrinsically natural that it does not call for any external enforcement. And, indeed, many of those who describe themselves as socialists accept Anarchism as their ultimate ideal, but think that a socialistic organization of industry is necessary as a preparatory stage.[2]

(2) It is necessary, further, to distinguish the more purely industrial question involved in the consideration

---

[1] The contrast between these two senses of the words has been well emphasized by Dr. Bosanquet (*The Civilisation of Christendom*, chap. x). Perhaps he has made the antithesis a little too sharp.

[2] I understand this to have been the view of William Morris, for instance.

of a socialistic method of organization from the more general question of the organization of human life. Apart from the industrial aspect of life, it may be urged that there are many activities that call for central organization. A state religion, for instance, or a general system of national education, or a national theatre or library or picture gallery, might be described as socialistic; but, as the good aimed at by such institutions is not an economic one, they have not much relevance to the purely industrial problem. They are concerned with things that are naturally common, and that are not, in general, destroyed by use. The same applies, though not quite so obviously, to the provision of public hospitals, free medical attendance, perhaps even free legal advice, old age pensions, and various forms of relief for the destitute. These are sometimes described as socialistic; but they are evidently quite compatible with the continued existence of private property and competitive methods of industry. Some of them would even be meaningless without it. The existence of competitive methods is not necessarily incompatible with Humanitarianism, or with the organization of this on a large scale. To provide life-boats is not the same as to say that we are not to venture on the sea. Rather it rests on the assumption that we do so venture.

(3) It is well to note also that the term "Socialism," even when applied to purely industrial organization, is still somewhat vague. It may mean what is more definitely expressed by the term "Communism"; or it may mean some form of Collectivism. Communism is the view that all property should be held in common, or, if not actually common, should be divided either equally or in proportion to the needs, or perhaps rather to the deserts, of those to whom it is assigned. Collectivism does not necessarily imply this, but only insists on the central control of industrial enterprise, which means mainly the abolition of the private ownership of capital. Such control may be that of a state or municipality, or it may be vested, as the syndicalists urge, in those who are concerned

with particular forms of economic work. Syndicalism may be regarded as an extension of productive co-operation and Trade-unionism. In any discussion of Socialism, it is important to know which of these methods of organization is intended.[1]

(4) With regard to the practicability and desirability of any such methods of organization, the questions involved are too large and complicated to be properly discussed here. But it may be noted that some kinds of industrial work lend themselves more readily than others to central control; and it may be doubted whether it is desirable that all kinds should be organized in quite the same way. The making and using of roads, bridges, and railways; the supply of water, gas, and electricity; the planning of towns and villages; postal and telegraphic communications; perhaps also the apportionment of land, are all operations on a large scale, affecting similarly a whole country or district, sometimes even the whole world, and it seems clear that the method of central control is specially applicable to such cases. Whether it could be as effectively applied to articles that are used in small quantities by a number of individuals, with different needs and tastes, is much more doubtful. Even with regard to the use of land, it has been urged with some force that personal possession and control of portions varying in size yields the best results; though there are also some pretty strong arguments on the other side. In general, when personal tastes and interests enter in, when invention or special forms of skill are important, it seems necessary to leave the control of the work mainly in the hands of those who are particularly adapted for it.

This is all that can be profitably stated at the present point. Some further considerations will be added later, in connection with the discussion of the problems of justice, equality, efficiency, and some others.

---

[1] Mr. G. H. D. Cole's book on *The World of Labour*, chap. xi, may be referred to on methods of industrial control.

9. *Work and Leisure.*—Though every one has his special place and task, it must not be forgotten, as we noted in the preceding chapter, that the requirements of his life are not exhausted in this way. If he is to be a good citizen, he must have some leisure for his general civic obligations and for the development of his own personality, as well as for the exercise of his special function. This involves the recognition that some limitation should be put to the time that is devoted to labour; and this is one of the things that it may be necessary to secure by some form of central control. The importance of this also will become more apparent as we proceed.

CHAPTER IV

THE STATE

1. *What is a State?*—It is not altogether easy to determine what is properly to be understood by a State.[1] The term is sometimes apt to be confounded with Nation or Government, and even with People or Country, and occasionally with some others. It will be well, therefore, to begin by trying to define several closely related terms. Those that it seems important to distinguish are Society, Community, People, Country, Race, Nationality, Nation, Government, State, and Sovereign State. Let us consider these in order.

(1) *Society.*—A society means any group of individuals brought together (not necessarily in close personal contact) for some particular purpose. There are debating societies, co-operative societies, scientific societies, etc., but a nation or a state may also be classed as a society. It is a general term, which is applicable to a great number of different modes of unity among individuals.

(2) *Community.*—A community is a society, the individuals of which live together in some sort of intimate contact—e.g. a socialistic community, a Moravian community, etc. The ancient Pythagoreans were, to some extent, a community; and some other philosophical schools—notably the Epicurean—had some tendency to

---

[1] The philosophical aspects of this subject are most fully expounded in Bosanquet's *Philosophical Theory of the State*; but Green's *Principles of Political Obligation* should also be consulted. On some special points, Bluntschli's *Theory of the State* and Sidgwick's *Elements of Politics* are still worth referring to.

form themselves into a community. The degree of intimacy in a community may of course vary greatly. Any society may be called a community when it is regarded as intrinsically bound together by some spiritual tie or common end. The whole human race, if regarded as essentially a brotherhood aiming at a common good, may be described as a community.

(3) *People.*—A people is a group of individuals, not necessarily living together, but having a certain unity of tradition or sentiment. The Jewish people does not live together, but it is bound together by certain strong traditions, by community of language, religious feeling, and many historical memories and associations. The Swiss people includes a diversity of races, differing in language and religion ; but they seem, on the whole, to have acquired a certain common sentiment. A nation does not always form a people. When Tennyson says

> We are a people yet,
> Though all men else their nobler dreams forget,

he implies that some nations are not peoples.[1] It is probably one of the elements of strength in Germany that, in spite of differences in religion and politics and even in race, the sentiment of the common Fatherland is unusually strong. What Carlyle hinted at [2] as the essential condition of a genuine friendship—" *except* in opinion, not disagreeing "—would seem to be applicable to the unity of a people as well. Sometimes a rather loosely associated people contains within itself groups that are more closely united. The ancient Greeks were a people, having a common language, literature, and religion, and historical associations ; yet the Athenian people was

---

[1] How far Tennyson was right in claiming that we are, in any specially emphatic sense, a people, is a question that we cannot here discuss. We are obviously not a very homogeneous people ; but it may be true that, for that very reason, we have learned, better than some others, to disregard minor differences when important issues are at stake.

[2] *Life of Sterling*, Part II, chap. ii.

very different from the Spartan. A somewhat similar but much slighter difference may be found between the English and Scottish peoples, and perhaps between the North and South Germans. Again, all the peoples in Christendom have a certain community of sentiment, though there are great differences between them; and there is some truth—though not as much as is often supposed—in the saying that " East is East and West is West," meaning that there is a certain like-mindedness throughout the East and throughout the West, and diversity of mind as between East and West. But perhaps this applies mainly to the differences between India and Great Britain.[1]

(4) *Country*.—A country is primarily a geographical expression; but countries are seldom marked off from one another by sharply defined physical features. Great Britain is pretty clearly marked as a country; but England and Scotland are regarded as distinct countries, because they were for a long time separate nations, and may still in some respects be regarded as separate. On the whole, a country may be said to be the place inhabited by a nation; but ancient Greece would generally be regarded as a single country, however sharp the distinction might be between the different states within it. On the other hand, however closely Ireland might be united with Great Britain, they could hardly be regarded as the same country. Yet we usually think of the Japanese islands as forming a single country. Such instances seem to show that the term tends to be used in a way that is partly geographical and partly political, and that it is, in consequence, somewhat ambiguous. It is of course often used as equivalent to nation.[2] In the sentiment of patriotism, the thought of the physical features of the country is generally combined, in a rather subtle and inextricable fashion, with that of the character of its

[1] Mr. Lowes Dickinson has urged this with some force. See *Appearances*, pp. 58–9, and *An Essay on the Civilization of India, China, and Japan*, p. 1.

[2] As in the exclamation ascribed to the younger Pitt, " My country! How I leave my country! " Even " land " is used in a similar way, as in Tennyson's " Love thou thy land."

people, their history, their customs, their traditions, and their institutions.[1]

(5) *Race.*—Some human beings are sharply distinguished from others by certain physical features, which are usually accompanied by some differences of temperament and perhaps by some more subtle differences in habits of thought, feeling, and action. There is a pretty obvious difference between a Negro and a Teuton; and a few other distinctions are hardly less obvious. It is somewhat difficult for those who are thus sharply distinguished to be sufficiently like-minded to form a single people;[2] but it can hardly be maintained that such differences form an absolute barrier. Jews, for instance, though marked off from the other inhabitants of the countries in which they live, not only by difference of race, but also by strong national traditions, appear to be capable, under favourable conditions, of an almost indefinite degree of assimilation to the others. Slavs in Germany are sometimes said to become "more German than the Germans"; and probably many similar instances could be adduced.[3]

---

[1] Shakespeare's famous passage may be referred to in this connection:

> "This happy breed of men, this little world,
> This precious stone set in the silver sea;
>
> . . . . .
>
> This blessed plot, this earth, this realm, this England;
>
> . . . . .
>
> This land of such dear souls, this dear dear land,
> Dear for her reputation through the world."

Compare Scott's "O Caledonia, stern and wild," etc., and Walt Whitman's panoramic views of America. See also Prof. Fleure's *Human Geography in Western Europe*.

[2] The difficulties have recently been urged in a striking way by Mr. William Archer in his book *Through Afro-America*. See also Bryce's *American Commonwealth*, chaps. xciv and xcv, and Dr. Beattie Crozier's *Sociology applied to Practical Politics*, Book II, chap. iv.

[3] Many of them are to be found in M. J. Finot's book on *Race Prejudice*, in which the comparative unimportance of racial differences is very fully brought out. It can hardly be doubted that national distinctions are due much more to environment and tradition than to race.

(6) *Nationality.*—A nationality is a group, not necessarily inhabiting a single country or bound by any common sentiment, but connected with one another by race or language or by some previous association. There are many people of Irish, German, Chinese, and other nationalities in the United States of America. Kant was partly of Scottish nationality, and George I was certainly of German nationality. Herr Houston Chamberlain, in spite of his Germanic sympathies and long residence in the Fatherland, must still be reckoned as being of British nationality.

(7) *Nation.*—A nation is a body of people, generally, but not necessarily, inhabiting a single country, and bound together by common laws and traditions. The Germans and the inhabitants of the United States are members of two distinct nations, though some of the former live in other countries than that occupied by their nation; and both groups contain members of several distinct states. Scotland, I believe, is still a nation, though it has ceased to be a state. If the Isle of Man could be regarded as a country, it would, I suppose, be a separate nation; but its smallness and its close connection with Great Britain prevent it from being so described. The term is of course often used as equivalent to "state," but the corresponding adjective at least is generally understood in a wider sense. Wales, which makes no claim to sovereignty and has not even a capital, has already a national Library, a national Museum, and a national University.

(8) *Government.*—Wherever there is a group with an orderly mode of life controlled by law, there must be some recognized authority that makes the laws and sees that they are carried out. Such an authority is a government. It may consist of a single individual or a number of individuals, and its authority may be absolute or subject to various restrictions. Its authority also may be exercised over a whole nation or only over certain parts of a nation, or it may extend over a number of distinct nations. What is called a local government is more or

less directly subject to the control of a central government. Even under a system of Home Rule, the national government would be in some respects subject to the imperial government; and even an imperial government may be controlled by constitutional rules. Sometimes when the term "state" is used, what is meant is the central government. When Louis XIV said, *L'état c'est moi*, he meant probably no more than that he was the supreme governing power in the state. But it is very confusing to identify the state with the government.

(9) *State.*—It seems best to define a state as a body of people subject to a government which is not itself directly controlled by any other authority. This excludes a district that has only some form of local government, subject to the authority of a central government. It does not, however, exclude a nation which is autonomous in certain respects, though not in all respects. The constituent members of the United States of America, or the separate kingdoms within the German Empire, may rightly be described as states, in so far as they have independent control over their internal affairs. It is, however, not easy to distinguish the position of such states quite clearly from parts of a nation that enjoy Home Rule, or colonial dominions with independent governments, which could hardly be called states. The essential difference lies in the extent to which the central government is entitled to modify or control the action of the subordinate authorities; and this may sometimes be open to doubt. Again, a state may be to some extent subject to control by states external to itself, which have a certain suzerainty over it, or which have restricted its actions by treaty. Belgium would appear to be an instance of this. Such states are not fully independent.

(10) *Sovereign State.*—A sovereign state, finally, is one that has complete independence. This does not necessarily mean that it possesses a government that is authorized to do whatever it pleases. Sovereignty, in the sense in which it is here understood, may or may not reside in the government. What Louis XIV appears to

have claimed is that it did reside in him; and in a pure autocracy this would no doubt be the case. Even such a government might be somewhat tempered by epigrams or by the fear of revolution; but in a constitutional form of government there are more definite restrictions. There may, as in the case of the United States, be a written constitution which limits the power of the government; or its power may be limited by the existence of separate organs of government which mutually restrain one another. In such cases, one or more of the organs of government are usually elected by the body of the people voting in accordance with certain recognized principles. The more fully such a system is developed, the more does it tend to be true that the ultimate sovereignty rests with the people, and that the government only acts on behalf of the people. It would usually be a mistake, however, to suppose that under such a system it is the people that governs. It is always possible that the elected government may not carry out the wishes of the people; and, indeed, most of the people might often wish that those who are elected should exercise their own judgment. Hence it seems desirable to distinguish the ultimate sovereignty in a state from the ruling power; just as, in the case of the family, we urged that there is a sense in which the child is the rightful sovereign, though it is the parents who rule. It is well to remember also that even a sovereign state may be restricted in its actions by treaties entered into with other states. All that is essential to its sovereignty is that the restrictions by which it is limited should have been voluntarily adopted. No doubt, in practice, it is sometimes difficult to determine whether this is actually the case.

It may be added that all the terms that have been here referred to are liable to be used in different senses. I have tried to define them in a way that is at least not far removed from the prevalent usage, and that serves to emphasize the most important distinctions. Further discussion would carry us too far from our present province.

Words that are familiarly used in ordinary discourse are liable to a considerable amount of ambiguity. It is not important that they should always be used in exactly the same sense, but it is important, for scientific purposes, that we should know in what sense they are being used at any particular time. The difficulties connected with the general conception of a state are most properly dealt with in treatises specially devoted to the science of politics.

2. *The Natural Basis of the State.*—It is chiefly in connection with the State that the question has been raised whether the fundamental modes of social unity are natural or artificial. That the Family is natural can hardly be seriously doubted; and it is not much less obvious that the requirements of education and the various needs to which industrial institutions minister lead naturally to certain modes of organization. It is only when such organizations are controlled by governments that arbitrary elements appear to enter in; and it is forms of government, in general, that are apt to seem arbitrary. They do not appear to spring spontaneously from the essential nature of man, but rather to be imposed by an external compulsion. And, of course, it must be admitted that they sometimes are so imposed. When one nation conquers another and forces some or all of its laws upon it, it is evident that these do not grow out of the nature of the conquered nation; and they may happen to be very foreign to its nature. But, in the same way, the burning of a fire might be said to be either spontaneous or artificial. It is natural for bodies of certain kinds to burn at a particular temperature; but the conditions by which that temperature is produced may be highly artificial and arbitrary. Similarly, it is natural for human beings to wear clothes, though the particular fashion in which they are worn may be very conventional. In Carlyle's *Sartor Resartus* all human conventions are very happily compared to clothes. But to wear some clothes is as natural as to eat and drink. When Rousseau said that man is

born free, and yet is everywhere in chains, he did not mean to deny the naturalness of certain forms of social control, but only to distinguish what is natural in this respect from what is artificial.[1] That it is natural, may be made apparent by noticing that it exists to some extent even among animals. Most herds have their leaders; and sometimes these not only lead, but compel. Some other ways of emphasizing the naturalness of control are no doubt less convincing. Such a method of argument as that which Shakespeare puts into the mouth of Ulysses [2] would not now carry conviction to many:

> The heavens themselves, the planets and this centre
> Observe degree, priority and place,
> Insisture, course, proportion, season, form,
> Office and custom, in all line of order;
> And therefore is the glorious planet Sol
> In noble eminence enthroned and sphered
> Amidst the other; whose medicinable eye
> Corrects the ill aspects of planets evil,
> And posts, like the commandment of a king,
> Sans check to good or bad.

The laws of nature are not now thought of as laws in this sense; and this change of attitude has somewhat weakened our belief in social law as well. In particular, the element of coercion, though still regarded as necessary in certain conditions, is generally thought of as an unfortunate necessity. But, even if coercion could be shown to be quite unnecessary, this would not render it any the less important, or any less natural, that there should be some method of central guidance and organization. How far any mode of government can be regarded

---

[1] The various ways in which society exercises control over its individual members are very fully expounded by Professor E. A. Ross in his book on *Social Control*. The State, as such, is of course only one of these controlling agencies; but perhaps Professor Ross has somewhat underrated its importance. See also MacIver's *Community*, pp. 153-8.

[2] In *Troilus and Cressida*.

as natural, would seem to depend a good deal on the extent to which its guidance is a simple response to the needs of those who are guided, and how far it is rather the imposition of an external force. Hence it may be well to inquire how far the conception of force is essential to the nature of the State.

3. *The State as Force.*—What seems to be specially characteristic of a state is that it contains a controlling power over the whole life of the community, a power that has an absolute and unquestionable authority while it lasts. Hence it has been urged, especially by H. von Treitschke,[1] that the essential feature of the State is simply force—*Der Staat ist Macht*; and this view appears to be widely held in Germany, where the emphasis on the State has for various reasons been unusually strong. Now, it certainly seems to be true that the State is an organized community having definite laws and aims which it is authorized, if necessary, to enforce. The force which it has to exercise has two main forms—that which is directed towards inner control, and that which is directed towards outward defence. Plato sought to bring this out by comparing the rulers of a state to watchdogs, which are friendly within their own household but aggressive towards strangers. But this is not a very good comparison. A wise ruler seeks friendly relations both within and without, and it is only when he fails to secure such relations that the exercise of force becomes necessary. Hence it can hardly be right to say that force is the essence of the State. Wherever there is government there is the possibility of resistance; and resistance may have to be overcome by force. Parents, teachers, and organizers of industry may have to exercise some form of compulsion; yet no one would maintain that force is the essential aspect of such relationships. The nearest parallel to the State in this respect is probably

[1] His book on *Politics* is now accessible in English, with an Introduction by Mr. Balfour. There is a good deal to be learnt from it, in spite of his prejudices and extravagances.

an industrial organization. The organizer of industry also has to maintain satisfactory conditions within and to contend against difficulties and dangers from without. In both cases this may involve some form of industrial strife; but such strife is generally a sign of defective organization either within the industry or in the surrounding social conditions. So it would seem to be with the State also. Where the laws are recognized as such, rebellion may be expected to be exceptional; and if a state is friendly to its neighbours, its neighbours may be expected to be friendly to it.

The emphasis on force is partly connected with the biological doctrine of the struggle for existence—a phrase which is somewhat misleading as applied to animal life, and still more misleading with reference to human life. What is urged is that the advancement of life depends on the survival of those forms that are best fitted to their conditions, and the dying out of those that are relatively less adapted. But even in animal life these results are not necessarily brought about by aggressive action; nor is the result necessarily the survival of the forms that are intrinsically highest. In human life the selection of the best forms is not brought about by struggle, but rather by conscious effort to promote the best. War, in general, tends to kill off the best. Disease and vice are more likely to be the means of eliminating inferior types. Some reference has already been made to this problem in dealing with eugenics; and to the special problem of war we shall have to return later. In the meantime it is sufficient to urge that the essence of the State is to be found in the element of central control—not in force, which is only an instrument of that control.

4. *The State as Law-giver.*—It thus appears that the primary function of the State is that of maintaining a certain form of organization within itself; and that its secondary function is that of defending this organization—or, as the Germans call it, this Kultur. Both these objects are secured by government, through its two main

organs—the legislature and the executive. The central control expresses itself in definite decisions and corporate actions. To the general nature of these some reference has already been made.[1] A state, however, has normally a very long life, and most of its actions involve or imply a mode of control that extends over many years, and is embodied in laws and institutions, by which the decisions that are made at particular times are governed. The more perfectly a state is organized, the more do its actions tend to be determined by the form of its constitution and by its more or less persistent laws, rather than by the momentary decisions of particular individuals and types.[2] The laws that it lays down need not be uniform throughout the whole body. Many details may be left to local government; and if different nations are included within a single state, the laws for each of them may be distinct; but they derive their authority and their sanctions from the central government. In general, however, the laws of a well-ordered state are such as not to require much in the way of direct enforcement. In the Great City, as Walt Whitman put it, the people "think lightly of the laws," feeling them to be simply the expression of their own purposes. But they would not be laws of the State at all if they were not enforced when necessary. They might be customs, rules, or moral injunctions, but not state laws. Thus it is true that force is always in reserve behind the activities of the State.[3]

We are thus enabled to see in what sense it is true that force is an essential element in the life of a state. Every real decision, whether by an individual or by a society, implies the use of the means that are necessary to render it effective. It would be madness for any

---

[1] Chapter III, § 5.

[2] There is a good deal of interesting discussion about this in Plato's *Statesman*, 294–302, and in Aristotle's *Politics*, Book III, chap. xv.

[3] This point has been very well brought out by Mr. G. G. Coulton in *The Main Illusions of Pacificism*, especially pp. 50–5. Some of the other contentions in that book are more open to question.

individual to form a decision which he obviously could not carry out; and the same is true of any organized society or corporation. Now, within a nation, the means of carrying out almost any action are dependent on the power that is supplied by the State. When an individual decides to make some use of his property, his belief in the possibility of carrying out that decision is dependent on his knowledge that he will be supported by the law of the land, backed, if necessary, by the force of the police; and the efficiency of these modes of control is ultimately contingent on the defensive forces of the army and navy.

Hence the repudiation of the idea of force as constituting the essence of the State does not imply any minimizing of the importance of force. Force is not a monopoly of the Prussians. Carlyle, who certainly did not regard force as the essence of the State, could be, at least in theory, as stern as any Prussian in its application. Even the apostle of " sweetness and light " quotes [1] with approval the utterance of his father: " As for rioting, the old Roman way of dealing with *that* is always the right one: flog the rank and file, and fling the ringleaders from the Tarpeian rock ! " There is not much sweetness in this. Rioting is nearly always due to the existence of some real grievance; and surely every other method of dealing with it should be first essayed. It remains true, however, that, in the end, force must be met by force; [2] and that it is among the duties of the State to protect its citizens and enforce its laws. Happily, when a sufficient force is in reserve, it is seldom necessary to employ it.

5. *The State and the Family.*—We have already noted that the Family and the State are the two most definite

---

[1] *Culture and Anarchy*, VI.

[2] This is very fully recognized even by so strong an advocate of peace as Mr. J. A. Hobson. See *Towards International Government*, pp. 87–9. Mr. Hobson objects, however (pp. 180–2), to the use of such phrases as " Great Powers," " Signatory Powers," etc. But, after all, States are Powers, and they are pledged to use their power in support of their treaties.

forms of unity that are almost universally present in human life, and that are concerned with all its main aspects. The Family is of course subject to the State. The State prescribes the conditions under which it may be formed and maintained and, if necessary, dissolved, though, in establishing its laws, it may make use of pre-existing customs or religious traditions. In general, however, the State leaves a large element of freedom within the Family, treating the parents as the guardians of its interests, and only interfering in cases of extreme injustice, or when a special appeal is made from within to its authority. It is recognized on the whole as forming an *imperium in imperio*, with a special function and interest of its own.

Nevertheless, the fact that both these modes of unity are, in a manner, concerned with the whole of life is liable to create a certain antagonism between them. This was a good deal emphasized by Plato, and was the real ground of his rejection of the family life in the case of the guardians, and of his attempt to assimilate the functions of men and women. But if we accept the view that the main end of the Family is the care of the early years of childhood, this appears to be a function that is of the highest importance to the State, and yet one that is naturally delegated to the parents, and especially to the mother. After the early period of childhood is past, the State naturally takes the education of the young more and more out of the hands of the parents. Even in early childhood it would seem that it rightly exercises some control over the parents in their treatment of the young; and it also controls their actions towards one another and in the disposition of their property. When properly constituted, the Family does not appear to be antagonistic to the State, but rather to be an excellent training-ground for the larger life of the citizen [1]—not least of the citizen who is to be largely concerned with the organization of the State.

[1] This is very well brought out in Mrs. Bosanquet's book on *The Family*, chap. x.

6. *The State as Educator.*—The work of the State being essentially that of organization, it is hardly to be expected that it can deal quite satisfactorily with the form and substance of education. It may provide suitable machinery both for the preparation of teachers and for the carrying on of the instruction of the young, and it may also exercise some supervision over the work, in order to ensure that it is efficiently performed. Beyond this, it may be doubted whether it is desirable that the State as such should interfere. Even if the officials of the State have had experience in dealing with children, and have studied the best educational methods, the fact that they are parts of a machine makes it difficult for them to enter sympathetically into the work of those who are in constant contact with the growing minds and changing conditions of the young. If the substance of instruction is provided by the State, it is pretty certain to be a lifeless substance. Its history is likely to be a perverted history, its religion an antiquated religion, its morality a conventional morality, and all the other subjects that it may undertake to deal with somewhat wooden. Its business is to provide a suitable stage for the actors rather than to take an active part in the performances.

7. *The State and Morality.*—There are two main ways in which it is important to consider the relation of the State to morality—viz. the sense and degree in which it is itself bound by moral considerations and the extent to which it is its function to promote morality in its citizens.

With regard to the former question, it has to be noted that those who represent the State as force tend to regard it as entirely outside the requirements of morality, or at least as being subject only to the one requirement of adequately maintaining its power. *Salus populi suprema lex.* That this requirement is important cannot be denied; but it has already been urged that it is an insufficient view of the State to represent it as simply a force. It is concerned with justice within its own borders, as well as with protection from without; and, for both purposes, it must have an adequate force at its disposal. But if it simply relies on force, it cannot easily maintain justice. If it urges, with regard to its own action, that "necessity knows no law," it can hardly expect that its citizens will not use the same principle with what they conceive to be their necessities. If it plunders its neighbours without scruple, it will only be by force that it can restrain its citizens from plundering their neighbours; and morality founded simply on force is the negation of morality. The distinction which Bishop Butler[1] emphasized between mere power and legitimate authority applies both to states and individuals. It is true, of course, that the functions of a state are different from those of an individual. The one may legitimately do things which the other may not legitimately do; but in each case there is a right and a wrong. The further consideration of this, however, must be left to treatises on ethics and politics.[2]

With regard to the second question, the answer to it is, to a considerable extent, implied in what was stated in the preceding question; for, if morality cannot, properly speaking, be enforced, the relation of the State to it is essentially an educative one. And I think it may be rightly urged that it is not the business of the State to promote morality in any direct way. Aristotle perhaps made the relation between ethics and politics too close in this respect—not unnaturally, in view of the complete way in which the life of the Greek citizen tended to be absorbed in that of the State. It seems clear that it is one of the functions of the State to provide education for its citizens; and this should include moral education. But it is probably not wise for the State to determine what form this education should take, except in a very general way. Educational institutions have their own special functions, just as the Family has; and, though

[1] *Sermons on Human Nature*, II

[2] But see the Note at the end of this Chapter and Book III, Chapter I., §5.

it is the business of the State to protect these institutions and to assure itself that they are performing their proper work, it is not its business to do their work for them. Again, legislation may aim at the reform of particular types of moral evil, such as those that interfere with the life of the Family, or with the life or property of individuals, or that, like intoxication, tend to lead to crime. But, in general, the State can only regard such actions from the outside, and mainly in the way of removing dangers and temptations. The active promotion of morality is only indirectly its function.[1]

8. *Forms of Government.*—Many different forms of government have been enumerated. Plato recognized five main types, and Aristotle six, while several modern writers have made more minute distinctions. If we were to consider all the possible variations, the number would be very large; but it is doubtful whether it is necessary to distinguish more than two fundamental forms—the oligarchic and the democratic. Though some governments are called monarchies, and these are distinguished from aristocracies, yet the ruling sovereigns are in practice guided by their counsellors; at least, where this is not the case—where the ruler can say, with any plausibility, *L'état c'est moi*—the community can hardly be regarded as forming a state at all. It is, in that case, controlled by what is substantially an external authority. Democracy, again, may be supposed to be, as Plato represented it, a mere anarchy, in which case it is not a form of government. On the whole, it seems true to say that, whenever there is a real state with a real government, the government is either a small number exercising independent authority or else a large number representing approximately the whole community. There are, however, different types of oligarchy and democracy. An oligarchy may be a genuine aristocracy—a government by those who are regarded as experts or wise men; or it may be

[1] See on this Green's *Principles of Political Obligation* and Bosanquet's *Philosophical Theory of the State*, chap. viii.

government by a hereditary caste, or by a military class, or by those who have property. A genuine aristocracy may be really representative of the whole people, and so approximate to a democracy. The other types approximate rather to despotism, i.e. to a government of the people by an authority that is essentially external to themselves. Democracy, again, may mean the rule of the majority, or of selected individuals who represent the majority, or who represent constituencies formed in a more or less arbitrary way. In a large community, it seems clear that it must be, in some degree, representative. Hence it tends to mean government by the rich or by experts or by orators. Thus the differences between types of government cannot, in general, be very sharply drawn. Any government that is well organized is almost bound to appeal in some degree to the mass of the people and to contain some degree of expert administration. It is mainly a question of the manner and degree in which these elements are combined and of the spirit in which the combination is worked. A recent writer [1] has stated that " an important lesson of history is that the value of a system of government does not depend merely on its form, but chiefly on its spirit." But the spirit is apt to be somewhat affected by the form. The lines of Pope—

> For forms of government let fools contest;
> Whatever is best administered is best—

can only be defended if form is understood in a very formal sense. The important contests about forms of government turn mainly on the question, which is likely to be best administered. But this does not depend so much on the general form as on the particular safeguards. It does not greatly matter, for instance, whether the chief executive officer in a state is called Emperor or King or President, so long as there is some adequate security that what he does will, in general, be in harmony with what is thought by the wisest and best informed

[1] D. J. Hill, *The People's Government*, Preface, p. vii.

of the citizens. All the devices of government, so far as they have any value, are devices for securing this; and it is a thing that is by no means easy to secure under any form of government, even one that is supposed to be the most democratic.

The phrase of President Lincoln, "Government of the people by the people and for the people," which is commonly accepted as a description of democracy, may be regarded, if broadly interpreted, as a characterization of any good government. On the other hand, if narrowly interpreted, it can hardly be applied to any government. The actual work of government can never be carried on by more than a small part of any people—if only for the reason that the work of government is performed at particular moments, whereas the life of the people extends through many generations. What is important is that the part by which the work is done should be fairly representative of what is wisest and best in the whole. To this subject we shall have to return in a later chapter.

9. *Local Government.*—The control of affairs within a large modern state is practically never wholly vested in a single central authority. There may, as we have already noted, be states within states; or there may be separate nations with a considerable measure of autonomy. In any case, there are municipalities and districts having some degree of independence in local affairs; and there are families, schools, churches, industrial and commercial organizations, and various other forms of social unity, which, within certain recognized limits, are allowed to exercise some self-control. Usually the methods of government within these reflect the general spirit of the larger government of the State. Under a paternal type of government, the father of a family will generally have a higher degree of authority within his little circle than one who lives under a government of a more popular type. But on such differences it is hardly necessary to dwell at present.

10. *The Evolution of the State.*—States have a general tendency to expand, and, in expanding, to undergo certain changes in their general character. The most important of these changes would appear to be the following:—

(1) In the relations of a state to its citizens there tends to be a certain advance from status to contract.[1] It is generally recognized that it is a mistake to look for any contract at the foundation of the life of the state; but as it grows, it tends more and more to establish contracts, some of which might no doubt be said to be implicit from the beginning. But, in general, it begins by accepting class distinctions based on custom or force and ends by the establishment of contracts based on law.

(2) Many early states are City States, like those of Greece, or at least small communities. These tend to fail from lack of sufficient power of self-defence, and partly from the want of a sufficiently varied internal life. Hence there is a progress towards a combination of states, at first somewhat loosely welded and gradually becoming more coherent. From this there is often a further progress to more extended empires, with colonies and dependencies attached. It seems to be more or less normal that this should be followed by a disruptive movement in the direction of local autonomy. The Empire changes into a Commonwealth, and perhaps eventually breaks up into separate states. Such separate states, will, however, generally retain some connection with one another, and may readily become federated for certain purposes. It is possible, for instance, for a man to be a " good European," partly because Europe retains some of the cohesion that was given to it by the Roman Empire.[2] From this kind

---

[1] In Maine's *Ancient Law* (chap. v) this tendency is perhaps somewhat exaggerated. See Note 4 in Sir F. Pollock's edition.

[2] It seems to be largely this circumstance that has made the recognition of international laws possible in Europe—this, at least, combined with the influence of Christianity. But these forces tend gradually to make themselves felt in regions to which they have not themselves, in any explicit form, penetrated.

of cohesion it may be possible to pass to a federation on a larger scale, including many nations not previously combined together, and perhaps eventually to a federation of the world. But this opens up a large and controversial subject, to which also we shall have to return in a later chapter. What it is chiefly important to recognize is that any real progress in the structure and relations of states depends on the extent to which they become the embodiments of what may be rightly characterized as a general will or common purpose, and on the extent to which that common purpose is directed towards the common good of humanity. Progress, in any other sense, may very well be progress backwards.

NOTE ON THEORIES OF THE STATE

THE full consideration of different theories of the State belongs properly to the science of politics. They can only be slightly touched upon in a general outline of social philosophy. But, in view of the special importance of having clear ideas about the State at the present time, it may be well to append some further remarks on that subject here. The chief views that it seems important to distinguish are the following: (1) the view of it as a personality, (2) the view of it as a superpersonal entity, (3) the view of it as an impersonal power, (4) the view of it as merely a mechanism for carrying out the purposes of the individuals who compose it, (5) the view of it as one among other natural modes of association, having a special value and special functions of its own. On each of these a few comments may be made.

1. *The State as Personal.*—The definition given by Bluntschli may be taken as a typical expression of this view. "The State," he says,[1] "is a combination or association of men, in the form of government and governed, on a definite territory, united together into a moral organized masculine personality." The last adjective here is due to Bluntschli's somewhat fantastic conceit, that the State is masculine and the Church feminine. This does not appear to be based on much else than the fact that in German one speaks of *der* Staat and *die* Kirche. No doubt it is true that the genders of words are not altogether arbitrary; and I suppose it may be admitted that some parts of the work of the State are

[1] *The Theory of the State*, Book I, chap. i, § 7.

naturally more the concern of men than of women, and that women are, on the whole, more deeply involved in the interests of the Family and the Church. But Bluntschli pressed this to an extravagant length.[1]

With regard to the personality of the State, it is obvious that it cannot be literally maintained;[2] and, on such a subject, it is dangerous to play with metaphors. It is true that the State has some of the characteristics that belong to a person. In particular, it can form decisions and carry out actions, for which it may be held responsible. But so can a bank or a football club, which, I suppose, no one would regard as persons. In the case of the State it is often difficult to say where the responsibility rests for particular decisions. In an autocratic government the monarch is naturally held responsible, though he may have been largely dependent on the pressure of his advisers. In our own country it is maintained that "the King can do no wrong"; and, in general, the responsibility for executive action is taken by the Prime Minister. But, in many important matters, the decision rests practically with some particular official, or with the majority in some special organ of government. In any case, it can be ascribed to some person or to some body of persons.[3] It is true that they are generally a good deal influenced—especially in democratic countries—by outside opinion; but this is often true of the actions of private individuals as well. It is particular persons who act on behalf of the State; and the State, as such, cannot properly be regarded as a person.

2. *The State as Superpersonal.*—The conception of the State as superpersonal is associated with the names of

[1] For some criticisms, see Mrs. Bosanquet's book on *The Family*, p. 286.

[2] It has already been noted (Book I, Chap. II, § 5) that it may be maintained by a legal fiction.

[3] It is worth noting that Dr. Bosanquet, who has been disposed to deny this, has recently been led to modify his view to some extent. See his *Social and International Ideals*, p. 290.

Fichte and Hegel; and I suppose Dr. Bosanquet may be taken as its best representative in our own country at the present time. Hegel even referred to the State as a God; and all the upholders of this conception represent it as the embodiment of all the best ideals of its individual members, with the possible exception (a large exception) of those that are definitely concerned with science, art, and religion. Matthew Arnold, who was a supporter of this view, described the State as the "organ of our collective best self, of our national right reason." For Dr. Bosanquet it is the expression of the "real will" of the nation, of which particular individuals represent only partial aspects. It has to be admitted, however, that such a conception, if applicable at all, is only applicable to the ideal State; yet the writers to whom I am referring are, in general, specially insistent in maintaining that ideals are not of much value unless they can be shown to be applicable to existing things. But is it even applicable to the ideal State? It seems to be admitted that the higher human activities in the development of science, art, and religion carry us somewhat beyond the legitimate sphere of the State; though it is surely part of its business to protect and encourage such activities. But the same considerations would seem to apply to all forms of creative work, such as invention, exploration, educational experiments, etc. These depend on individual initiative; and even the most ideal of states would probably be well advised to leave them to that. It cannot make poets, prophets, or thinkers. It is well if it does not crucify them, or allow others to crucify them; and it is still better if it can give them some positive encouragement. But they are likely to draw their inspirations in the future, as they have done in the past, from far other sources than those with which the State is concerned. The State, as such, has to confine itself, in the main, to the making and enforcement of laws, the organization of collective enterprise, the maintenance of internal peace, the prevention of remediable sources of distress, and the protection and encouragement of all forms of work that have been proved to have social value. This is surely enough for any state, however ideal. To create is the work of individuals and of voluntary associations: it is for the State to protect, to encourage, and to organize.

3. *The State as Power.*—The view of the State as essentially force has been already discussed in the text, but we may notice here its relation to the conception that has just been referred to. The doctrine of Treitschke and others is sometimes said to be derived from that of Fichte and Hegel; and I believe there is a certain amount of truth in this. They were all greatly influenced by the special conditions that affected Prussia in their times. It is a great mistake, in general, to interpret the utterances of social and political philosophers without reference to the circumstances of their time and place. Even the greatest philosophers—even Plato and Aristotle— were not supermen. They were just human beings thinking, and thinking with their eyes on the changing world in which they lived. Hegel at least was well aware of this. Both Fichte and he wrote at a time when it was necessary to get the German people to realize their national unity, and to place themselves under the political direction of Prussia. Treitschke wrote at a time when this had been accomplished, partly by the help of his own influence. Hence they all laid special emphasis on national unity and the importance of State control; and it is probably true that they all used somewhat exaggerated expressions. Treitschke, however, carried his exaggeration farther than either Fichte or Hegel. He was a public orator and historian, rather than a philosopher; and even for his exaggerations there was some excuse. If we are to give the State so important and unique a place as that which was claimed for it by Fichte [1] and Hegel, it is pretty clear that its importance depends mainly on

---

[1] For some discussion of Fichte's view, reference may be made to the Appendix to Professor Vaughan's edition of *Rousseau's Political Writings*.

its power. Leisure (to use Aristotle's expression), on which all the higher activities of humanity depend, can only, on any large scale, be won and protected by the power of the State. It is only a slight exaggeration of this to say that the State *is* essentially Power; and it is an exaggeration into which it is very natural to fall in Germany, where circumstances have made this particular aspect unusually prominent. The unity of Germany was secured very directly by " blood and iron." Moreover, it was not secured completely. Germany, so far from being the ideal State, is still, in some respects, hardly a State at all. Rather, as Mr. Belloc and others have well urged, it is an aggregation of states under the domination of a military autocracy; or, at best, it is what Plato called a Timarchy. Of *such* a state it is practically true that its essence *is* force; and Treitschke was simply interpreting what he found. But it is just this circumstance that has made Germany, in spite of its many excellences in other respects, so terrible a menace to the civilization of the world.

Hegel certainly did not maintain that the State is force. Dr. Bosanquet has recently called attention to passages in which he emphatically repudiates the claims of force. It is well to remember, however, that even Treitschke did not support the claims of *any* kind of force, but only the force of a well-organized state, supporting a high civilization. Though he held that every state must be a Power, he did not hold that any kind of power constitutes a state. Hence it is perhaps hardly fair to instance Hegel's condemnation of the force of Napoleon. Treitschke might very well have made the same condemnation—especially in view of the fact that the force of Napoleon failed in the end. Napoleon could hardly be said to be the representative of the power of a state. He was the terror of states; and his admirers were, in general, the enemies of national domination. It is true, however, that Hegel did not identify the State with force, even in the sense in which Treitschke did so. Indeed, Treitschke bases his theory quite explicitly on the repudiation of the Hegelian conception of the State.[1] But Hegel did emphasize the importance of the State in such a way as to discredit attempts to secure any larger mode of unity, and, on the whole, to represent war as being necessarily a permanent institution. Dr. Bosanquet does not follow him entirely in this, but he appears to do so to a considerable extent.

Carlyle is sometimes brought into comparison with Treitschke; and such a comparison is not without foundation. But Carlyle was not a great believer in *states*. It was rather the power of the individual hero that he glorified; and, as heroes are persons, they are of course amenable to moral judgment. In this respect he is more nearly akin to Nietzsche, with his worship of the superman, than to Treitschke. But he was a good deal more guarded in his utterances than either of them, and can hardly be properly classed along with them. Nor indeed should Nietzsche and Treitschke be classed together, as they so commonly are.

Hobbes is another writer who laid much emphasis on the power of the State. He represented the State as the source, rather than the subject, of the ordinary obligations of morality. But he valued the State mainly for the security that it gives against the egoism of individuals; and his attitude cannot properly be identified with that of any of the Prussian writers. Yet, so far as his theory bears upon international relations, the results to which it leads would seem to be substantially the same as those that are set forth by Treitschke.

It would, however, carry us too far afield if we were to attempt to consider in detail the doctrines of particular philosophers.

4. *The State as Mechanism.*—In our own country the tendency has been, in general, to think somewhat lightly of the State, and to value rather the liberty of the individual.[2] The State has generally been thought of mainly

[1] *Politics*, Book I, chap i.
[2] The contrast between the British and the German attitude

NOTE ON THEORIES OF THE STATE

as a means for securing this. It thus tends to be regarded as little more than a mechanism, and a mechanism whose functions should be reduced to a minimum. Its powers for the encouragement of good have been minimized; and sometimes even its powers for the resistance of evil have been disregarded or condemned. This is probably quite as great an error as that of the Prussians, and perhaps almost as mischievous. In particular, the extreme doctrine of non-resistance to evil can hardly be too strongly repudiated. Like the other extreme, it is based largely on the teaching of earlier prophets, without sufficient regard for the circumstances in which they spoke. One at least of these prophets gave very definite warning that his words should not be taken too literally. What seems to be important is that, when evil is resisted, the resistance should be of such a kind as effectively to remove the evil, and overcome it with good. Very often the resistance rather perpetuates or increases the evil.

The doctrine of non-resistance, as applied to social problems, takes several different forms. For a long time its most conspicuous form in this country was to be found in the general conception of *laissez faire*, which has now been very largely discredited. The extreme opposite of this is State Socialism. But some socialists have also tended to preach the doctrine of non-resistance in a different form, viz. that of the rejection of force as an instrument for the defence of national life and for the maintenance of social order. But when force is repudiated in one form, it generally reappears in another. As against the force of the State, there has recently been a tendency to advocate sectional violence.[1] The philosophy of M. Bergson has been taken as a foundation for this; but it has also been connected, in a less extreme way, by Mr.

towards the State is well brought out by Professor Sorley in the volume of lectures on *The International Crisis: the Theory of the State*, especially pp. 34-55. See also Mr. Hugh Eliot's *Herbert Spencer*, Introduction.

[1] The most striking statement on this is to be found in M. Sorel's book, *Reflections on Violence*.

Russell with a very different type of philosophy.[1] What these philosophies have in common is the distrust of reason as the basis for the unity of human life, and the tendency to fall back upon particular impulses, passions, and interests.[2] As against such views, the emphasis on the unity of the State may very well be pressed. It is only by the co-operative action of a whole people that we can expect right reason to prevail against the apparent interests of individuals and sections. The well-organized State exists, as Matthew Arnold insisted, "on behalf of whatever great changes are needed, just as much as on behalf of order." For this purpose it must be provided with adequate force. Even if we were to succeed in establishing some sort of federation of the world, it would still be necessary to have a strong police force for its maintenance; and certainly, as long as the present anarchy in the relations between states continues, it seems essential that a strong defensive force should be kept in existence. This has been pretty fully recognized by the leading continental socialists;[3] but there has been some tendency to deny it in our own country.

5. *The State as a Mode of Social Unity.*—We can best avoid these pernicious extremes by holding fast to the conception of the State as one of those modes of social

---

[1] *Principles of Social Reconstruction*, p. 97.

[2] In connection with this, reference may be made to an interesting paper on "Realism and Politics," read to the Aristotelian Society in March 1918 by Mr. J. W. Scott.

[3] The most notable instance is that of Jaurès, who, in his book on *L'Armée Nouvelle*, advocated a system of defensive military organization on the Swiss model. The main parts of this book have been made accessible to English readers by Mr. G. G. Coulton as *Democracy and Military Service*. See also Liebknecht's *Militarism and Anti-Militarism*, Part II, chap. vi. Of course, even if these writers are justified in their recommendations for continental countries, it does not follow that what they suggest would be suitable for the very different conditions of our own national life. I am inclined to think that a carefully limited system of training would be beneficial even here; but certainly my opinion on such a subject is not of much value.

NOTE ON THEORIES OF THE STATE

unity by which the idea of a common good is made effective. Like other modes, it is a natural and vital growth, and not merely a mechanical instrument; but, like other modes, it has its special functions and its special limitations; and it best fulfils the end that is implied in its nature when it has constantly before it the larger interests of humanity that it subserves. This I take to be the view that is presented to us by T. H. Green; and it is the view that I have tried to expound in the text. Dr. Bosanquet's view appears to me to be, to a large extent, identical; but I think he has tended to revert rather too much to the older doctrine of Hegel. Green has adopted most of what is best in Hegel's theory.[1] He was not as great a philosopher as Hegel, just as Wordsworth was not as great a poet as Goethe; but in both cases we have perhaps some reason to be not altogether discontented with our own. Dr. Bosanquet himself has given us a vigorous defence of the British intellect;[2] yet he seems to me to defer a little too much to the views both of Rousseau and of Hegel. The British intellect is perhaps not equal to the German in the thoroughness of its grasp of large conceptions, just as it is probably inferior to the French in lucidity; but it is sometimes more finely balanced than either; and, though such a balance is apt to look like vacillation and inconsistency, it is not always a sign of weakness. Human society, like the universe in general, is a very complex structure, and has to be looked at from many different sides. I gladly admit, however, that the special emphasis that Dr. Bosanquet has laid on the conception of the State[3] may have been needed as a prophylactic against the prevalent individualism, which is still our besetting sin.

[1] Which, indeed, as Sir Henry Jones says (*The Working Faith of the Social Reformer*, p. 212), " is little more than a modern version " of the fundamental conceptions of Plato and Aristotle.

[2] *Social and International Ideals*, pp. 17-18.

[3] For some further discussion on this subject, reference may be made to Professor MacIver's book on *Community*, Appendix A. With regard to Hegel, it should be noted that he was denounced in his own country (by Schubarth) as an enemy of the Prussian State.

CHAPTER V

JUSTICE

1. *General Conception of Justice.*—In view of what has already been urged, we may perhaps be allowed to assume that the primary aim of a well-constituted state is to establish and maintain justice within its borders. But the conception of justice is not altogether easy to make clear. The word means originally what is commanded by some governing power; and hence some have been led to maintain, with Thrasymachus in Plato's *Republic*, that what is just is simply, on the whole, what is in the interest of the strong—i.e. of those who happen to possess the power of government. This view is not quite identical with the general principle that Wordsworth ascribed to Rob Roy—

> The good old rule, the simple plan,
> That they should take who have the power,
> And they should keep who can.

It differs from this in recognizing that human beings are members of a community, subject to a controlling power; but it ascribes to that controlling power the same principle as that by which Rob Roy is supposed to have been guided. But even the view that justice is the interest of the strong raises the question, What is the true interest of the strong? And, as the strong are after all human, this question tends to resolve itself into the deeper one, What is the Ultimate Good of human beings?[1]

[1] This is, of course, the main point of the discussion in the first Book of Plato's *Republic*.

And, if we recognize further, as surely we must, that it is not the proper function of the controlling power to pursue its own interest, but rather to promote the good of the whole, it becomes still more apparent that the underlying problem is that of determining what constitutes the human good. This problem, however, is a difficult one ; and it is the special business of the science of ethics to deal with it.[1] It must suffice for our present purpose to note that such expressions as Happiness, Welfare, Well-being, Self-realization, the Development of Life, and others, have been used to characterize the good at which human beings aim ; and that probably we shall not be far wrong if we interpret it as meaning the realization of those capacities that are most distinctively human. Justice would then have to be taken as meaning, not what the governing power commands with a view to its own interest, but rather what it ought to command with a view to the realization of the good of the citizens over whom it exercises control. A little reflection, however, suffices to show that a controlling power can hardly by itself secure the well-being of the citizens. A large part of the well-being of individuals can only be secured by their own efforts. It may even be said that their effort is part of their well-being. It has been urged, for instance, that the pursuit of truth is better than its possession ; and though this is open to doubt, it seems at least to be the case that the value of those things that human beings seek depends largely on the fact that they are appreciated and chosen. Hence they cannot simply be given to people by any external power. And so, what we have to ask here is not, How is the good of the whole people to be secured ? but rather, What can the controlling power effect **towards** the securing of that good ? This is a somewhat narrower question, though still a sufficiently large and searching one.

The general answer to this question would seem to be, that the controlling power cannot secure everything that is good ; but that it can do much to establish and main-

[1] My own view is summed up in my *Manual of Ethics* (5th ed.), Book II, chap. vi,

tain the kind of social order that is best adapted to enable individuals to secure what is best. As Aristotle pointed out,[1] this problem has two, or it may be better to say three, main aspects. The first question is, What is the best arrangement of society that a state can establish? The second is, How can it be best maintained under changing conditions? And the third is, How can it best be restored when it is disturbed? The first question is said by Aristotle to be concerned with distributive justice, the other two with corrective justice. In the case of corrective justice, however, it seems desirable to distinguish, as Aristotle did, the somewhat different conceptions of exchange and reparation. But it may be best to begin with a general explanation of distributive and corrective justice.

2. *Distributive Justice.*—The essential question here is, What is the best arrangement of society, with a view to securing the greatest good of the whole? Various answers might be given to this; and it is not possible, within our present limits, to discuss them all. It must suffice to state here that the best general answer appears to be that which was given by Plato. According to him, the best arrangement is that in which every one is placed in the position for which he is best fitted, adequately prepared to fulfil his function in that place, and supplied with the materials and instruments that are necessary for its proper discharge. If, however, we accept this as a general basis for the conception of distributive justice, there are some additions or qualifications that it seems desirable to insert.

In the first place it must be admitted that, in any large modern state, it would be impossible to secure all that is implied in Plato's conception. It may be doubted whether it would have been really possible even in such a small community as he had in mind. This need not, however, make it any the less true that it is the object that the State should have in view; and that, in so far

[1] *Ethics*, Book V, especially chaps. ii–v.

as it is not secured, there is some degree of injustice. It is probably true that all ultimate aims are impossible of immediate fulfilment; and this at least was very fully recognized by Plato. It is the object, for instance, of the medical art to secure that every one is in perfect health, but the approximation to this that is immediately possible is certainly a very imperfect one. So it is with justice. The State cannot secure that every one is in the place for which he is best fitted; but it can to a considerable extent secure that no unnecessary obstacles are placed in the way of each one discovering for himself what is the position for which he is best fitted, and eventually gaining that position. The development of his powers by education will be a considerable help in this. So will the provision of access to the land, the establishment of labour exchanges, and many other devices. But, even with such aids, Dr. Johnson's weighty line, " slow rises worth by poverty depressed," may long retain its force—though we may perhaps venture to hope that such a case as that of Chatterton will not recur again. In like manner, the State cannot secure that every one, even if he finds the position for which he is best fitted, will properly fulfil his functions. But it can provide methods of supervision and inspection; and it can secure the establishment of a thorough education, which will not only develop his natural powers, but instil something of the spirit of civic obligation. This was, of course, a very essential part of Plato's scheme. Again, the State cannot ensure that every one has the necessary materials and instruments for the proper discharge of his functions; but it can do something at least to remove such extreme poverty as would prevent him from securing them, and such extreme wealth as might tempt him to waste them. It can do something to provide suitable house accommodation, a suitable supply of water and light, libraries, art collections, facilities for travel, and many other conveniences; and to make them accessible to all. Plato was not unaware of the importance of such provisions for the realization of his plan.

Another qualification that has to be made on the general principle laid down by Plato is that, so far as it implies definite State regulations, it can only be accepted as general, not as applying to every individual instance. The laws of a state, as Aristotle urged [1] can only provide for what is best in general. This is probably truer in a large modern state than it might be in a small Greek community. The State can hardly be expected, for instance, to provide the best kind of education for a Shakespeare, a Wordsworth, or a Watt. It may be doubted whether even a private institution could do that. Nor can the State, in other matters, provide the best arrangement for cases that are exceptional, or even that deviate in some comparatively slight degrees from what is normal, unless the deviation occurs in a number of instances of a definitely recognizable type. As an example, we might take the case of the inheritance of land. Sometimes it is provided that large properties descend to the eldest son. Now, it is pretty certain that this does not always result in the property coming into the hands of the person who is best fitted to make a good use of it in the public interest. But it might be urged [2] that, in general, it would lead to a better result than could be expected from any other definite arrangement. There may be grounds for thinking that the property would suffer by being divided up into small holdings; and there may be grounds for thinking that the eldest son, having grown up all his life with this prospect in view, may be more likely, in general, to fulfil the function satisfactorily than any other who could be discovered by a universally applicable method. A similar justification may be made for the hereditary principle in monarchy; though here also it would be generally allowed that it does not always lead to the best results. On the other hand, if a system

---

[1] *Ethics*, Book V, chap. xiv. Plato had previously emphasized this in his *Statesman*, 294.

[2] This is only used as an illustration. How far this contention could be justified, is too large a question to be properly discussed here. Its answer depends a good deal on changing conditions.

of peasant proprietors were instituted in the case of the land, or of an elective president in the case of the ruler, it is pretty certain that these methods also would not be the best in every individual instance. Laws, in general, can only provide for what is best in general. How individual difficulties are to be met is a different question.

There is still another objection that might be made to the Platonic principle. It might be urged that it tends to subordinate the individual life too completely to the service of the State. The work of an individual may have little direct reference to the life of the community in which he lives, and yet may be of lasting value to the world. Spinoza's philosophy was for the world, rather than for his particular country; and even in the world at large there were but few who could appreciate it. Similar remarks might probably be made about Browning's "Grammarian" and about many eminent mathematicians, artists, and others. Yet it may be urged that a wise state should encourage such work, which in the end advances its culture and redounds to its glory. Plato would not have denied this; but it may be urged that in practice, the attempt to apply his principle would tend to exclude it. Again, even in the event of incapacitation for service, it may be urged that the State has an obligation to care for its citizens. Here Plato seems pretty definitely to demur. He certainly appears to suggest that, as soon as any one is unfitted for the discharge of his particular function—even if only temporarily—he should be left to his fate. Most people in modern times would regard such a doctrine as inhuman; but some might urge that it is not the business of the State, but rather of private individuals or religious institutions, to make the necessary provision for such cases. This is a question to which we shall have to refer again later.

But, whatever force there may be in these objections and qualifications, it can hardly be doubted that the Platonic principle furnishes us with the right basis for the general conception of distributive justice.

3. *Corrective Justice.*—Even if justice in distribution has been tolerably secured within a particular community, various circumstances may arise to disturb it; and the right way of meeting such disturbances was referred to by Aristotle as corrective justice.[1] The disturbance may take place by accident (i.e. without the choice of any individual), by agreement between individuals, or by the interference of one individual or group with another. The individuals or groups may be members of a different community; but this involves international relations, the consideration of which had better be postponed for the present. Accidents can be to some extent compensated by insurance; and provision is sometimes made for this by the State. Agreements are best dealt with in a separate section, as justice in exchange. Injuries inflicted by individuals on each other are the kind of derangement with which governments are most directly concerned. The injury may consist in breach of contract, robbery, or personal violence (which may be either verbal or physical). Breach of contract may be met by enforcing its fulfilment, perhaps with compensation for loss of time or opportunity (which seems to be the essence of interest). If the loss of time has been fatal, or the goods cannot be restored, it becomes to all intents a personal injury. The same applies to robbery. For personal injuries, in general, no compensation can be made. An eye cannot be restored, nor can any real equivalent be provided for it. The principle of "an eye for an eye and a tooth for a tooth" is not one of compensation, but revenge; and two wrongs do not make a right. All that the State can do is to try to prevent such action by some form of protection (e.g. the police), by deterrence through the prospect of various forms of punishment, by special restrictions (e.g. on the sale of intoxicants or of lethal weapons), and by moral education. The consideration of such devices is beyond our scope; but it seems important to say something about justice in exchange and about the general place of reward and punish-

[1] *Ethics*, Book V, chap. vi.

ment. Aristotle's treatment of these subjects is rendered, in some respects, almost ludicrously inadequate through his effort to represent personal injury and its punishment as cases of exchange and compensation.

4. *Justice in Exchange.*—It would be rather misleading to represent fairness in exchange as coming under the head of corrective justice.[1] To speak of it in this way would be to assume that the commodities that are originally distributed are definitely fixed, and that exchange involves a disturbance of this distribution. But most of the exchanges that actually take place are exchanges of services, and are essentially a part of distribution. People do not, as a rule, exchange their tools or instruments of production, but rather the products of their labour; and it is by such exchanges that they secure food and clothing and the other things that are necessary for carrying on the work of their lives. Hence the problem that is involved in exchange is a part of the problem of distributive justice. Now, the State might conceivably organize this aspect of distribution, just as it might deal with the parcelling out of the land and other more permanent possessions. It might take action to secure that the citizens produce in the right quantity all that is necessary to supply one another's needs, and that each receives just what he requires to enable him to carry on his work. Some writers have endeavoured to picture ideal communities in which all this would be arranged; but it may be doubted whether any one has succeeded in explaining a scheme that would be practicable in a complex society. Pending the production of such a scheme, the adjustment is somewhat roughly made by people finding out for themselves what they are fitted to do, and bargaining for the disposal of their products in exchange for the things that they need. To facilitate such exchanges, an elaborate system of money, securities, and various forms of credit has been devised, involving highly complex

---

[1] Aristotle distinguished the two things pretty clearly.

banking arrangements. How the forces of demand and supply work with the help of this elaborate system, it is one of the chief tasks of the science of economics to explain; and we are not concerned with this problem here. The only question that concerns us here is with regard to the justice of the arrangements that are thus brought about. If we were right in the view that we adopted with regard to the general conception of justice, a just arrangement would mean one in which each one does efficiently the work for which he is fitted, and receives what is necessary to enable him to continue his work. His needs, however, may have to be taken to include what is required for the support of his family, and at least for the early part of the education of his children. Now, it is pretty obvious that there cannot be any guarantee that the action of demand and supply will lead to justice in this sense. The utmost that can be urged is that it does roughly tend to do so—possibly with as close an approximation as any other general method could be expected to yield. The chief defects in its working are due to the fact (*a*) that people do not always find the work for which they are best fitted; (*b*) that they do not always put their best energies into it; (*c*) that sometimes there are too many working at one kind of employment, and not enough at others; (*d*) that men's demands are not always for things that they really need—sometimes they are even for things that are positively hurtful; (*e*) that sometimes things of the greatest value are very little in demand. Among the means that may be used to remedy these defects may be mentioned (*a*) good methods of technical instruction; (*b*) efficient labour exchanges; (*c*) State control of the supply of some of the more important needs; (*d*) taxation or restriction of articles that are of little value, or that are apt to be positively injurious; (*e*) education in the appreciation of real values. It would not be possible, within our present limits, to consider the detailed application of these various modes of treatment; but some further reference may be made to them at a later stage.

5. *Reward and Punishment*.—The best way of regarding reward and punishment, so as to bring out their social significance, is to say that they consist in the award of positive or negative values as marks of approval or disapproval. Usually a reward gives pleasure, and a punishment gives pain; but this is not necessarily the case. A man may very well dislike to have a reward, when he conceives that he has done nothing more than his duty; and yet it may be socially important to give some mark of approbation. Similarly one may be pleased by punishment if it is regarded as one's due. One may even conceive that he has a right to be punished, and, in default of an external authority, may inflict it on himself. One may do penance, and derive satisfaction from the act.

When positive or negative value is awarded simply as compensation, it is hardly right to describe it as reward or punishment. The pension that was given to Dr. Johnson was no doubt partly a mark of approval; but it was partly a recognition that he had not been properly paid for his work. On the other hand, when " damages " are inflicted, they are partly a deferred payment; though they may be intended also to mark disapproval. Hence Aristotle's treatment of rewards and punishments as simply compensation is unsatisfactory, and in some cases becomes quite absurd.

Rewards and punishments given to animals are also not quite properly so called. They are usually intended to induce the animals to perform certain actions and abstain from others. In the ordinary life of animals, this purpose is served by success and failure, usually accompanied by pleasure and pain respectively, and leading to the formation of certain dispositions to action and the inhibition of others. The so-called rewards and punishments that are given to them are a more artificial way of securing the same results. Many of the rewards and punishments given to children are in the main similar. They are stimulants, rather than marks of approval or disapproval. They may be compared to the hanging of a carrot in front of a donkey, or the spurring of a horse.

These are hardly to be called rewards or punishments; though no doubt the element of approval or disapproval is often to some extent present, but usually in a very subordinate way, in such cases. When, on the other hand, a statue was erected to Nelson, or when the bones of Oliver Cromwell were exhumed and hung up, these acts were intended as marks of approval and disapproval; and they might properly be described as reward and punishment, though there was neither pleasure nor pain given to the persons who were thus treated.

Now, when we inquire into the justice of rewards and punishments, it is important to bear in mind the distinctions that have now been indicated between the different senses in which these terms may be understood. When we are dealing with cases of compensation (as we are, for instance, in what are commonly classed as civil injuries), the general principle is clear enough. It is a case of corrective justice, in the sense in which this was understood by Aristotle. It is an attempt to provide an equivalent for what has been wrongly lost—to give to him who had too little, and take from him who has had too much. To estimate the right amount is not always easy, especially as it is not possible in some cases to find any exact equivalent of the same kind. But some way of rendering a sort of rough justice is generally obvious enough. On the other hand, when what are called rewards and punishments are intended as stimuli, they are essentially means for a particular end; and, assuming that the end is good in itself, and one that the power that rewards or punishes is authorized to promote, their justification lies in their suitability for the promotion of the end in question. If we are justified in training animals to perform tricks or to render services, we are justified in stimulating them by any effective methods that are not cruel. If we are justified in giving children particular kinds of training and instruction, we are justified in stimulating them also by methods that are not cruel or degrading. In the case of adult human beings, it is always doubtful whether we are justified in choosing ends for them which they do not choose for themselves; but self-discipline at least is not open to this objection. Finally, in the case of rewards and punishments in the stricter sense, the object in view is that of making clear both the fact of approval or disapproval and the grounds on which such approval or disapproval rests; and here, once more, the reward or punishment is justified when it is the best means for attaining this end, when it is not cruel or humiliating, and when it is applied by an authority that has a right to express approval or disapproval of the kind of action in question.

Punishment naturally calls for more attention than reward. In dealing with adult human beings, it is, in general, true that the only suitable reward for right action is to give it "the glory of going on and still to be." It is wrong action that calls for special treatment. Now, the various theories of punishment that have been put forward connect pretty obviously with the various types of action and ends that have just been referred to. The preventive theory is applicable to them all. The compensatory theory of Aristotle applies specially to the first type. The deterrent theory, and also the theory of natural resultants, as formulated by Rousseau or Spencer, apply specially to the second type. The retributive theory, in the sense in which it is also reformative or educative, applies specially to the third type. But the discussion of these theories belongs to ethics, the philosophy of law, and the science of education, rather than to social philosophy. At least it is beyond the scope of the present outlines.[1]

6. *Equity.*—It is apparent, from what has been already stated, that not everything that is legally just is just to particular individuals or socially beneficial in particular

---

[1] Reference may be made to Green's *Principles of Political Obligation*, L; to Bosanquet's *Philosophical Theory of the State*, chap. viii, § 7; to McTaggart's *Studies in Hegelian Cosmology*, chap. v; to Rashdall's *Theory of Good and Evil*, Book I, chap. ix; and to Spencer's *Education*, chap. iii.

cases. The generality of the law prevents it from taking full account of special circumstances. Hence the conception of equity has been distinguished from that of legal justice.[1] An equitable arrangement, in this sense, is one that is strictly just when all the circumstances are taken into account. Not only is it impossible for law to secure what is equitable in this sense, but it would hardly even be possible to devise any method by which it could be accurately determined. Of course, even in legal decisions it is sometimes possible to take account of special circumstances. One who has committed a crime may be wholly or partially exonerated on account of extenuating circumstances; and, on the other hand, one who is notoriously incapable or negligent may be debarred from what would otherwise be his legal right. But less obvious cases cannot be legally dealt with. Hence it falls rather upon private individuals or voluntary associations to make good certain deficiencies of the law. Churches and similiar institutions, as well as private benefactors, can sometimes secure for individuals privileges to which their merits entitle them, but to which they have no legal claim; and, on the other hand, popular reprobation may often inflict a deserved punishment which the law has no authority to enforce. But these are somewhat incalculable agencies, and there is seldom much guarantee for the equity of their decisions. Some further considerations bearing upon this will have to be brought forward at a later stage.

It may be well to notice that the word "equity" is in some danger of conveying a misleading impression. It suggests the idea of equality. Now, there is, of course, a sense in which not only what is equitable, but even what is legal, involves equality. They both involve that cases that are essentially the same have to be dealt with in the same way. But this does not imply equality where the cases are different. The fine saying of Walt Whitman [2]—

---

[1] See Aristotle's *Ethics*, Book V, chap. xiv. The recent statements on this subject by Professor Kojiro Sugimori in *The Principles of the Moral Empire*, chap. v, are worth referring to.

[2] *Song of Myself*, 24.

"I will accept nothing which all cannot have their counterpart of on the same terms"—can hardly be quite literally applied. One who is blind cannot have any real equivalent for sight ; and one who is deficient in any capacity cannot have any definite equivalent for that which such a faculty enables one to enjoy. The saying can only be applied to arbitrary or artificial advantages, not to those that rest on natural differences ; and even to the former it would often be very difficult to apply it. But the general subject of equality will be more fully dealt with in the next chapter.

7. *Natural Rights.*—Legally people have a right to what is enforced or permitted by the State, or by some authority recognized by the State. Morally their rights are determined by such general considerations as those that have been already mentioned in connection with justice and equity. If the legal rights do not coincide with the moral rights, it is incumbent on people to use any legitimate means that may be at their disposal to bring about reform. Whether active resistance to the government is a legitimate means, and, if so, in what circumstances, is a difficult question, which could not be satisfactorily discussed here. All that can be said is that it depends on a balancing of the evils of an inequitable or unjust arrangement against the evils of anarchy, civil war, or general insecurity—a balance which can never be exactly measured, but may be approximately estimated. What is specially important for our present purpose, however, is simply the recognition that the rights involved in the constitution of a well-organized community may properly be described as natural. But natural rights have often been understood in a somewhat different way. They have been connected with the conception of a " state of nature " as existing prior to the formation of any organized states. Hobbes, for instance, whose view on this subject is the most definite and extreme, contends [1] that " every man by nature hath right to all things, i.e.

[1] *De cive*, I. 10.

to do whatsoever he listeth to whom he listeth, to possess, use, and enjoy all things he will and can." It has already been urged that this conception of a state of nature is fictitious, and that there is no real ground for thinking that the existence of organized communities is not essentially natural to man. We may speak of natural impulses that are prior to any definite organization; but even among animals natural impulses are subject to some restraint, and it is much more decidedly natural for human beings to restrain them by reference both to individual good and to the common good. On the whole, it seems truest to say that natural rights are simply those that it is right for a well-constituted society to grant.[1]

8. *Rights and Obligations.*—It is evident that a right, whether equitable or legal, is in some degree dependent on the fulfilment of certain obligations by the person on whom the right is conferred. This is especially clear in the case of equitable rights. According to the Platonic conception of justice, the rights that are due to any one are simply those that are involved in the performance of his civic duties. This view may, as we have seen, be regarded as somewhat too extreme. It may be recognized that individuals have some right to freedom for self-development, as well as to the opportunity of performing their more purely civic obligations; but it remains true that the granting of rights rests on some presupposition that they will be employed for the furtherance of some desirable end. The non-fulfilment of this obligation may fairly be held to annul the moral right; though it may only be in cases of flagrant abuse that the legal right can be withheld. It would be an intolerable tyranny for the State to determine the exact way in which individuals employ the rights that are conferred upon them; yet it

[1] D. G. Ritchie's book on *Natural Rights* contains the fullest discussion of the whole subject, but is perhaps a little too negative. On the more positive side, reference may be made to Professor W. J. Roberts' article on "The Appeal to Nature in Morals and Politics," *International Journal of Ethics*, April 1910.

is implicitly assumed that they are employed in some legitimate fash'on. Frequently, in purely legal considerations, it is held that the only obligation that is implied in the possession of rights is that which is imposed on others than those who enjoy them. Thus the right to particular kinds of property involves the obligation on the part of others to " keep their hands from picking and stealing." Obligations, thus regarded, tend to be conceived as almost purely negative ; and no doubt, for legal purposes, it is seldom possible to go much beyond this. The more positive obligations can seldom be defined with sufficient accuracy to be capable of legal enforcement. But it is important to remember that some obligations are implied on the part of a person who enjoys a right ; and occasionally they are so obvious that even the law can take account of them. The expressions " perfect obligation " and " imperfect obligation " are sometimes used to distinguish those that can be legally enforced from those that either cannot be enforced or could only be enforced at the expense of some grave enfringement of individual liberty. Legally, for instance, a man may " do what he likes with his own," so long as he does not infringe the legal rights of others ; but few things can be regarded as so entirely a man's own as to absolve him from all obligation in his use of them. He may possess animals, for example ; but he is not at liberty to treat them with cruelty, although animals can hardly be said to possess any legal rights. Even the wanton destruction or abuse of inanimate things may very well be prevented by legal enactments. This might be otherwise expressed by saying that the community reserves some rights over the things that it permits its citizens to possess ; but this is only another way of saying that the rights that they enjoy imply some obligations with regard to the manner of their use. To this extent at least the Platonic conception appears to be a thoroughly sound one.

CHAPTER VI

SOCIAL IDEALS

1. *The General Significance of Ideals.*—Societies, like other aspects of human life, are essentially progressive; and it is important that we should try to understand not merely what they are, but what they have it in them to become. This applies, indeed, in some degree, to all things that live and grow. The curious phrase of Aristotle, τὸ τί ἦν εἶναι (the being what a thing was), seems to be intended to bring this out. In studying such things, we have always to bear in mind their potentialities of development. But in most living things there are pretty definite limits to such potentialities. A seed unfolds into a particular type of plant, and an embryo into a particular type of animal; and the modifications that can be made in them are comparatively slight. The same applies to the more purely physical aspects of human life, and to all that depends on these. We cannot, by taking thought, add a cubit to our stature; nor does it seem possible to make much change in the general characteristics of our temperament and endowments. But, apart from this, we can hardly set any limits to the possibilities of the human race. Our knowledge of ourselves and of the world in which we live may grow indefinitely, and may yield an indefinite advance in the control of our material conditions and in the improvement of our social relations. In these respects at least it is true to say that "man partly is, and wholly hopes to be." No doubt this very fact makes it impossible for us to forecast the future; and sometimes it may be rightly said that "a

man never goes so far as when he does not know where he is going." Yet we can certainly look ahead to some extent, and partially define the general direction in which we seek to move. We may, accordingly, now note some of the chief ways in which attempts have been made to indicate the ideals at which a society should aim. These are partly connected with the main conceptions of government, and may consequently be characterized broadly as the aristocratic and the democratic ideal. But they may be more definitely expressed by noting what precisely is aimed at by these two forms respectively. In general it seems true to say that the aristocratic ideal aims chiefly at efficiency and at a high type of personal development, while the democratic ideal has for its watchwords Liberty, Equality, and Fraternity. We may first consider the two ideals in general and afterwards the special aims that they imply.

2. *The Aristocratic Ideal.*—The nature of this ideal is well seen, in its most inspiring form, in Plato's *Republic* and in the writings of Carlyle and Ruskin. In a more extreme, paradoxical and repellent form, it is presented in the works of Nietzsche. Its motto may be found in the Homeric phrase, αἰὲν ἀριστεύειν καὶ ὑπείροχον ἔμμεναι ἄλλων (always to excel and surpass the others), and in the modern *noblesse oblige*. Its exponents love to dwell on the virtues of godlike and heroic men, men who "live dangerously" and achieve great things for the race, or who, like Goethe, raise the pyramid of their being as high as possible. Their object is, in general, to secure the most capable men as servants of the community, and especially those who are most capable of ruling. We have seen that the general principle of securing those who are most capable for the discharge of each particular function is involved in the Platonic conception of justice; and in this sense we have accepted the principle. But, in this sense, it is not specially aristocratic, since every one is assumed to be capable of exercising some function; and the subordination of one to another is not necessarily

involved. The principle becomes definitely aristocratic only when it is applied specially to the rulers, and elevates them over others as a superior caste. No doubt, the best exponents of the aristocratic ideal tend to mitigate its rigour by emphasizing the conception of *noblesse oblige*. The Christian injunction, "if any will be chief among you, let him be your servant," is partly anticipated by Plato in the rigid discipline that he imposes on his guardians, and in his exclusion of them from many of the privileges that are allowed to the commercial and industrial classes. Carlyle says [1] that "it is the everlasting privilege of the foolish to be governed by the wise." The conceptions of chivalry, whether as seen in the mediæval knights or in the Japanese Samurai, show a similar balance of dignity against privilege. It is well to remember that "knight" means originally a servant, and that some princes have taken as their motto "*Ich dien*." But, as a velvet glove may cover a mailed fist, so a humble device may sometimes veil an insolent spirit. Still, it must be admitted at least that the aristocratic ideal contains a noble aim. A finely developed personality can hardly be too highly prized; and efficiency in a leader is of more supreme importance than in any other. Next to the efficiency of the ruler (if indeed it should be placed second), the efficiency of the educator is probably the most important.

3. *The Democratic Ideal.*—The democratic ideal is sometimes taken to mean the government by the lower class in the community or (what is almost the same thing) the government by the majority. It is in this sense that the conception is understood and attacked by Plato, and in modern times by Carlyle, Ruskin, and Sir Henry Maine. J. Austin [2] defined Democracy as "any government in which the governing body is a comparatively large fraction of the entire nation." But hardly any of its advocates would accept this as a true account of the ideal at which

---

[1] *Latterday Pamphlets*, I.

[2] *A Plea for the Constitution.* See also his *Lectures on Jurisprudence* and Maine's *Popular Government*, Essay II.

they aim. The phrase of President Lincoln, "Government of the people by the people and for the people," would be generally accepted as a more correct description. But the first and the last part of this expression apply to all good government. The advocates of an aristocracy aim at the government of the people, and conceive that such government is for the people's good. Their contention is that what is called democracy tends to be hardly a government at all, but only a thinly veiled mode of anarchy; and that it is not really for the good of the people, but at most for those parts of the people that happen, from time to time, to acquire power and influence. The advocates of democracy reply that these defects are not necessary aspects of a democratic system; and, on the other hand, that there is no real guarantee that an aristocracy will be either an efficient government or one that consults the well-being of the people as a whole. To secure this, they urge that the government should be not merely of the people and for the people, but also by the people.

Now, this raises again the question, to which we have previously alluded, What is the people? It may be well to add a little more at this point on that subject. A people would seem to mean a body of individuals in close association aiming at a common good. The chief difficulty is that, if we interpret it in this sense, we can seldom be sure that in any nation a people is actually to be found. We are told of a time in the history of the Jews when there was no king in Israel, and every one did what seemed right in his own eyes; but, if we substitute the people for the king, it would seem to be quite possible to have a state of affairs in which there is no people, and every one's hand is against his neighbour. Of approximations to this it would be easy to point to many unhappy instances. When this is the case, such government as there is will tend to be one of some people by other people, probably in the main for the interest of the latter group. Usually it will become, in some degree, a plutocracy. Do not, it may be asked, almost all governments that are described as democracies tend in effect to become plutocratic oligarchies? It has to be observed further, that, even at the best, the people by whom a government is carried on can seldom be quite the same as the people for whose benefit it exists. A government, and especially a democratic government, is apt to be short-lived. It is generally a party government, and one party rapidly gives place to another; and each party aims, to some extent, at the obstruction of the other. The people, on the other hand, if there is a people, continues from generation to generation. The good that it desires is the good, not merely of those that are now living and able to take some active share in the work of government, but also of the young who are only being prepared for citizenship, and of their still unborn posterity. What guarantee have we that the contending parties can have any clear vision of the good of all this people? Is it not rather likely that their government will prove as short-sighted as it is short-lived? Hence the phrase "government by the people" is apt to be highly misleading. What it is meant to emphasize is that a good government must imply a people having a common good; and that we can only be sure of such a government if this common good is, in some degree, clearly apprehended and chosen by all. This is somewhat further emphasized in the motto "Liberty, Equality, and Fraternity." But, in order to bring out the significance of these terms, it may be most convenient to consider them in the inverse order. After dealing briefly with them, it will be easier to see the value of the conceptions that underlie the aristocratic ideal, and to discuss the possibility of combining the various aims.

4. *Fraternity.*—Fraternity may be regarded as the essential basis of any social ideal. Any conception of a genuine social unity implies, as we have seen, a certain like-mindedness in the people and a certain recognition that their good is a common one. This was emphasized by Plato in his account of the organic unity of the State;

and it was even more definitely brought out by Aristotle in his contention that friendship is the basis of justice. Modern statements of this conception can hardly be said to have added much to the general theory of the subject; but the underlying principle gained an additional force from the cosmopolitanism of the Stoics and from the more deeply spiritual interpretation of human brotherhood that underlies the teaching of Christianity. Every other genuine ideal for the unity of society may be regarded as growing out of this central conception, and as seeking to make its implications more apparent. It is evident, for instance, as Aristotle urges,[1] that friendship or brotherhood implies a certain kind of equality; and this is the conception that is naturally taken next in order.

5. *Equality.*—Equality may be interpreted in a number of different senses; and we must try to see which is the clearest and most fundamental. It may mean equality of possessions, equality before the law, or simply the denial of the ultimate importance of such distinctions as those of caste, race, sex, nationality, education, ability, character, and the like. A few words on each of these meanings may be useful.

(1) Equality of possessions is advocated by some of those who are called communists or socialists.[2] It is a view that connects itself naturally with the conception of brotherhood. According to the old saying, "Among friends all things are common." Of course, as a gospel for immediate application, it is open to the objection that all are not friends, but at the most may gradually become so; but this fact need not prevent us from accepting it as a counsel of perfection, to be applied as far as possible. A more serious objection is that which connects

---

[1] *Ethics*, Book VIII, especially chap. ix.

[2] Certainly not by all. It is sometimes difficult to determine how far particular socialistic writers have this in view as an ultimate ideal. Among prominent socialists at the present time, Mr. Bernard Shaw is perhaps the one who has made the nearest approximation to it.

itself with the Platonic conception of diversity of function. Those whose vocations are different have different needs. A poet, a speculative philosopher, or a religious teacher may have need of little for himself beyond the bare necessities of existence, together with leisure for his own free perceptions, thoughts, or intuitions, and perhaps some books, which he might be able to consult in a public institution. An inventor, on the other hand, or a student of natural history may want some elaborate machinery or a large equipment for an exploring expedition ; and he may require to have these at his free disposal. Even if they were provided by the public (as they sometimes are at present), they would be essentially his possessions for the time. Others would not be entitled to use them. And even a friendly public might not be willing to entrust such possessions to him until he had justified their confidence by some smaller adventures at his own risk.

Again, if all had equal possessions, it would seem to be practically necessary that all should render equal services ; and this could not readily be ensured. Services cannot be as easily measured as goods can. It seems to be assumed by those who advocate equality of goods, that the goods at present in existence would be available for distribution. But the labour that produces these goods is at present dependent on the fact that it is only by such labour that goods are procurable. If every one were to have an equal share, without the condition of equal service, it would certainly not be easy to establish such an organization, even among the most well-disposed people, as would ensure that the necessary goods were forthcoming. The truth seems to be that such an arrangement is not sufficiently rooted in nature to have much prospect of success. It is natural for men to put forth effort to secure those things that they need or value. They may do this directly by actually producing them, or indirectly by producing other things and effecting an exchange. But men have no natural stimulus to pursue ends that are beyond their vision or power of valuation. No doubt, if we were to suppose them all to be endowed with such vision, the case would be different. Perhaps the application of the principles of eugenics, together with a very perfect system of education, may produce such a race of people; but it hardly seems worth while at present to speculate about the social organization of supermen. In the meantime, it is hardly true that, even in the best ordered families, the principle of equality of possessions is observed, though here there is certainly some approximation to it. Rather the tendency is, on the whole, to adjust possessions to needs and capacities. This is simply the application of the Platonic conception of justice, which, as we have seen, does not involve equality.

(2) Equality before the law is, of course, involved in the idea of justice; but, as we have already noted, it means only that, when the relevant circumstances are the same, the treatment is the same. Law is no respecter of persons, even when equity might call for some differentiation in their treatment. The conception of equity itself, however, is apt to give rise to some confusion. It is apt to be thought that it implies equality, in a sense in which it hardly seems to do so. Spencer, for instance, appears to have over-emphasized [1] the connection between equity and equality. This is, I think, partly due to a misconception. It is sometimes thought that the conception of equity is derived from that of equality; whereas it would seem that the reverse is rather the case. The original meaning of *æquus* appears to have been what is just, or perhaps at first what is plane or level. It then came to mean what is equal, because this is just when there is no special ground for discrimination. But to say that is not to say or imply that there never are special grounds for discrimination.

(3) The third meaning of equality is the most important for our present purpose, and is the one that connects immediately with the idea of brotherhood. What is involved in it is the recognition that the things that distinguish men from one another are insignificant in

[1] *Data of Ethics*, § 60.

comparison with the things that unite them. This is, indeed, generally true whenever we are dealing with beings of the same kind. There are many different types of dog; but probably their common doghood counts for more in the determination of their modes of life than the special features that distinguish them. At any rate, it may be pretty safely maintained that it is our common humanity that gives us our unique position in the universe, and that all other differences are comparatively insignificant.[1] "A man's a man for a' that." It remains true, no doubt, that some differences are more fundamental than others. In Burns's song it is differences of rank and fortune that are declared to be insignificant. The possession of "sense and worth" is still recognized as a legitimate basis of distinction. But at least, when we acknowledge the essential unity of mankind, sharp distinctions of caste can hardly be admitted. Here most people in modern times would feel that Plato was at fault, with his "noble falsehood" about some people being of gold, some of silver, and some of baser metal. Aristotle is rather less inclined for such a differentiation, but recognizes a pretty sharp barrier between those who are by nature free and those who are by nature slaves. Stoicism and Christianity did much to break down such distinctions; though they have reappeared in Nietzsche's antithesis between the morality of masters and that of slaves. Even Carlyle's insistence on "the infinite difference between a good man and a bad man" is certainly somewhat contrary to the spirit of Christianity, and is probably indefensible in itself. Most men at least are neither black nor white, but rather various shades of grey. Even the superman—if this means a large-natured man like Shakespeare or like Walt Whitman—is "not as God, but then most godlike being most a man." At any rate, it is only on such a view that the general view of human brotherhood can be maintained. Equality, in this sense,

[1] I may remind readers of the constant emphasis that is laid on this conception in the writings of Walt Whitman, and, more recently and more explicitly, in those of Mr. G. K. Chesterton.

is thus a necessary implication of fraternity, and simply serves to make the meaning of the latter a little more determinate. But it is well to bear in mind that it does not involve the denial of differences, nor need it even lead us to desire to "rub each other's angles down." There are two ways of removing angularities. We may cut off the angular points, or we may expand the remainder of the surface. The one method leaves us with a somewhat contracted sphere, the other with an enlarged one. It would seem that the latter is what we ought to aim at. In religion, for instance, it may be doubted whether it is wise to seek to eliminate the aspects in which different types of religion differ. It is probably better to try to develop the deeper unity of principle that underlies them; so that gradually the points of difference may be seen to be insignificant. But this is only an illustration; and we need not dwell upon it here.

6. *Liberty.*—The considerations at the end of the preceding section lead us directly to the conception of liberty. The liberty that is demanded in an ideal society is sometimes thought of as meaning the complete independence of individuals, except in so far as their liberty interferes with the liberty of others. It was in this way that it was put by Kant, and more recently by Spencer. But it may be questioned whether this limitation is quite adequate. There may be forms of licence that it is desirable to check, though they are quite compatible with a similar licence on the part of others. Even the principle that "they should take who have the power, and they should keep who can" leaves every one free to pursue it; and the conception of pure *laissez faire* in industry is a more limited application of the same principle. The real limitation to freedom is to be found rather in the idea of a common good. Among brothers freedom of action is limited, not merely by the desire not to restrict one another's freedom, but by the desire not to interfere with any real good. It would seem that, if there is any reality in the conception of the brotherhood of mankind,

a similar limitation must apply to the larger community as well. Hence it may be doubted whether any satisfactory ground can be given for particular forms of liberty, except the ground that the possession of them does more good than harm; in other words, that they are rights that may be expected to carry with them their corresponding obligations. Freedom of speech, for instance, is properly claimed as a right in a civilized community; because any check upon it would more often hinder the utterance of things that it is well to utter than of things that had better be left unsaid. But this is probably true only when people in general have reached a certain level of self-restraint in speech; and, even in such a people, there may be circumstances in which it ceases to be true—e.g. in a state of war. Even in peace there may be limits to the desirability of complete freedom in this respect. Dr. Johnson said that every one had a right to say what he thought, and every one else had a right to knock him down for it. But this would hardly conduce to social order and brotherhood. It seems better to say that, in general, the simple expression of an opinion does no harm to any one; and that to leave the control of such expression in the hands of any kind of official (such as a literary censor), or to try to determine by law what sort of opinion is fit to be uttered, would often lead to the suppression of new and important ideas or of valuable forms of literary art. But it may be right to introduce some qualifications even in time of peace. It cannot well be recognized that any one has the right to describe another as a liar or murderer, at least without the production of very ample evidence. It is doubtful also whether it should be regarded as allowable that any one should express opinions in a needlessly offensive way, or shout them too loudly from the housetop; though, in these cases, it may be difficult to determine the degree of offensiveness or loudness that should be prevented. Perhaps limitations of this kind should be regarded rather as moral restrictions than as restrictions that are properly imposed by law—at least in a community in which most people have learned to exercise self-restraint. But we cannot pursue this subject here into further detail.

In general, it seems clear that the claim to liberty is implied in the principle of fraternity. Those who have a regard for one another as persons will not seek to place restraints on one another's activity, except for some very sufficient reason. But there are cases in which such sufficient reason may be adduced—viz. when it is apparent that some particular form of freedom is liable to be used in such a way as to be prejudicial to the common good. All that can properly be said, without a thorough discussion of detailed instances, is that the *onus probandi* rests with those who seek to restrain any particular form of activity.[1]

7. *Personal Development.*—The conception of freedom may be taken as giving the transition from the democratic to the aristocratic ideal; for, the freer people are, the more do they tend to exhibit their relative superiority and inferiority; and, in general, those who are superior in any respect (especially in those respects that are somewhat prominent and forcible) are apt to acquire some degree of dominance over those who are inferior. The aristocratic ideal grows out of the recognition that modes of superiority ought to be encouraged. This is not contrary to the spirit of fraternity; though, as Aristotle urged, it is difficult to have a genuine friendship where there is conspicuous inequality. It is not, however, impossible; and, as long as there is real inequality among human beings, any genuine brotherhood of humanity must involve the toleration of such inequality, and the recognition of the natural leadership of the superior in any particular respect. Such a recognition does not necessarily lead to an aristocratic type of society; but it very readily does so, especially if there are any cir-

[1] Mill's book *On Liberty* is probably still the best general statement that we have on this subject. Spencer's *The Man versus the State* is very one-sided; and so, I think, are some of the recent utterances of that most amiable of anarchists, Mr. G. K. Chesterton.

cumstances that lead to special emphasis being laid on some particular form of superiority—such as military skill or the possession of some form of knowledge, such as the ancient classics. The saying of Spinoza, that "the highest good is common to all, and all may equally enjoy it," is subject to the qualification that some of the finest things are only appreciated after a considerable degree of effort. Such an aristocracy as that which is advocated by Plato is based upon the conviction that the highest good can only be properly understood and appreciated by the few; and, even by them, only through a long course of training and instruction. Those who have not been so disciplined must, he thought, be subject to external control. The chief objections to such a view are (1) that no sharp division can be drawn between those who are capable and those who are not capable of appreciating the higher values; (2) that the appreciation of them is often cultivated fully as well by the experience of life as by any special method of training and instruction; (3) that the recognition of the brotherhood of humanity is itself (as Plato allows) one of the most important of the higher values, and that any sharp division of classes puts a fatal barrier in the way of such recognition. But these objections need not prevent us from acknowledging that some are superior to others in certain important respects, and that every kind of superiority gives a title to some form of leadership. A career should be open to all the talents, in order that all the important ends of life may be served in the most efficient way. And thus we are led to notice the ideal of efficiency, which is naturally connected with that of free development.

8. *Efficiency*.—It seems clear, from what has been already stated, that the conception of a just order of society involves that of efficiency, as well as certain forms of equality and liberty; and thus implies elements that may be properly described as aristocratic, as well as those that are more purely democratic in their tendency. The common good, it would seem, is best promoted by placing

every one, as far as possible, in the position that he can most efficiently fill; and it is, no doubt, true that this is specially important in the positions of greatest responsibility and most far-reaching influence. It has always to be remembered, however, that efficiency must mean efficiency for the common good. A ruler may be very efficient in his actions, and yet may be essentially pursuing his own private good or that of some limited class with which he happens to be associated. Merely to say, as Carlyle was prone to do, that the "canning man" should be the king,[1] is not very satisfactory. Carlyle's view depended partly on his disbelief in specialized forms of ability, and in any ultimate distinction between capacity and goodness. But at least what Bacon called "wisdom for a man's self" is pretty clearly distinguishable from wisdom for the community. The ability to lead an army to victory does not always imply either the ability or the will to make the best use of victory. It remains true, however, that in large and important enterprises, especially where swift decisions are necessary, it is essential that the most capable man should have the leadership, and should be given a free hand in his action. It is in such circumstances that the Homeric saying applies most forcibly, οὐκ ἀγαθὸν πολυκοιρανίη· εἷς κοίρανος ἔστω (the rule of many is not good; let one be chief). But even Homer recognized that, in deliberation, the leader should be subject to the guidance of his council. It is chiefly in the details of executive action that the swift perception and prompt decision of a single capable mind is required. Comte laid special emphasis on the necessity for making a distinction, in this respect, between the requirement of deliberation and that of executive action; and his disciple, Mr. F. Harrison, has summed the matter up by saying [2] that "on the one hand we must have real

[1] I am afraid this is one of Carlyle's fanciful etymologies. King seems to be connected with kin, and probably referred originally to noble birth.

[2] *Order and Progress*, p. 382. See also Sir Chas. Waldstein's *Aristodemocracy* and *Patriotism, National and International*, Postscript to Preface; also *A Defence of Aristocracy*, by A. M. Ludovici.

leadership, on the other we must have genuine consent." This implies a certain combination of the characteristic features of Aristocracy and Democracy.

9. *General Summary on Social Ideals.*—We may now sum up briefly with regard to the two main types of social ideal.

(1) The purely democratic ideal tends to over-emphasize the conception of equality, and thus to neglect the importance of having in every position the man who is fittest and best for the discharge of its functions. It is thus apt to be lacking both in efficiency and in the development of the highest types of personality. It seeks, in Browning's phrase, to have "no more giants," but rather to "elevate the race at once." But the race can only be gradually elevated, and a chief factor in its elevation is the presence and influence of men of high ability and character, occupying the positions for which they are best fitted.

(2) The aristocratic ideal, on the other hand, suffers from the following disabilities: (*a*) It has never been adequately explained how the best rulers are to be discovered and put in their proper place. The most efficient to rule are not always the most efficient to secure their right position. Hence Plato was led to urge that the best ruler would have to be *compelled* to rule. In times of crisis the most capable man is sometimes pressed forward, almost against his will; but it is to be feared that this is not very often the case. (*b*) Even a very efficient ruler needs some guidance and control. The very fact that he is elevated above others makes it difficult for him to understand the needs of those over whom he rules—unless he is in a very small community, where he can have constant intercourse with those who are below him. It may be doubted whether even the good Haroun Alraschid was successful in finding out everything that it was important for him to know.

Hence it appears that a genuine ideal must contain elements of both aristocracy and democracy; and in what proportion they are to be combined must depend largely on circumstances of time and place. In general, it is probably true to say that, the less fully a people is educated and united, the more necessary is it that it should be guided from above by the best and fittest who can by any means be discovered and brought forward. When the people becomes more of a real unity, when it has well-established traditions and widely diffused knowledge, it becomes more possible to give the democratic elements in its constitution a continually increasing prominence.

The attempts that have been made, from those of Campanella and More to those of Bellamy, William Morris, and Mr. H. G. Wells, to sketch what are commonly called Utopias—i.e. imaginary conditions of a perfect social unity—suffer, in general, from the impossibility of forecasting the exact directions in which human life may be reasonably expected to advance. They are often, however, highly instructive, especially when several of them are compared with one another. Their interest is often mainly historical, indicating the main defects that were felt to be present in the existing social order at particular times, and suggesting ways in which these defects might be removed.[1] Hence they are generally most valuable when, like Plato's *Republic*, they are not pure Utopias, but rather definite attempts to study some existing form of society, and to bring out the elements of strength and weakness that are contained in it. Plato's *Republic* is based on the study of the types of community represented by Athens and Sparta, and is an attempt to combine what is best in each, with a few additions that

[1] The same purpose is often served even more effectively by somewhat satirical pictures of imaginary societies, such as those of Rabelais and Swift, or, in more recent times, Samuel Butler's *Erewhon* and M. Anatole France's *Penguin Island*. Actual attempts to establish small ideal communities are also of great interest. C. Nordhoff's book on *The Communistic Societies of the United States* and *The History of American Socialisms* by J. H. Noyes have a special value from this point of view, as bringing into somewhat vivid contrast the more successful and the less successful types. There are some good remarks on Utopias in Dr. Beattie Crozier's *Sociology applied to Practical Politics*, Book II, chap. i.

are suggested by reflection on the combination. Studies of this kind enable us to see a little way in advance, which is perhaps all that human beings can fairly hope to do.

One of the chief difficulties, however, in considering the best way of organizing any particular community, lies in the fact that we have to take account of its relations to other communities, by which it is liable to be affected both in the way of friendship and of enmity. This is a consideration to which we may conveniently pass in the next chapter.

BOOK III
WORLD ORDER

CHAPTER I

INTERNATIONAL RELATIONS

1. *General Statement.*—So far we have been considering mainly the constitution of isolated or independent communities, organizing their internal relations and providing for external defence. Writers on social and political theory have, in general, been rather too prone to confine themselves to such considerations. Plato, for instance, assumed that the ideal community that he was depicting would, on the whole, be self-contained and self-sufficient —except that its relations to other Greek communities would be, in some respects, more intimate than its relations to the surrounding "barbarians." This was, of course, a very natural assumption for him to make. He was not constructing an ideal in the air, but rather interpreting the conditions that he found in the actual City State with which he was familiar. Subsequent writers have not the same excuse; and, no doubt, some of them have referred a good deal to international relations; but it is probably still true to say that such relations have seldom been sufficiently emphasized.[1]

It is evident, as we have already noted, that modern states at least are not self-sufficient, but form parts of a larger community, by their relations to which their mode of existence is profoundly affected. The larger modern states are, in general, combinations of separate

[1] Opinions on this subject are, no doubt, a good deal affected by individual bias. I must confess that I have always been a believer in the *orbis terrarum*, much more than in the contributions of particular nationalities.

countries, sometimes only held together, by force or temporary necessity, and remaining to some extent distinct nations, in spite of the fact that they have a common central government. It not infrequently happens that the relations of these countries to other states are almost as close as those that bind them to the particular state within which they are politically included. Even after Scotland was definitely included within Great Britain, it continued to have some intimate relations to France. Ireland has kept up a good deal of intercourse with the United States of America. Wales has long had many cordial relations with Brittany. England itself has, until quite recently, had a strong infusion of German influence, by which it has been greatly affected both for good and for evil. The Poles have been divided between Russia, Germany, and Austria, but have not ceased to have independent national aspirations of their own. The Jews, when they are treated with toleration, become, in general, good citizens of the states within whose territories they happen for the time to be living, but are also bound to one another by certain common traditions. In almost all European nations there have been a considerable number of people who have tended to think of themselves as "good Europeans," rather than as specially devoted to the institutions and traditions of their particular countries; and the interests of some have been even more widely cosmopolitan. And it would certainly be difficult to overrate the extent to which the whole of our Western civilization is based upon that of Rome, of Greece, and of Judea. Many other instances might be adduced to show that we cannot lightly assume that the life of any nation or state is homogeneous, independent and self-contained. It is important, therefore, to consider some of the chief ways in which the general activities of an organized community are affected by its relations to other communities.

2. *International Morality.*—If there is any truth in the conception of the brotherhood of mankind, it is evident

that the foundations of morality must be held to be common to all nationalities. Indeed, it is pretty clear that, on any intelligible view of human nature, this must be the case. It does not fall within our scope here to discuss different theories of morality; but, whether we suppose that morality consists in the promotion of happiness or perfection, whether we suppose that it rests upon the intuitions of conscience or the decisions of reason, it can hardly be disputed that its basis lies in something that is essentially common to humanity. It has to be admitted, however—again, on any theory—that the moral ideas by which human beings are actually guided in their practice do not quite correspond to the ultimate principle by which they are justified, and do vary somewhat from time to time, from place to place, and even from individual to individual. Particular duties and particular virtues are more highly prized and more uniformly practised and cultivated by some than by others. Some attach more importance to courage, some to temperance or self-control, some to truthfulness, some to loyalty, some to benevolence, some to industry, some to the pursuit of knowledge or wisdom, some to the suppression of desire. But those who specially admire and cultivate particular modes of excellence would seldom be found to deny that the modes of excellence that are pursued by others are also, in some degree, good. It is sometimes urged, however, that each people has a special civilization or, as the Germans express it, a special Kultur of its own, to which a certain system of moral excellences belongs; and that it is the business of a nation as a whole, in its corporate capacity, to maintain and advance its own special type of civilization. According to those who hold this view, in its most extreme form, the individuals within any state are under the obligation of fulfilling certain duties and cultivating certain virtues; but the State, as such, has no duty but that of maintaining, defending and advancing the mode of life that specially belongs to it. It is justified, they conceive, in any action —however objectionable it might otherwise be—that is necessary for this purpose. Such necessity "knows no law." There is no higher principle by which it could be legitimately constrained. A view of this kind is evidently very closely connected with the doctrine, to which reference had already been made, that the State is essentially force. The latter doctrine has been maintained, and has been applied in the manner that has just been indicated, by certain Prussian writers on the theory of the State, of whom H. von Treitschke is the most notable. It seems to have been so widely adopted in Prussia that it is hardly unfair to characterize it as the Prussian theory. It is not, however, altogether peculiar to Prussia. It has been, to some extent, accepted in theory, and perhaps still more extensively acted upon in practice, in other countries as well.[1] Also, some Prussian writers—notably Kant and, I believe, Paulsen—were far from subscribing to it.[2] But the successful application of it by Frederick the Great and Bismarck, and the eloquent exposition of it by Treitschke and others, have evidently given it a certain dominance in Prussia in recent times, and even in Germany as a whole, such as it has never had in any other time or country. It is not a doctrine that can be thoroughly discussed here; but a few remarks upon it may be useful and timely, especially as it is generally believed to have been one of the chief causes—some would say, essentially the only definite cause—of the present great European war.

It has been urged already that it is erroneous to regard force as the essence of the State; but it has been conceded that the possession of force is one of its essential features. That that force is to be used for the support of its life, and of all that is valuable within that life, is obvious enough. What is not obvious is, that it may legitimately

[1] For illustrations of this, reference may be made to Mr. J. A. Hobson's *Towards International Government*, p. 179, and to Lord Acton's Introduction to Machiavelli's *Prince*, pp. xxviii–xxxiii.

[2] Even those who may, on the whole, be said to subscribe to it, nearly always admit some qualifications in its application. Kant and Paulsen were not purely Prussian; but neither was Treitschke.

be used for this purpose in contravention of every other obligation. It may be conceded that circumstances are conceivable in which the object in view would be of such supreme importance as almost to override every other consideration. If we could conceive a country with so high and unique a civilization that it would be to the obvious advantage of the world to have it universally imposed, and if it were clear that it could be imposed by force, it might be difficult to point to any obstacle that should be allowed to stand in its way. Some peoples in the past would appear to have been animated by such a conviction. In ancient times, the Jews seem to have thought that any amount of violence against neighbouring peoples was justified by the supreme value of their religion and its associated customs. The Mohammedans appear to have had a somewhat similar persuasion; and, indeed, a belief of this kind would seem to be implied in almost all wars that have a distinctively religious character. The Romans, again, based their claims—not altogether without reason—on the excellence of their government and their system of laws, and conceived that, on these grounds, *regere imperio populos* could be taken as their legitimate mission. Alexander the Great probably believed that he was spreading what was best of the civilization of Greece among the barbarians; and Napoleon may have set out with the object of establishing the humane principles of the French Revolution. Many modern nations have felt themselves entitled to take up what has been called "the white man's burden." Now, it is certainly arguable that, if the ends thus aimed at could have been successfully achieved by violence, and could not have been achieved in any other way, almost any amount of violence might have been justified by the achievement of some of them. In like manner, if any individual were so much wiser and better than all the other people in the world that it would be for the general advantage that he should become their absolute ruler, one might pardon almost any device that he might adopt to attain that position. But to argue in this way is to ignore the actual conditions of human life. It would be rather absurd, in any age, to suppose that any one nation or any one man has so great a superiority over others as to justify so extreme a measure; and, the more the world advances in its general civilization, the more absurd does such an attitude become. In the modern world at least, the civilization of any one country and the excellence of any one individual are inevitably shared with others, to a very large extent, without the use of violence. When their advantages become apparent, our means of communication carry them rapidly from one to another; and, in some cases at least, they are only too readily appropriated. Sometimes, no doubt, their adoption is resisted by vested interests and by the power of selfish individuals or classes, and against these some force may have to be applied; but the application of such force would be limited by the nature of the purpose in view. It would not be a force that "knows no law." Finer manners, for instance, can hardly be promoted by methods that are brutal. In a world in which peoples mix so freely and may understand one another so readily, it seems clear that any nation that seeks to impose its civilization on others, without restraint or scruple, cannot be regarded as benefactor, but rather as the enemy of the human race, even if it be true (of which, at any rate, it can hardly be entitled to be the sole judge) that its civilization is, on the whole, superior to that of others. Indeed, a claim of this kind is in pretty manifest contradiction to the general principle from which it sets out—viz. that *every* state has the right to maintain and defend its own civilization. It may, of course, be admitted that there are circumstances in which a state may lose this right, through some failure to fulfil the corresponding obligations. If its government were so flagrantly unjust that it could not properly be regarded as a state at all, it can hardly be denied that other states would have the right to interfere and, if necessary, to apply force for the restoration of order; and it must be confessed that the precise circumstances in which this becomes legitimate cannot be easily determined. This is one of the problems of international law to which some reference will be made in the following section.

It should be added that it is not to be denied that the moral consideration by which states are properly guided in their corporate actions are not quite the same as those that govern private individuals. Even the duties of individuals vary with their conditions and functions. Any one, for instance, who is in the position of an agent for others is subject to conditions that do not apply to one who is acting independently on his own behalf; and this distinction applies emphatically to the case of a government acting on behalf of its people. But the detailed consideration of such differences would carry us too far into the province of applied ethics. It is enough to state here that the recognition of these differences does not in any way interfere with the validity of moral principles. Duties vary, but they are none the less duties on that account. The conception of the common good of mankind remains the supreme guiding principle throughout.

3. *International Law.*—The real difficulty about international relations is not with reference to morality, but rather with reference to law. The hold of moral principles upon individuals, and still more upon groups, is apt to be rather weak when they are not embodied in legal enactments and supported by adequate sanctions. Hence attempts have been made, not altogether without success, to construct a coherent body of international regulations.[1] The Congresses at The Hague have been of the greatest service in this work. It is not intrinsically much more difficult to draw up suitable laws for the conduct of states than for the conduct of individuals; but it is obviously much more difficult to enforce them. Now, those at least who hold that the State is essentially force

---

[1] The extent to which this has been done is fully set forth in W. E. Hall's *International Law*, 5th edn. (ed. Dr. A. Pearce Higgins). See also *The Confederation of Europe*, by W. A. Phillips.

are naturally inclined, if not even logically bound, to consider that international agreements without adequate sanctions are only " scraps of paper." Even with regard to the actions of private individuals, there are many who are prone to think that laws have no real authority except the force that is behind them. Yet the force behind all laws is ultimately dependent upon the recognition of their authority. The mightiest monarch cannot enforce obedience except with the help of those who acknowledge his right to their obedience. The acknowledgment may be somewhat reluctant, extorted by a variety of arts and conceded from a variety of motives ; but it can hardly be dependent upon simple force. But between nations, when there is no spontaneous recognition of the authority of law, hardly any method of persuasion, other than the exercise of force, is available. Sometimes a common religion, or even a common language, or common traditions, or the relations that are brought about by trade or travel, may create a body of sentiment, such as is usually to be found within a single nation, which may render the actual exercise of force unnecessary or exceptional. But international jealousies and fears make the operation of such sentiments, even when they exist at all, somewhat precarious in their operation. It has to be recognized also, not merely that the authority of international law is more difficult to establish than that of the laws within a particular state, but that it is also more difficult to arrive at an agreement with regard to the laws that are to be adopted. Even within particular States, there is generally a minority that is opposed to the exact terms of any particular law ; but rough justice can usually be arrived at by discussion and compromise. The differences of view between independent states, each of which is accustomed to regard itself as sovereign, and each of which has its own peculiar traditions, and its own methods of thought and expression, cannot be so easily adjusted. Hence international law tends to remain much more flimsy in its texture, and much less definitely binding, than the laws of particular states. Improvement may be hoped for in these respects ; but, before considering the possibility of this, it may be well to notice at least one other prominent way in which nations tend to be bound together—viz. by trade.

4. *International Trade.*—Besides the presence of international morality and the rudiments of international law, there are several other influences that contribute to unity among states. The most important of these are probably community of religion, of race, of language, of general culture, and the relations brought about through industrial and commercial intercourse. Community of language is comparatively rare, and need not be specially considered here. It was a considerable bond of union between the separate states of ancient Greece ; it contributes to the friendly relations between Germany and Austria, between France and Belgium, between Switzerland and several other countries ; and the relations between our own country and the United States are materially affected by the fact that, in Wordsworth's phrase, both of them "speak the tongue That Shakespeare spake ; the faith and morals hold Which Milton held."[1] Also, as we noted previously, the use of Latin, and later of French and English, for international intercourse in Europe, has served as a unifying agency. Unity of race is probably not very effective, except when it is accompanied, as it commonly is, by some degree of unity in speech and in religion or cultural traditions. The influence of religion and general culture may be best reserved for later treatment. For the present, we may confine ourselves to the influence of international trade.

The potency of this factor is very obvious, and perhaps the tendency in recent times has been, on the whole, to exaggerate it. Cobden, and those who co-operated with him in the establishment of the general principle of Free

[1] It is obvious that the first clause in this statement would be much less effective without the addition of the second. A common outlook on life is a much stronger tie than a common language ; but the two things have some tendency to go together.

Trade, had the highest hopes of the beneficial effects that it would produce in removing the jealousies and friction that are caused by competing tariffs. In a more general way Herbert Spencer emphasized [1] the antithesis between military and industrial stages of civilization, and contrasted the harsh antagonisms of the one with the friendly co-operation of the other. More recently, Mr. Norman Angell has urged [2] that a true understanding of the economic interdependence of separate states would naturally result in the cessation of international strife. That there is some truth in all these contentions cannot, I think, be denied; but, certainly at the present moment, it is difficult to believe that they have much real weight. This is partly due to the fact that the benefits resulting from Free Trade have not been so generally recognized as Cobden and others anticipated, but probably still more to the fact that the influence of purely economic considerations is not quite as dominant as some have supposed. Several writers on the economic interpretation of history, led by Karl Marx, have represented industrial and commercial conditions as the underlying explanation of all the great movements in human affairs. It seems truer to say, with Professor Marshall,[3] that the economic factor has been the strongest, next to the religious; but it has to be added that there are other factors, such as race, language, and the general manners and traditions of different peoples (depending on a variety of circumstances), which cannot safely be ignored. So long as different states feel themselves to be distinct in other respects, the possession of those economic advantages that make for national strength—such as a plentiful supply of coal and iron and of the prime necessities of subsistence—becomes a ground of competition and antagonism, and

---

[1] *Data of Ethics*, § 50.

[2] *The Great Illusion.* Mr. Angell's statements are, however, open to a good deal of criticism. They are vigorously assailed, for instance—perhaps a little too vigorously—by Mr. G. G. Coulton in his book on *The Main Illusions of Pacificism*.

[3] *Principles of Economics*, at the beginning.

counteracts the unifying tendency that economic influences might otherwise have. German writers, in particular, have laid stress on this; and Germany at least is not a good instance in support of Spencer's contention, that a highly developed industrialism is opposed to militarism.

Still, after such qualifications have been made, it remains true that industrial and commercial intercourse has a real tendency to promote international unity. It is substantially true of some economic goods that they are, in Spinoza's phrase, " common to all, and all may equally enjoy them," though it is by no means true of all; and industrial strife, both within and between states, is largely dependent on this distinction. Some commodities can be indefinitely multiplied and exchanged all over the world; and it is to the advantage of every one that they should be freely moved. Others are definitely limited in amount or confined to particular regions, and it is to the economic advantage of particular men or particular nations to possess them. The detailed consideration of this must be left to writers on economics and politics. So far as goods are readily exchangeable, the traffic in them tends to promote friendly relations, and leads to other modes of unity. Men have to learn something of the languages and modes of thought of those with whom they deal. They have to assimilate their methods of business and their instruments of communication, such as the post, the telegraph, and the means of transport. The regulations of these necessarily become, to a large extent, international; and in these respects the boundaries between different nations begin to appear somewhat artificial. Labour also passes, though not as easily as many other things, from one country to another; and the populations of most countries lose a great deal of their rigid distinctions. All this is pretty obvious, and need not be further dwelt upon.

5. *War and Peace.*—The difficulties that have been indicated in the way of the establishment of a firm body of international law, together with the qualifications

that have to be conceded to the contention that industrialism promotes international unity, compel us to recognize that conflicts between separate states must still be regarded as probable. Conflicts within states can generally be avoided, or reduced to moderate dimensions. Almost all quarrels between individuals or small social groups can be settled in well-ordered communities by the authority of law. Duelling and "lynch law" tend to disappear in civilized countries. The former is still practised and defended in some places, when what is called "honour" is at stake, for which it is held that law can make no adequate provision; but most people are coming to see that even cases of this kind can be at least better dealt with by law or mediation than by an appeal to violence. Industrial disputes, in which large bodies of people are involved, are often more difficult to adjust. Strikes are sometimes described as a species of industrial war; but they seldom involve much actual bloodshed, or even serious injury to property; and the disputes that give rise to them can usually be settled by arbitration. Civil war, however, is not unknown within states, especially when the states contain distinct nations that lay claim to some degree of independence; but in most cases the threat of such conflicts is enough to lead to some method of conceding what is reasonable in the claims that are put forward—except when other independent states become involved in the quarrel. In general, it is only between independent states that actual warfare is to be apprehended; and this is sometimes said to be inevitable in certain circumstances, owing to the fact that there is no higher authority to which sovereign states can appeal. How far this difficulty can be met we shall have to consider shortly. In the meantime, we have to notice some arguments that have been put forward in support of the view that it is not even desirable to provide any method of solution, other than that of war, in the case of sovereign states.

This view depends largely on a special emphasis being laid on the conception of sovereignty. It is urged that any attempt to appeal to a higher authority would imply the abnegation of the sovereign right to maintain and defend the well-being of the community. This is of course true; but the question is precisely whether it is desirable to preserve the absolute sovereignty of the State in this extreme sense. This is a question to which we must return shortly. Granting, however, that some limitations may rightly be put upon the sovereignty of the State, we have still to face the argument that there are large questions, affecting the well-being of the community, which no self-respecting state could properly submit to the decision of any external body. When a dispute arises with another state, in which an issue of this kind is involved, it is contended that the state is entitled and, if possible, is even bound to uphold its own conviction at any cost. It is sometimes added that, in such a case, its might constitutes its right, and provides its only legitimate limitation. A view of this kind is closely connected with the doctrines, to which reference has already been made, that the essence of the State is power, and that it is not subject to moral considerations; and often it is not easy to make any clear distinction between these doctrines. But they are not necessarily to be identified. It may be admitted that the use of force is only one aspect of the State's activity, and that in the exercise of that force it should be governed by moral considerations; and yet it may be maintained that there are special cases in which the welfare of the community is the only consideration that can be legitimately taken into account. In such a case it would be true that *salus populi* is the *suprema lex*. What the State has the power to do for this supreme object would be what it is right for it to do. It is not right, it would be admitted, to attempt what is manifestly impossible; but when something is supremely desirable, and there is power to accomplish it, it is right to do it; and the State ought to see to it that it has the necessary power to do all that is essential for the maintenance of its highest ends. I take this to be what was meant by Carlyle and Treitschke in the general identification that they tended to make between *right and might*.[1] But it is at least important to be clear as to what things are really essential to the well-being of a community, and also as to whether it would not be better, where possible, to secure them with the consent of others, rather than in antagonism to them. Those who deny this believe that, at least in certain circumstances, war is in itself a good; and we must notice the grounds on which this view is defended.

Those who hold that war is good support their case, in general, by contending that it calls forth certain virtues which, in times of peace, are apt to languish and lose their vigour. It evokes courage, self-sacrifice, the spirit of comradeship, devotion to a common good, and even gives fresh scope for pity, chivalry, and magnanimity. This much may be allowed, though it is to be feared that, in the midst of the actual stress and horror of warfare, some of these noble qualities tend to be forgotten.[2] It is urged, further, that what is most sublime in literature and art is dependent on that heightening of the emotional life which can only be fully realized through the presence

---

[1] It is perhaps not quite fair to associate the names of Carlyle and Treitschke in this way. The general tone and attitude of the two are very different, Carlyle always put right in the foreground, and insisted that it is the rightness of an action that gives it might. But, if it is maintained that the two things always go together, as Carlyle often seems to maintain, and, if it is held, as he also appears to allow, that rights cannot be definitely ascertained, whereas mights can, it would seem that there can be little, if any, practical difference between the doctrine that Right is Might and the doctrine that Might is Right. They are practically different only when exceptions or limitations are allowed. This whole subject is very much bound up with the question, how far we are entitled to regard the universe as a Cosmos—a question that lies outside our present scope. Carlyle's attitude with regard to Right and Might is very well discussed by Professor H. L. Stewart in the *International Journal of Ethics*, January 1918.

[2] War has often been compared, in these respects, to earthquakes, shipwrecks, and other great disasters; but there is the important difference that, in these cases, the heroic efforts that are called forth are entirely for the saving of life, whereas in war they are mainly for its destruction.

or the imagination of extreme peril and violent endeavour. Even Ruskin was forced, somewhat reluctantly, to admit an element of truth in this; and it is in this sense, I suppose, that the saying of Nietzsche [1] is to be interpreted, that " a good war sanctifies any cause." It adds the touch of self-devotion to what would otherwise be little more than a cold approval. That there is some force in all this can hardly be denied. There is nearly always some soul of goodness in things evil; and it is in consequence of this that some of those who are most eager for the abolition of war have had to admit the necessity of looking for something that could be taken as its " moral equivalent." Probably this is a case in which we have to recognize that human life suffers from the fact that it has grown up from a lower level. We have grown up through

---

[1] It is not easy to know how the cryptic utterances of this rhapsodist are to be interpreted. They have probably been a good deal misunderstood. A paradoxical and impassioned writer cannot properly be read if his statements were mathematical propositions. One has to consider the general impressions that he seeks to convey. Nietzsche certainly tends to express himself in a provocative and bellicose fashion. This, however, is not uncommon among teachers of the prophetic type, who generally feel that, in some sense, it is not their function to send peace on the earth, but rather a sword. Some of his sayings, with a little change of phraseology, are not very unlike those of Emerson, and may be understood in a similar sense. The chief difference between them is that between sanity and hysteria. Nietzsche foams at the mouth, whereas Emerson might almost be charged with being too much at ease in Zion. The latter charge could not be made against Whitman, who, with some resemblances, is on the whole the antithesis of Nietzsche—the pure democrat against the pure aristocrat. It may be noted that both Emerson and Nietzsche appear to have been a good deal influenced by Montaigne. I suppose the best authority in English on the work of Nietzsche is now Mr. W. M. Salter. At least, he is the most exhaustive, if not the best balanced. Dr. Wolf's *Philosophy of Nietzsche* gives the main points in a more compact form; and Mr. A. M. Ludovici has dealt in a striking and suggestive way with several aspects of his teaching. To all writers of this kind the saying of Emerson appears to be applicable, that their utterances are " good for this trip only." They at least stimulate thought.

struggle, and we cannot readily devote ourselves to anything that does not involve some struggle. *Nitor in adversum* expresses an attitude that is natural to man. If we are not fighting against our enemies, we must at least be " fighting the good fight " in some other form ; and unfortunately there is no other form that can be so easily realized by the generality of mankind. And this leads us to another ground on which war is sometimes defended.

It is urged that, according to the modern doctrine of evolution, the development of the higher forms of life is dependent on a struggle, in which the lower types are destroyed and the higher preserved. Against this it has to be pointed out that there is no guarantee that those that survive are the higher, but only that they are the fitter in the particular circumstances. It would certainly be hard to show that the destruction of the ancient Greek states or of the Roman Empire was for the good of humanity ; and at least with reference to individuals, it is in most wars the strongest and noblest who perish. It has to be added, further, that, as we advance in the development of life, it is more and more true that it is by conscious selection and effort that the higher level is secured. It is to a sound education, to better conditions of life, and possibly in time to the application of the principles of eugenics, that we have to look for the advancement of the race.

This subject has been very fully discussed by Mons. J. Novicow.[1] His main contention is that the real struggle for existence, on which human progress depends, is the struggle against the forces of nature, not against our

---

[1] *La Critique du Darwinisme social.* It is on the struggle against natural forces that the stress is laid also in Professor Haycraft's *Darwinism and Race Progress.* Some good remarks on the right interpretation of the struggle for existence will be found in Professor Chalmers Mitchell's book on *Evolution and the War,* especially in chapter ii. The subject is also well discussed in Mr. G. G. Coulton's *Main Illusions of Pacificism,* especially pp. 93–114. Huxley's *Evolution and Ethics* is still worth referring to. So, indeed, is Darwin's *Descent of Man,* Part I, chap. v. and Professor Hobhouse's *Social Evolution and Political Theory,* chap. ii.

fellow-men. It was the struggle against nature also that William James suggested as the moral equivalent for war,[1] and, indeed, this suggestion was partly anticipated by Carlyle in his emphasis on Captains of Industry and Regiments of Labour.[2] The more recent suggestion of industrial strife as a substitute for international strife is more open to objection.[3] It is to be feared that such strife would be lacking in those more generous impulses that are often to be found in international struggles. In any case, it would hardly be an equivalent for war, but rather war itself in a new form.

We cannot pursue this subject farther at present. It seems clear that war is not in itself good. It may be conceded that, as things stand, it is productive of some good, as well as of much evil, and that it would be foolish for existing states to count too rashly on its elimination. The old saying, *si vis pacem para bellum*, retains some force; not, of course, in the sense that we should prepare to make war, but that we should not altogether neglect to be in readiness to meet it. This does not mean that we should be already " in shining armour," but only that we should have enough foresight and imagination to realize the dangers that may confront us, and not to be lulled to sleep with " the unlit lamp and the ungirt loin." With still more confidence may it be affirmed that, if peace is to be permanently established, it must be a peace that is not simply the negation of strife, but is itself a struggle for the higher ends of humanity, achieving " victories not less renowned than those of war." Then indeed we may be able to substitute for those military ideals that

[1] See essay on this subject in his *Memories and Studies*.
[2] Chiefly in *Past and Present* and *Latterday Pamphlets*.
[3] M. Sorel makes this claim for the general strike: " Strikes have engendered in the proletariat the noblest, deepest, and most moving sentiments that they possess; the general strike groups them all in a co-ordinated picture, and, by bringing them together, gives to each one of them its maximum of intensity; appealing to their painful memories of particular conflicts, it colours with an intense life all the details of the composition presented to consciousness " (*Reflections on Violence*, chap. iv, p. 137).

Nietzsche seems to express—*Live dangerously* and *Be hard*—the more pacific ones, *Live strenuously* and *Be hopeful*. As Aristotle put it, "there is no leisure for slaves." "Bondage with ease" is certainly not to be preferred to "strenuous liberty." Peace and liberty are only possible where there is a constant effort to secure and maintain them.

6. *Progress in International Relations.*—If we are right in thinking that such a peace as that to which we have referred is what is to be aimed at, it is important to consider how it is to be achieved. Obviously there are difficulties in the way; and, in the previous section, I have sought rather to emphasize them than to represent them as negligible. That some progress may be made, however, is surely apparent enough. The more thorough development of international law may be of great service, but it seems clear that adequate sanctions are required, and that these can only be provided by the great Powers. Hence it has come to be generally recognized that a League of Nations is the kind of authority that is needed.[1] But objections to such a scheme readily present themselves. In particular it has been urged that it would interfere with the sovereignty of independent states. This is not an objection that can be lightly set aside; but in answer to it, we may again note that no sovereignty can be absolute. The distinction between a sovereign state and one that is not sovereign has only a relative validity. A sovereign state is one that is not subordinate to any definite authority. Now, it is not proposed that a League of Nations should constitute such an authority. A

[1] The writings on this subject are too numerous to mention. Probably most of them are somewhat ephemeral. *The Choice Before Us*, by Mr. Lowes Dickinson, is certainly one of the most interesting. His book on *The European Anarchy* is also worth referring to; so are *The Morality of Nations* by Mr. C. D. Burns and *The Principles of the Moral Empire* by Prof. Sugimori. See also Green's *Principles of Political Obligation*, § 175, and Mr. A. J. Toynbee's *Nationality and the War*, chap. xii.

federation of the world is not in contemplation. Anything of that kind would amount to the establishment of a single sovereign state, to which all others would be subordinate. It may be taken as certain that the world is not ripe for this. Perhaps it never will be. It may be best that a number of distinct peoples should develop along somewhat different lines. But, apart from the establishment of a single superstate, it would seem that even sovereign states have to admit certain restrictions. Even the great State of Germany is somewhat restricted by the right of the little states within it. Every treaty puts some limits to the complete independence of the nations that sign it; yet it is evident that without some sort of treaties there can be no security; and it is surely evident also that treaties are worthless unless those that sign them are pledged to unite in their support. Again, no nation in modern times thinks of entering upon a great war without the support of some allies. That also is a League of Nations. Now, it may be well to inquire what it is that makes such Leagues of Nations possible. The general answer would seem to be that it is the recognition that certain states have a common good to pursue. The more nations there are that acknowledge a common good, the more extensive may a League become; and, if there is any good that is common to every nation, they may all combine to pursue it. Now, every state that values its sovereignty does recognize a certain good that is essentially the same for all—viz. the freedom to maintain its own civilization. But, in order that all nations may have security for this, peace is a necessary condition. Hence it may fairly be maintained that peace and freedom are two closely related goods that are common to all nations alike; and all might very well combine to defend them. To do this is not in reality to sacrifice sovereignty, but rather to secure the necessary conditions upon which alone the essentials of sovereignty can be maintained. The only ground for apprehension is, that a League formed for such a purpose might gradually be led to pursue other purposes instead. It might seek to restrict freedom, instead of to promote it. That there is this danger, cannot be altogether denied. Even to maintain the freedom of some states, it might be necessary to restrain the actions of others; and there is an easy transition from necessary restraints to those that are vexatious and pernicious.[1] But a League of Nations for Peace and Freedom would at least be nominally committed to these objects. They would be the sole grounds for its existence; and, if its constitution were carefully framed, it would have the wisdom of the whole world behind it. If water chokes us, with what shall we wash it down? If the wisdom of the world is not enough, where are we to look for a better wisdom? Well, we may, of course, try to make the world wiser; and some ways of doing this will be considered in the following chapters. But, at any particular time, we can only use the wisdom that is present. It is obvious that no mechanical device can solve such a problem as this; but mechanical devices may not only serve to give effect to the desires of peoples, but may also help very largely to cultivate these desires. The details of the constitution of a League of Nations do not, of course, concern us here. It is the business of practical statesmen to draw them up. What the social philosopher has to consider is only the general principle on which the conception rests; and what has now been stated about that must for the present suffice. In time it may lead to larger issues, to a more complete removal of national barriers, to the distant dream of " the parliament of man, the federation of the world." But I have thought it best to confine myself, for the present, to more immediate issues.

[1] It is, of course, obvious that such a League would need to have at its disposal some force for the establishment of its aims. But it would be essentially a police force for the maintenance of peace and order. The scheme does not involve the beating of swords into ploughshares, but only the transformation of the soldier into the policeman. The distribution of this force among the different nations would be a difficult problem, but surely not beyond the wit of man.

CHAPTER II

THE PLACE OF RELIGION

1. *The Meaning of Religion.*—Various attempts have been made to define religion. They are rendered difficult by the great variety of phases that religion has assumed, and it would be out of place to discuss them here.[1] It must suffice for our purpose to state that religion, at least in its most developed forms, seems to mean essentially a certain absolute devotion to what is recognized as highest and most valuable.[2] It is hardly true to say, with Carlyle, that "Work is Worship"; but the spirit that inspires the best forms of constructive or creative work may be properly described as religious. Christianity, in particular, perhaps more than any other of the great world-religions, seems to have meant mainly a spirit of devotion to the ideal of social unity, and to all that is essential for its promotion and maintenance; and it is, at any rate, this aspect of religion that is specially important for our present purpose. It is clear, for instance, that, without such a spirit of devotion, it would be vain to look for those advances either in national life or in international relations which have been emphasized in the preceding chapters. With reference, in particular, to the growth of international unity and the establishment of the peace of the world, Mr. Dickinson has recently, in the book referred to at the close of the last chapter, given a very

[1] The discussion in the first chapter of E. Caird's book on *The Evolution of Religion* is probably the best.

[2] "Wherever we have devoutness, devotedness, devotion, we have the primary features of religion" (Bosanquet's *Value and Destiny of the Individual*, p. 25).

striking illustration of the service that may be rendered by a genuinely religious attitude. It relates to the way in which in 1900 the outbreak of war between Argentina and Chile was prevented by an emphatic appeal to the underlying principles of Christianity.[1] Such instances are rare. Mr. Dickinson says that they may be almost described as " miraculous." But the influence of religious ideas may be noticed, not merely in the Crusades and other movements generally described (perhaps not quite properly) as religious, but in such reforms as those that were inaugurated by the French Revolution. The Religion of Humanity, which can hardly be called a world-religion, and which probably owes some of its chief features to Buddhism and Christianity, has fixed upon this social aspect of the religious spirit almost to the exclusion of the other aspects by which it is in general characterized. It is probably true that, in order to complete such a religion, we ought at least to add to it some such worship of nature as we find in the poetry of Wordsworth and Shelley, and perhaps some more definite attempt at a coherent view of the universe as a whole, such as we find in the writings of Plato and other constructive thinkers. But, for our present purpose, it may be enough to regard religion as meaning the spirit of devotion to the perfection of human life. Looking at it is this way, we may connect it with the general analysis of human nature that was given in the earlier chapters of this book. Even from this point of view, however, religion has some distinguishable aspects to which it is well to call attention. It cannot be narrowly interpreted without serious loss.

2. *Chief Aspects of Religion.*—In the earlier chapters of this book it was urged that human life has three main aspects—the vegetative, the animal, and the more characteristically human. The more purely human aspect, depending on the presence of rational choice, modifies and gradually dominates the other two; and the consideration

[1] *The Choice Before Us*, pp. 165-6. The passage is too long to quote, but it may be consulted with great advantage.

THE PLACE OF RELIGION

of social institutions and modes of unity, with which we have so far been concerned, has been mainly occupied with the ways in which conscious choice operates upon our lower needs and impulses. What we have now to notice is the operation of that ideal aim which belongs more distinctively to the purely human side of our complex nature. This purely human aim shows itself in the pursuit of what is true, what is beautiful, and what is good; and it is with the highest forms of these that religion, in its most complete manifestations, would seem to be concerned. It is chiefly what is good in social action that is of interest to us here; but the other aspects cannot be altogether ignored.

When the bearing of religion upon social activity is specially emphasized, religion seems to be hardly distinguishable from morality, in the highest sense in which that term is used. Matthew Arnold said [1] that religion is essentially "morality touched by emotion"; but all morality that is good for much has a touch of emotion. What is described as the Ethical Movement seeks to identify the higher morality with religion. But this identification, like that contained in Positivism, tends to exclude from religion the worship of nature and the conception of an intelligible cosmos.[2] It may be said that morality, in its highest sense, means the pursuit of everything that is true and beautiful. But, at any rate, it is the *pursuit* of these; whereas in religion they are rather thought of, I believe, as, in some sense, eternally realized, or involved in the nature of things. Moreover, morality is generally understood to mean devotion to and pursuit of what is recognized as true and beautiful at some particular time and place; whereas in religion there is an aspiration after the absolute ideal. Morality tends to be interpreted as being, in some degree, conventional. It may be said that the same is, more or less, true of religion; but at least it aims more definitely at what is absolute and complete. It may be characterized as the spirit that

[1] *Literature and Dogma*, chap. i.
[2] See my *Elements of Constructive Philosophy*, Book III, chap. iv.

animates progress in morality. But it also animates progress in art and philosophy, which, in their highest forms, become religious just as morality does. The enjoyment of what is beautiful, and the contemplation of what is true, appear to be essentially religious attitudes; just as the impassioned effort after the maintenance of what is true and beautiful, which is the essence of morality, is also a religious attitude. Religion thus combines the true, the beautiful, and the good, in a way in which they are not combined either by science, by art, or by morality, however true it may be that the highest forms of philosophic contemplation, poetic creation, and moral endeavour are all essentially religious.

3. *Religious Institutions.*—It is natural that the religious attitude, especially on its more social side, should lead to the establishment of special institutions for its support and application; just as the other aspects of human nature do. It is natural also that these institutions, like others, should contain elements that may be characterized as conventional. The most obvious of these are the various churches and other sectarian associations, ranging from such elaborate organizations as that of Catholicism to such simple unions as the Society of Friends. Sometimes the social aim is, to a certain extent, obscured or subordinated in such institutions. They may give more attention to the promulgation of particular doctrines, the observance of particular ceremonies, or the cultivation of the individual life, than to the ideals of social unity; but the fact that these ends are pursued in common entitles us to regard them, even in such cases, as having a distinctly social significance. It is true that religion is sometimes conceived as an almost purely personal concern. Individuals are sometimes thought of as taking up religion, as they might take up painting or music, and finding in it a kind of satisfaction or a kind of discipline, which has but little reference to social obligation; but these individuals do not, in general, connect themselves closely with religious organizations. Oriental mystics,

mediæval hermits, and "beautiful souls" (such as the one depicted by Goethe) are illustrations of such tendencies. But even those who adopt attitudes of this kind generally find it useful to have some fellowship with those who are like-minded. Masonic lodges and similar institutions, especially when they are inspired by such conceptions as those that are expressed in Goethe's Masonic hymn, may be noted in this connection. Indeed, even painters, musicians, and speculative thinkers band themselves together occasionally, and devote themselves to the common pursuit of their special interests with an enthusiasm that may almost be called religious. It is somewhat difficult to determine whether such an association as that of the Pythagoreans should be described as a philosophical brotherhood or a religious sect. Similarly, those who devote themselves specially to the advocacy of social ideals, and form themselves into associations for this purpose, may often be regarded as religious in spirit, even if their aims are not such as would be commonly classed as religious. Expressions are sometimes used, such as "American democracy as a religion" or "the religion of socialism," which indicate that political or social ideals may be pursued with so whole-hearted a devotion as to be regarded as what is highest and best in life. Again, educational and charitable institutions are often founded and supported by those whose aims are mainly of a religious character; and such institutions may sometimes have to be treated as essentially religious. Thus religious institutions must be interpreted in a somewhat wide sense for our present purpose. Even when particular institutions can hardly be said to be in themselves religious, religion may have an important place both in their spirit and in their work. Even drudgery, we have been told, may in this way be made divine. Hence we have to take note of the connection of religion with most of the other important aspects of social life.

4. *Religion in Education.*—If it is recognized that the essential spirit of religion is a fundamental aspect of the

pursuit of the common good, it is evident that it ought to have a prominent place in the education of the young ; and this would probably be universally recognized if it were not for the difficulties that are created by the diversities of religious belief. Those who are strongly convinced of the importance of particular creeds or ceremonials or modes of religious belief, are naturally anxious that these special forms of religion should be impressed upon the minds of any young people whose education they control ; and those who think differently are naturally opposed to this. Hence, where there are many varieties of religious conviction there is a tendency to eliminate religion from school work, or to reduce it to very small dimensions. It is not within our present scope to attempt to solve this difficulty, but some remarks about it may be of use.

The attempt to impart particular creeds to immature minds is evidently open to serious objection. If it succeeds in its object, it tends to produce an attitude of mind to which religion is rather a deadening tradition than a living inspiration, and a force that separates the individual from his fellows instead of uniting him with them. But it is perhaps just as likely to fail in its object, and create a distaste for every form of religion. In any case it violates what is now generally recognized as an essential principle of education—a principle to which attention has already been called—that it should be, as far as possible, a development from within, not simply an imposition from without. Yet it is evident that it is not possible to guard the young altogether from the influence of the religious (or irreligious) atmosphere by which they are surrounded. In this respect, as in many others, they are necessarily affected for good or ill by the attitude of their parents or guardians, and of any religious organizations with which these are connected. I have already insisted upon the autonomy of the child, and have urged that the control of the parents should only be regarded as a delegated authority. But such influences as I am now referring to could not be prevented without a degree of interference with the life of the family which, even if it were possible at all, would probably be more harmful than beneficial. Even in the school, the views held by particular teachers can hardly fail to have some influence; though in this case there is at least a better chance that any influence of this kind may be counterbalanced by divergent influences. At any rate, such an influence is only one of the many ways in which the growing mind is necessarily affected by its human environment. The question that remains is, whether these inevitable influences need to be supplemented by more direct efforts to give instruction in particular forms of religion, or to cultivate a particular type of religious attitude.

That there must be some instruction in religious ideas seems clear enough. History would be unintelligible without some understanding of the conflicts between different religious conceptions; and literature would be to a large extent meaningless without an appreciation of the religious ideas by which great writers have been inspired and without some knowledge of the sources from which they drew their inspiration. But to know and appreciate the ways in which men have been affected, it is not necessary to commit oneself to their particular views. On the contrary, natural though it is to take sides, and right as it may often be, it is yet important to understand and appreciate a number of divergent attitudes. To know about the Greeks, for instance, one must have some sympathy with their outlook on the universe; and so it is with any historical records or literary expressions. Such study of religious ideas and attitudes is entirely favourable to human fellowship, and can hardly have any prejudicial effects; and the same applies to the attempt to understand and appreciate the various religious influences that exist at the present time. To do this is one aspect of that regional survey which is beginning to be recognized as an important element even in education of an elementary character.

What is important, beyond this, is to imbibe something of the essence of the religious spirit. If we are right in thinking that this spirit is that of devotion to what is true, beautiful, and good, it is evident that there are many ways in which this may be effectively cultivated. The study of the sciences, in particular, cultivates the love of truth; that of the arts, the love of beauty; and the intelligent study of history and literature leads naturally to the admiration of what is good and the hatred of what is evil. In view of the more directly practical importance of goodness, both in its more purely personal and its more social aspects, it may be urged that some more direct attempt should be made to bring its more important phases clearly before the minds of the young, in a way that would engage their sympathies and develop their practical activities. But it is surely obvious that this ought to be done, as far as possible, in such a manner as not to represent any of these excellent things as dependent upon the acceptance of particular creeds or theories of the universe, or upon the observance of particular ceremonies; so that, whatever views may be ultimately adopted by those whose minds and hearts are being cultivated, whether they accept or reject the doctrines of their elders, they may always be able to fall back upon those eternal values, to realize that truth is intrinsically preferable to falsehood, beauty to deformity and good to evil. The spirit of religion would thus become a perpetual possession, whatever special form it might afterwards assume. This seems to be the essential point; its detailed consideration we cannot here pursue.

5. *Religion and Social Service.*—It would obviously be a very narrow view to take of religion if we were to suppose that it is only to be found in definite connection with creeds and churches. As we have already noted, it may show itself in devotion to education or charitable work, in political ideals, in the service of art and science, and in many other ways. But it is perhaps more particularly seen in efforts to improve social conditions, and that is at least the form in which it is of most interest to us in our present study. Even in the best organized societies, as we have seen, the ideals of justice and equity can hardly be fully

realized; and even what is essentially equitable may involve limitations and hardships that it is desirable to remove or mitigate. Still more true is this in societies that are not organized in the most perfect way. In such cases the spirit of devotion to the good of humanity shows itself in efforts to improve the conditions. In times of war the importance of such efforts is specially apparent; but in peace-time also there are constant occasions for beneficent work in hospitals, prisons, slums, etc.; and in attempts to bridge over the gulfs that are created between individuals and classes by differences in position, possessions, education, and other circumstances. University Settlements are a notable example of the way in which such efforts have been developed in recent times. Such work is, of course, not always undertaken with any explicit reference to religion; but certainly, in a broad sense of the word, it must be inspired by the religious spirit; and, indeed, many churches seem to be tending to regard such work as a main part of their function. It is probably important that this side of their work should be more definitely developed and recognized; since it does not fall within the scope of the State or local government, and is apt to be inefficiently carried out when it is left to purely private effort. The difficulty in this, as in many other things, is mainly due to the disunion of the churches. But the gradual recognition of what constitutes the essence of religion might be expected to lead to unity of effort in this particular direction. Differences of opinion in matters that are speculative, or that depend on taste and sentiment, need not prevent co-operation in practical endeavours.

6. *The State and Religion.*—As religion is an important element in education, both in the narrower and in the wider sense, as well as in social organization and in the promotion of the spirit of devotion to the common good, the State can hardly be indifferent to its maintenance. But there are great difficulties in determining the exact relations between the State and religion; and with these

we cannot deal adequately in a book of this kind. Some general principles, however, may be laid down.

The main work of religious institutions is evidently education. Hence the general conditions that apply to the State's relations to education are applicable also to its relations to religion. The State is naturally called upon to see that this aspect of education, as well as others, is adequately provided for; but that it should actually seek to carry it on, or to determine the substance and method of the teaching, would seem to be beyond its legitimate province.[1] In practice, this would appear to mean that there ought not to be a State Church, but that, if necessary, religious institutions that are recognized as meeting a national need should receive some endowment from the State. But, of course, it is much more difficult in the case of religion than in most other forms of education to determine what institutions can be fairly regarded as supplying a national want. It does not appear that any definite principles can be laid down with regard to this. It has to be decided, from time to time, by the changing conditions of opinion and feeling within states.

The question is further complicated by the fact that it is not a purely educational problem. The highest ideals of national life are closely connected with religion, and naturally seek a religious expression. State ceremonies are often of a religious character, and it is almost inevitable that they should take their form and colour from some particular type of religious organization. All that can be urged is that, so far as possible, the ceremonies that are adopted should be such as are congenial to, or at least not actually repellent to, the chief forms of religious

---

[1] The arguments put forward by such very different writers as Matthew Arnold (*Culture and Anarchy*) and Dr. Stanton Coit (*National Idealism and a State Church*), not to mention the earlier statements by Hume and others, are certainly impressive; but I doubt whether they really carry us any farther than what is indicated above. The view that I have sought to urge is very well emphasized in Professor Kojiro Sugimori's *Principles of the Moral Empire*, pp. 214-16.

organizations that exist within the country. This would seem at least to be the ideal that ought to be aimed at, though it may be only very imperfectly realizable.

Another difficulty arises from the fact that some types of religious organization are to a certain extent hostile to the life either of the State in general or of some particular states, and tend to interfere with their sovereignty. A strongly international religion, like Catholicism, is apt to claim a jurisdiction above that of any particular state. The mediæval ideal was, on the whole, that of a single State and a single Church in close relation to each other.[1] On the other hand, more individualistic types of religion, such as the Society of Friends, tend to hold themselves aloof from the State altogether. Between these two opposing tendencies, the State has to steer its course as best it may, recognizing as sympathetically as it can any differences of opinion that exist within it, so far as they do not actually prevent it from exercising any of its necessary functions. When the State seeks a larger control than this, religion is apt to become perverted to the service of the magistrate. According to Gibbon,[2] "The various modes of worship, which prevailed in the Roman world, were all considered by the people as equally true ; by the philosopher, as equally false ; and by the magistrate, as equally useful." But the magistrate is seldom so tolerant as this. He will generally prefer a religion of terror to one of love, a religion of convention to one of free inquiry. But this leads us to the general question of religious toleration, to which it will be well to devote a special section.

7. *Religious Toleration.*—The problem of religious toleration is, of course, part of the general problem of freedom of opinion, and of its public expression, to which we have already referred ; but there are special difficulties in this

[1] Dante is the most conspicuous representative of this view. His attitude is most definitely explained in his treatise *De Monarchia*, but it is also very apparent throughout his *Divine Comedy*.
[2] *Decline and Fall*, chap. ii.

case that require consideration. Differences about religion tend to mean, and indeed, if they are sincerely and earnestly held, and are really differences about religion—not merely about the modes of its expression and organization—must mean, a certain divergence in the whole outlook upon life. Differences of this kind are not simply differences of opinion, but of practice as well, and almost inevitably lead to serious conflict. They have been among the most fruitful sources of war, both international and civil; and, even when they do not issue in actual strife, they engender hatred and antagonism. Hence it is difficult for any society that is aiming at a common good to regard such differences with complacency. Indifference to differences is only possible when they make no difference. But it is at least possible to narrow the issue by trying to distinguish between what makes a real difference and what does not. Differences, for example, about ceremonial or church government, though they may be closely connected with differences of a more fundamental kind, are in themselves negligible. Nor do differences about purely theoretical questions of doctrine present any real difficulty from the point of view of the State. Even differences about the rightness or wrongness of certain modes of conduct, such as the use of animal food, the practice of vivisection, the enjoyment of dancing, sport, or theatrical performances, the utterance of oaths, the observance of distinctions of rank, the employment of corporal or other forms of punishment, the relative obligations of parents and children, the equality or inequality of the sexes, etc., though they interfere seriously with the likemindedness that is necessary for friendly intercourse, do not necessarily present any insuperable difficulty in the way of toleration. With reference to such questions, it is comparatively easy to recognize that what is right for one need not be right for another; though, of course, in practice this would not always be allowed. Real difficulties arise chiefly when rights are claimed or duties acknowledged that interfere directly with the apparent rights or obligations of others, or with the sovereignty of the State. Most of the differences that have just been referred to might, if absolutely pressed, lead to such difficulties. They only avoid such difficulties when it is allowed that different people may have different standards of conduct. The two things that it is most difficult for a state to tolerate are intolerance and insubordination; and any extreme differences in religion are apt to involve one or other of these—very often both.

It is clear that it can hardly be possible for a State to tolerate intolerance, or to refrain from interfering with interference. The right to have one's own opinion tolerated involves the obligation to tolerate the opinions and respect the rights of others. The Thugs could not be tolerated, however sincere one might believe their convictions to be, because action in conformity with these convictions would involve the violation of the rights of others. Nor can any belief be tolerated which involves the attempt to enforce it upon others, unless the belief is held only as a pious opinion, not to be immediately put into practice. Even in the latter case, it is difficult to tolerate such beliefs, unless the authorities of the State have some assurance that the beliefs will never issue in action, or are convinced that, when they do, the action could be easily checked.

Similarly, it is difficult to tolerate insubordination; since, so far as it goes, such an attitude nullifies the authority upon which the very existence of the State depends. Any one living in the territories within which the jurisdiction of the State extends is assumed to recognize its sovereignty. Yet, in this case also, there are degrees of insubordination that may evidently be tolerated. If some citizens regard a particular law or executive decision as unjust, they may sometimes be permitted to disobey it, if they are in other respects law-abiding, and if their disobedience does not make the law of no effect. If, for instance, in war-time a state adopts conscription, and if some citizens refuse to undertake military service, either because they think that particular war unjust, or because they believe that all war is wrong, they may be exempted from such service. This would hardly be possible if they were so numerous that their exemption would prevent the successful prosecution of the war, or if their insubordination in this particular implied a general disregard of the authority of the State. Similar considerations might be applied to the refusal to pay a particular tax, on the ground that it was levied for an undesirable object. But it seems clear that exemption could not be allowed merely on the ground that those who claimed it were members of a minority whose views had been overruled. It could only be granted on the ground of the violation of a principle that is regarded as sacred—i.e. a ground that is essentially religious.

This may suffice to bring out the difficulties involved in the problem, and to point to the general consideration by which they may be removed. Here, again, a more detailed treatment would carry us too far.

8. *International Religion.*—It is evident, from what has been already stated, that the religious spirit, as here interpreted, carries us beyond the limits of any particular state. Many of the older religions were essentially tribal. The object of worship was thought of as the power that supports and defends the national life, in opposition to surrounding peoples. It would seem that in modern Prussia there is a curious survival of this conception. But all the great religions have broken away from it. It was one of the essential features of Christianity that it broke down the barriers between Jew and Greek. The Stoics, who certainly had a strongly religious spirit, rendered a similar service to Greece and Rome by their conception of cosmopolitanism. Before these, Socrates and Plato did much to break down the limitations of the City States by moralizing the conception of the divine, and by attempting to combine the conflicting ideals of Athens and Sparta. Catholicism aimed at being a worldwide religion, but, by combining this aspiration with that of establishing a world-wide empire, lost something

of its religious character. It could hardly serve both God and Cæsar. It seems clear, however, that if there is ever to be a genuinely world-wide organization, it must be supported by the spirit of unity in the pursuit of a common good; and such a spirit would be, in its essence, religious. Merely mechanical devices cannot put an end to international strife. Hence there have been many attempts to bring together East and West, and to evolve from their union a genuinely world-wide religion. The danger of such attempts is that they may only succeed in evolving a new sect, in opposition to those that already exist. It is probable that the end aimed at can only be attained by the gradual evolution of the existing religions, each of them learning to subordinate what is merely traditional in its doctrines and observances to those more essential elements that can be recognized as eternally true, beautiful, and good.[1]

9. *Defective Religions.*—It is implied in what has just been stated that all existing religions have their defects and limitations; and this, I suppose, would be generally acknowledged by all who have studied them with care. It would be out of place here to point to the particular defects that may be found in any of them; but it may be worth while to try to enumerate the main defects to which religions appear to be subject.

(1) *Superstition.*—Most religions contain some elements of superstition—i.e. doctrines or observances that cannot really, on careful reflection, be believed or justified.

(2) *Idolatry.*—Most religions are not altogether of the nature of devotion to the truest and best that is known, but combine this with the worship of things that are either only symbols of what is good or limited modes

---

[1] The true conception of a world-religion seems to me to be admirably set forth in the little book by Harendranath Maitra on *Hinduism: the World-ideal*. *The Principles of the Moral Empire*, by Professor Kojiro Sugimori, may also be referred to. The Concordia Movement, recently initiated by President Naruse in Japan, seems to promise well for the cultivation of the spirit that is desired.

of existence that have some excellence in themselves (such as the State), but are not deserving of complete devotion.[1]

(3) *Dogmatism.*—Most religions contain doctrines that cannot stand the test of rational reflection, but are accepted on authority, and can only be justified by an appeal to that authority.

(4) *Sectarianism.*—Most religions embody the traditions of some limited circle of people, who are either unable or unwilling to appreciate what is worthy of admiration in other traditions. It is to such limited circles, in their more extreme forms, that the biting words of Swift are applicable—" Some people have just enough religion to make them hate one another, not enough to make them love one another."

(5) *Fanaticism.*—When the limited outlook of some particular sect is not merely accepted as worthy of devotion, but as worthy of absolute devotion, as against every other outlook, we have what seems to be most properly characterized as fanaticism.

(6) *Hypocrisy.*—It is difficult to be quite sincere in devotion to anything that is essentially limited and imperfect. If it does not commend itself to our whole nature, we can only devote ourselves to it by some sort of " make-belief." Hence fanaticism passes easily into hypocrisy. Make-belief is not far removed from pretended belief.

(7) *Individualism.*—Some escape from the limitations of tradition by setting up a private religion of their own. Unless they are great geniuses, or at least men of remarkable spiritual insight, such an attitude is apt to be even more limiting than tradition.

(8) *Mysticism.*—A purely individual religion is apt to be mystical—i.e. to lay an almost exclusive emphasis on the more recondite and incomprehensible aspects of what

[1] What is commonly called idolatry is essentially symbolism; and there is no real harm in it, so long as it is properly understood. Harendranath Maitra has some excellent remarks on this in the book that has just been referred to, pp. 25-7.

is highest and best, and so to lose contact with the upward struggle of humanity.[1]

(9) *Conventionalism.*—When men begin to realize the defects in existing religions, and fail to see how these defects can be removed, they sometimes adopt the attitude of accepting some form of religion, not as containing anything that is worthy of absolute devotion, but rather as a tradition that is not worth setting aside. This is not far removed from pure irreligion. It has been expressed by saying that a man " gives up religion, and begins to go to church."[2]

(10) *Irreligion.*—If religion means devotion to what is highest, irreligion would seem to be the attitude of not recognizing that anything is worthy of complete devotion. It is the attitude of *nil admirari*, the conviction that " there is nothing new and nothing true, and it does not matter."

10. *Progress in Religion.*—The general conclusion to which this survey points is that we can hardly expect to find a perfect religion, or at least not speedily to give it a universal currency ; but that the defects in different religious or irreligious attitudes may be gradually corrected. If we are right in our general conception of what the essence of religion is, it may be said that all genuine religions aim, more or less consciously, at the apprehension and realization of that which has an intrinsic and absolute value ; and that there are few of them that do not at least contain some elements that have real value. Hence it would seem that all of them that are to retain a truly religious spirit must be essentially progressive,[3] learning by degrees to

---

[1] This is the general defect of the purely Oriental types of religion. But I think Harendranath Maitra has succeeded in showing that it is much less serious than is commonly supposed.

[2] This attitude is strikingly depicted, in sharp contrast with a different one, in *The Conventionalists*, by R. H. Benson. It is also well shown, on a larger canvas, in Trollope's Barchester series.

[3] The progressive character of religious thought is admirably brought out in Edward Caird's two books, *The Evolution of Religion* and *The Evolution of Theology in the Greek Philosophers.*

set aside what is limited or imperfect in their attitude, and concentrating their attention on a more and more comprehensive ideal—" weaning themselves," in the language of Goethe,[1] " from that which is partial, and living resolutely in the whole, the good, the beautiful."

[1] Sich vom Halben zu entwöhnen,
Und im Ganzen, Guten, Schönen,
Resolut zu leben.

CHAPTER III

THE PLACE OF CULTURE

1. *The Meaning of Culture.*—It has been our aim throughout to show that society, in its various forms, is not an artificial excrescence, but is based on the essential nature of man, and that its end is the perfecting of that nature. Hence we are brought back to the individual. Society is made for man, not man for society. This is sometimes forgotten by enthusiasts for particular forms of social unity, especially by enthusiasts for such large organizations as those of the Church or the State. It was not forgotten or overlooked by Plato and Aristotle, though it is sometimes supposed that it was. Plato, after completing his account of the ideal state, recognizes that it is not a state that can ever be expected to exist on earth, but rather one of which the pattern is laid up in heaven. In other words, it is the ideal by which the best human beings are inspired, which they may hope to realize gradually without, in proportion as they have first realized its essence within. Accordingly, the closing part of the *Republic* is occupied, not with the ideal state, but rather with a somewhat allegorical representation of the progressive development of the individual soul.[1] Aristotle, in like manner, after giving us his sketch of the civic virtues, contends that the highest achievement for man is to be found in what he calls [2] the " theoretical life "— for which, however, the life of practical social activity is to be regarded as the necessary foundation. Such a

[1] Some further remarks on this will be found in the Appendix.
[2] *Ethics*, Book X.

view does not contradict the contention that the good that is sought by human beings is a common good; for it is precisely in the cultivation of the individual personality that we escape from the region of conflicting ends, and find a happiness in which all may share. Now, it is this kind of achievement that is best expressed by the term "Culture," which is generally taken to denote education in its larger sense—the sense in which it is the end of life, rather than the preparation for life.

The distinction has already been noted between the narrower and the wider sense of education. In the narrower sense it is to be regarded mainly as a process of initiation into the life of the community: in the wider sense it is rather the development of the spiritual nature of man, of which the life of the community is an instrument. The former is the pre-condition of the latter. One has to learn to be a citizen of a particular society, with a particular station and particular duties within it, before he is free to advance to become a citizen of the universe; but it is a terrible disaster for any one when his education is completed in the former process. Goethe is probably the finest example in modern times of one who never completed his education, but was always pursuing a more extensive culture, seeking to "raise the pyramid of his being as high as possible." No doubt if such an effort is divorced from the conception of social purpose, it may become little more than a refined form of egoism. Even Goethe has been accused of this, chiefly on account of his apparent lack of interest in the political development of his country, and a certain tendency to treat persons rather as types and influences than as independent beings; but, if this is a just accusation [1] it points to a

---

[1] Goethe defended himself against the charge by affirming (certainly with truth) that he was never guilty of envy ("Auf'm Neidpfad habt Ihr mich nie betroffen"). But this is not wholly convincing. A genuine egoist is too self-satisfied to envy any one. On the whole, however, there seems to be very little foundation for the charge. The egoism of Goethe meant simply, in the main, that he knew his vocation, and confined himself to it. His apparent

limitation in his self-culture. The richer humanity of Shakespeare, or perhaps of Plato, might be a better illustration of culture in its most complete sense. Such completeness is, of course, impossible for most of us. The kingdom of the universe is reserved for the select few; but we may all have a place in the sun. There is a tendency, however, to use culture in a sense that makes it a special privilege. It is sometimes spoken of as a " fine flower,"[1] and regarded as the special prerogative of one who can be properly described as a "scholar and gentleman." As against this, T. H. Green, referring to the wish of Moses that " all the Lord's people should be prophets," expressed the hope that the time would come when every Englishman would recognize himself and be recognized by others as being in the truest sense a gentleman.[2] But perhaps this term has been too much soiled by ignoble use, and is too suggestive of a special leisured class. The German use of *Kultur* avoids this error, but seems to have the opposite defect. It is applied to the general basis of a particular type of civilization, and does not specially emphasize the cultivation of the individual.[3] If our use of Culture is too much assimilated to that of horticulture, the German use may be charged with a connotation suggested by agriculture. The cultivation of a human personality is not properly to be compared either to that of a flower or of a field. A better comparison might be to the growth of a fruit, attached to the body of a tree, but developing a certain independent

---

deficiency in patriotism is largely accounted for by the fact that he was one of the chief prophets of international unity. It is probably true that he did not adequately realize the value of such a nationalism as that of Mazzini.

[1] One of the best uses of this comparison is to be found in Tennyson's description of Lushington—

" bearing all that weight
Of learning lightly, like a flower."

[2] *Collected Works*, vol. iii, pp. 475–6.

[3] The German *Bildung* corresponds more nearly to what we understand by Culture.

life of its own. Matthew Arnold (following Swift) characterized the essence of culture as consisting in a certain kind of " sweetness and light." The phrase has become a little vulgarized, but it serves at least to bring out both the social and the more individual aspect of it. But it may help us to understand its nature more clearly if we consider its particular content and relations.

2. *Culture and Pedantry.*—The significance of culture may be more definitely brought out by contrasting it with pedantry. The pedant is one who has acquired a certain knowledge of particular things that have value, but who has no proper appreciation of their value, and cannot distinguish between what is important and what is unimportant. It is to be feared that even Browning's " Grammarian " was something of a pedant ; though he may have been saved from its worst effects by the fact that his concentration on small details was with a view to the important end of interpreting significant records. But it is dangerous to determine "not to live but know ". Specialization is apt to lead to pedantry.[1] It is not confined to scholars. One whose talk is of oxen may be essentially pedantic. The object with which pedantry is concerned is not badly characterized as " shop." One's shop may be oxen, or it may be general information or some special department of study. It is shop if it is not seen in its right proportion and relations—in other words, if it has been duly assimilated. The cultivated man is one who has certain kinds of valuable knowledge, which he rightly values and puts in their proper place. A musician may be a pedant if he can think of nothing but his special art. Milton at least knew better.

> He who of these delights can judge, yet spare
> To interpose them oft, is not unwise.

[1] Cambridge is sometimes compared unfavourably with Oxford in this respect—how far with justification I am not prepared to decide (I think, with some). But at least we have compensations. Wisdom is justified of all her children ; and every form of culture is liable to degenerate into pedantry.

But even the refinement of culture may be essentially pedantic, when it loses its spontaneity and becomes a pose. The æsthete may be as truly a pedant as the philologist. Even religion becomes pedantic when it is petrified into a rigid creed. The truly cultivated man is the amateur—the lover—rather than the "expert."[1] "The great things of history have been done by the great lovers, by the saints and men of science and artists."[2] The love of a person may be a liberal education; and indeed nothing can give a liberal education unless it is loved almost as if it were a person—as Wordsworth, for instance, loved Nature. But perhaps it would be pedantic to pursue this topic further.[3]

3. *The Place of Science.*—Science is sometimes apt to be conceived as rather antagonistic to culture; and it must be confessed that the study of it is often pursued in ways that can hardly be described as cultural. So is the study of literature; but it is perhaps somewhat easier to divert scientific study from its finer purposes. This is the case chiefly when its subject-matter is treated merely as an accumulation of facts or as a basis for technical applications. But the failure to recognize its cultural significance is largely due to the narrow way in which the term is generally used. Scientific study is the attempt to gain accurate and systematic knowledge in some particular department. The mathematical sciences are the

---

[1] Of course an amateur is generally understood to mean one who loves something only a little—not enough to pursue it thoroughly. On the somewhat similar ambiguity in the term "expert," see the statement in the Appendix, p. 266.

[2] Clutton Brock, *The Ultimate Belief*, p. 99.

[3] Montaigne's *Essay on Pedantry* (I. xxiv) is worth referring to; but he does not very clearly distinguish between the right and the wrong use of learning; and he fails to notice that other things, besides learning, may be pursued with equal folly. It may be true, for instance, that the culture of the Germans has been somewhat spoilt by pedantry, but it is quite possible to pursue wealth or fashion or amusement or military service with an equal disregard of their proper use and ultimate value.

most typical and complete in this respect. But it is mainly to the natural or physical sciences that the term is commonly applied. The Germans use *Wissenschaft* in a much more extended sense.[1] Human nature, human societies, human institutions, human history, human languages, form subjects for scientific study, quite as truly as what concerns the forces of inanimate nature or the lives of lower organisms. Even if it were true (which I think it is not altogether) that the proper study of mankind is man, it would still be desirable that this study should be pursued scientifically. It is true that the more humane sciences cannot, in general, be made quite as exact as those that are concerned with the lower forms of being, or with general conceptions—like mathematics or metaphysics. But there are degrees of exactness even in the natural sciences, and, as Aristotle urged, it is an important element in culture not to expect more exactness than the nature of a particular subject permits. Suspense of judgment, tentative hypotheses, are the constant accompaniments of genuinely scientific investigation. To learn to distinguish clearly between what we know and what we only guess is one of the most valuable lessons in life; and science, when it is properly studied in any of its leading departments (including history), serves better than anything else to bring home this lesson. But, in order to secure the full cultural results that scientific study can yield, it is important that the relations between the different sciences should be understood. It is probably true that, in early education, it is best not to begin with the specialized study of particular sciences, but rather with a general study of the objects around us; and it is probably no less true that, after the study of some special

---

[1] Professor Burnet, in his very interesting book on *Higher Education and the War*, calls attention (especially on pp. 78–97) to the confusion that is apt to result from this difference of usage. He notices also a similar difference in the use of the term "Philology," which in this country is understood to mean linguistic studies, whereas in Germany and most other European countries it means literary studies.

sciences, it is very desirable to reconsider their general relations, and to try to disentangle their fundamental conceptions. This leads naturally to the study of logic and metaphysics. It is hardly to be supposed that such a method of study can be satisfactorily completed in any courses that are supplied in schools and colleges.[1] Scientific study (even apart from original research) has to be regarded as a life-work; and the attainment of clear knowledge and insight with regard both to human nature and to the structure of the world in which we live may be rightly characterized as one of the supreme ends of human existence. It is the purely intellectual end; and, though some recent writers have quite properly insisted that the intellectual end is not the only end, yet it is surely one of its ends. As rational beings, we cannot but be continually seeking for "more light." The recent tendency (largely due to the pragmatists) to scoff at "intellectualism," and the frequent use of "rationalism" and "free-thought" as terms of reproach, must, on the whole, be stigmatized as deplorable. There are other things that have value as well as knowledge; but, when we are concerned with knowledge, it is essential that we should "play the game," following it with whole-hearted devotion, and going, as Plato would say, wherever the argument leads. The will to seek is better than the will to believe.

4. *The Place of Art.*—Art is at once more individual than science, and more creative. While science is in the main analytic, art is in the main synthetic. It is an individual's perception of something that has value,

[1] Plato thought that (quite apart from the more purely philosophical part of it) it should be continued up to the age of thirty; and, though modern methods of study may provide more compendious synopses of the important aspects of particular subjects, this must surely be counterbalanced by the greater extent of the material. But, of course, every one now recognizes that there are many important things of which he must be content to be almost or even quite ignorant.

combined with his creative interpretation of it—an interpretation which gives it an appeal to others, and makes of it "a joy for ever." In music, as Browning put it, two sounds are converted into "not a third sound, but a star." In some of the simpler forms of art, and also in some of the greatest and most perfect, the artist's interpretation is so clear and inevitable that it comes home to almost every one at once. In other cases, a special education is needed for the proper appreciation of the result. But in all cases it is the creative interpretation of one mind that makes its appeal to others.

As the aim of science is truth, so that of art would appear to be beauty.[1] The objects with which it deals may, indeed, in themselves be ugly—in what is called realistic art they very often are so—but they are rendered beautiful through an artistic construction. It may even be urged that it is only in this way that any of the higher types of beauty are ever apprehended. The beauty of some colours and sounds, and some simple visual forms, is, no doubt, so directly apparent that it can hardly be missed. Hence the simpler types of music and painting make a ready appeal even to the uncultivated mind. Other kinds of beauty are more difficult, and require both the experience of life and some cultivation of artistic taste. The beauty that we have learned to see in nature was not apparent to more primitive minds—in some cases it is not even apparent to highly cultivated minds that have not been taught to regard it in a particular light. It has to be looked at with an artist's eye, either from a natural gift or through the influence of artistic expression. Hence, if it is admitted that the pursuit of beauty is one of the main functions of human life, this form of culture must be regarded as, in some degree, essential. There is probably a sense in which it is true to say that beauty —what the Greeks called τὸ καλόν—is the highest end

[1] Tagore and some others appear to deny this; but I think it is only when beauty is understood in a somewhat limited sense that it can be denied. Mr. R. H. Caritt's book on *Theories of the Beautiful* may be referred to on this subject.

of all. We can hardly maintain straight off, with Keats, that truth is beauty; but at least it may be urged that truth gives us no complete satisfaction until we can see that it has beauty. It is not folly to be wise even when ignorance is bliss (if it ever is); but certainly wisdom could not be taken as an ultimate good if it only enabled us to say that all is vanity and vexation of spirit. We pursue truth in the hope that we shall find the world to be an orderly and intelligible system; and we accept beauty as a foretaste of that wished-for discovery.

5. *The Place of Literature.*—Poetic literature is, of course, to be classed as art—probably as its highest form; and even prose literature, when it is properly to be called literature at all, has a certain artistic quality. Coleridge held that the opposite of poetry is not prose, but science. Goethe's *Dichtung und Wahrheit* expresses essentially the same antithesis. But most literature combines some of the characteristics of art and science. It shows us what is beautiful; but it does not simply express it, as pure art does, but, to some extent, explains and analyses it. This is true even of a good deal of literature that is in poetic form, such as the greater part of the work of Pope, a good deal of French poetry, and, in a somewhat different way, the more reflective and argumentative writings of Browning. Such poetry can hardly be regarded as pure art. Literature also deals more directly with what is good—as distinguished from what is true or beautiful—than is generally possible either for pure science or for pure art. Hence it is, on the whole, the most completely human of all the instruments of culture, and is aptly characterized as "humanity" or *literæ humaniores*. It explains the value that art expresses, and gives expression to the truth that science seeks.

It is chiefly by literature, in this wide sense of the word, that like-mindedness is promoted among those who have a common speech, and even to some extent among those who have not this advantage. Sometimes, no doubt, the like-mindedness is apt to be of a rather trivial kind.

The morning paper that circulates throughout a large part of the country, and that has its information distilled in the evening or weekly papers and in more remote journals, may give to large bodies of people very superficial and perverse views of the things that are important; and the popular books of the hour may not be on a much higher level. Hence some writers, such as Ruskin, have been inclined even to deplore the multiplication of cheap literature. But at least even such literature is generally a little better than the gossip of a village, and does to some extent enable people to realize that they are citizens in a large community. Such a realization leads almost inevitably to the desire for a fuller understanding of what is contained in the life of that community, and for a critical estimate of its value; and thus prepares men's minds for the study of science and art, which could hardly, by themselves, fulfil this preparatory office. Tolstoy's dissatisfaction with the higher forms of art was probably due in part to the comparative lack of this preparatory kind of literature in Russia, and to the absence of a sufficiently diffused education to enable what there is of it to be properly appreciated. He wanted all art to be milk for babes; whereas only some art can properly have that character. Even in our own country, the deficiencies of popular education have gone far to prevent literature from serving, in any adequate degree, the function for which it is fitted.[1]

6. *The Place of Philosophy.*—Philosophic literature is the kind of literature that most fully fulfils the function that has just been referred to. It puts the crown on science, and enthrones her with poetry and religion.

---

[1] Victor Hugo, in his *Notre Dame* (Book V, chap. ii), has a striking passage on the way in which cathedrals and other forms of architectural art served some of the purposes that are now served by literature. But they served it in a more restricted, though possibly in a more impressive, way. The general social significance of literature is well emphasized by D. G. Brinton, *The Basis of Social Relations*, pp. 164-7.

Parts of what is usually included in philosophy are, of course, purely scientific. Logic and psychology, in particular, are so; and so are many of the discussions in metaphysics and ethics. But the more speculative aspects of philosophy aim at a comprehensive survey of the universe, which brings them into close relation to the larger utterances of poetry and the deeper kinds of religion. Poetry, as Aristotle said, is more philosophical than history: it expresses the significance of that of which history is the record, and thus prepares it for philosophical interpretation. In the same way, it is more philosophical than the special sciences of nature, or at least than those that are rightly described as natural history. The ceremonies, the emotions, and the aspirations of religion aim, in like manner, at the cultivation of that kind of insight into the deeper secrets of human life and of the life of the cosmos, to which philosophy endeavours to give a scientific form.

7. *The Place of Individual Experience.*—A large part of the value of all the instruments of culture to which reference has now been made lies in the way in which they enable individuals to make use of their own immediate experience. We all have sources of culture and self-development continually around us and within us, in the products of nature, in the lives of our fellow-beings, and in the workings of our own minds and souls; but most of all this would remain dark to us without the interpretations that are given to it by science, art, criticism, and philosophy. These also, however, are dark and lifeless until they are assimilated by the individual intelligence, and brought to bear upon his own more direct experiences. Life without culture is barbarism; culture without life is pedantry. Much of what is called education is rendered futile by the failure to bring about this necessary contact; and this applies not only to the education that is given in schools and colleges, but to that which we might be gaining for ourselves throughout the whole of life.

8. The Social Significance of Culture.—Culture is primarily an individual possession, and may be only the property of the few. Yet it is evident that the good at which it aims is not in its essential nature exclusive. It is not like the possession of rare jewels, for which people may compete, and which only the special favourites of fortune may win. Rather it is that which is most emphatically human, and most emphatically that in which all may share. It is not naturally a source of strife, even in the sense in which religion may be said to be so. It does not naturally lead men to condemn one another, even in the sense in which morality may be said to do so. Nor do men or nations fight for books or pianos, for museums and laboratories, as they fight for food and clothing, for coal and iron; though there are perhaps quite as many for whom the former kinds of goods are not sufficiently accessible. There are, indeed, opposing schools in some of the sciences, in most of the arts, and most conspicuously in philosophy; but their conflicts are, in general, bloodless and unembittered; except when differences of opinion or feeling or mode of utterance in these departments of culture are connected, as they often are, with differences in morals or religion. The essentially communal character of culture is generally apparent in its initial stages. The simple artist and the primitive bard, the early songs and dances, are essentially social phenomena. The first beginnings of the study of natural objects and of the chronicling of the doings of men and peoples are also, in general, made by groups, rather than by individuals, and are valued as studies that give dignity to the group. Later, however, culture tends, in some degree, to become more purely individual, or at least to be more definitely confined to a select few. The more complex forms of science can only be apprehended and appreciated through a long course of study; and the same is true of the more complex forms of art, literature, and philosophy—especially when these are imported from distant ages or foreign countries. Hegel is said to have declared that only one man understood his philosophy—

and he did not understand it. But there is a certain return from the complex to the simple. After the more elaborate harmonies of Shakespeare and Milton we may enjoy the simpler poetry of Burns and Wordsworth. The results of science also tend to be made simpler and more accessible when their fundamental conceptions are more thoroughly grasped. Literature and philosophy pass from the learned languages and a somewhat affected obscurity to clearer interpretations in the language of the people. Tolstoy, no doubt, in his ultrademocratic revolt, went too far in his denunciations of Homer and Shakespeare, and in his contention that all genuine art must be popular.[1] This is somewhat on a par with the view that the Kingdom of Heaven is only to be entered by children. The finest results of human effort may be, in some degree, made accessible to children; but they have first to be won by the labour of years. Even in the more material goods of life, almost every one may now possess many things for which, in an earlier age, kings might have longed in vain; and this is, to some extent, true of spiritual goods as well. Yet it is well to insist that the hope of the future lies in rescuing culture from its aristocratic exclusiveness. The Pyramids, the Cathedrals, the Epics, the *Principia*, and the other lordly edifices of science and art, were on the whole the glories of an earlier age. It is doubtful whether, in general, they will or ought to be the models for the culture of the future. Instead of or at least along with a few cathedrals, we may hope to see a large number of beautiful and healthy cottages. Instead of or along with the epics of godlike heroes, or the mirth and sorrows of "ladies dead and lovely knights," we may look rather for some treasures of the humble in the midst of a surrounding squalor that may be gradually removed. With the mechanical aids that we now possess for the diffusion of all the best achievements of the human race, there is no

[1] See his book *What is Art?* As a counterblast to this—perhaps also a little one-sided—reference may be made to Sir Rabindranath Tagore's lecture on the same subject in his book on *Personality*.

longer any real reason why the labouring man or the busy mother of a family, with little leisure for science and art, should not be enabled to become, in the truest sense, cultured and refined.

9. *Culture as the End of Human Life.*—We now see in what sense education may be described as the end of life, rather than as the preparation for it. If we are right in thinking that the ultimate good for man lies in the perfection of the higher elements of his nature, and in the control of the lower by means of them, it is evident that it is in the various forms of culture that we find the gradual realization of this. The truly cultivated man has achieved the best of which human nature is capable. For, as we have urged, the truly cultivated man is not one who possesses particular kinds of knowledge or particular examples of beautiful things. He is rather one who has developed a certain attitude towards such objects. He is essentially the amateur, the lover, the man who appreciates what is finest in nature and in human life, and by appreciating owns it. Even if he has nothing, he may yet possess all things. Even if he seems to have failed, he may have won a glorious victory. For, as Browning says,

> In love success is sure
> Attainment—no delusion, whatsoe'er
> The prize be: apprehended as a prize,
> A prize it is.

CONCLUSION

GENERAL RESULTS

1. *Summary.*—We have now completed our survey of the social life of humanity. What we have sought to bring out is that the general structure of society, as distinguished from the details of its arrangement at particular times and places, rests throughout on the essential nature of man. It has its primary basis in his vegetative or economic nature; this is reinforced by his animal impulses; and society receives its final form from the controlling power of reason, which is the essence of his special constitution as man. Thus regarded, society cannot be treated as a statical or invariable mode of unity, but rather as one that is necessarily undergoing development. It is only by slow degrees that our rational nature gains dominance over our vegetative needs and our animal impulses; and reason is itself a power that is constantly pursuing ends that are not immediately realizable. Hence our goal is to be sought, not in any state that can be directly pictured, but rather in an ideal that is indeed definite and fixed in the general principles that underlie it, but subject to indefinite modification in its particular content. In this, as in other aspects of human life, the characterization of Wordsworth still holds good:

> Our destiny, our being's heart and home,
> Is with infinitude, and only there;
> With hope it is, hope that can never die,
> Effort, and expectation, and desire,
> And something evermore about to be,

Hence we cannot expect to have any definite guidance on the particular steps that we have to take in our onward course, but only general suggestions with regard to the direction in which it is desirable to move.

2. *Practical Value of Social Philosophy.*—In view of what has just been stated, it must be confessed that social philosophy, like philosophy in general, has no directly practical results. It " bakes no bread "; it cannot tell us, in any detailed way, what course it is best to pursue. But to admit this is not to say that it has no practical value. It does help us to see what are the guiding principles by which our course has to be directed. It is well to emphasize this, because some philosophical writers appear to be disposed to deny it. The fact that ordinary scientific study is concerned simply with the effort to ascertain what is, has led some to assume that the study of human life is similar. Such a view may be said to be the converse of that which held that human life is not capable of being an object of scientific study at all, because it is variable. It *is* variable; but it is variable mainly on account of the presence of an ideal to which it constantly looks and tends. We may say that, in studying this ideal, we are studying what is; but at least it is not what is, in the sense of present existence. It is rather τὸ τί ἦν εἶναι, what it has in it to become.

The difficulty in applying definite principles to the details of social life is due to its complexity. Some of the earlier writers on the subject tended to ignore this. They thought that it is enough to treat human life as the life of reason, and to lay down somewhat abstract principles for its guidance. It is in this sense that there is some justice in the criticisms (usually too violent) that are passed on rationalism or intellectualism. The Encyclopædists, Rousseau, Paine, Godwin, and the Utilitarians may be charged with this defect; perhaps even, in a different way, Kant and Hegel. Burke's protest, though somewhat prejudiced, has some value in this connection. " We are afraid," he says, " to put men to live and trade each on his own private stock of reason; individuals would do better to avail themselves of the general bank and capital of nations and of ages." We have always to remember that man is midway between an animal and a god, and is not wholly subject to the conditions of either. On this account all the aspects of his life have to be studied with imaginative insight, as well as with scientific precision. The experience of life has to be called in, as well as the deductions of speculative thought. The poets and the prophets have to be called to our aid, as well as the more abstract thinkers.

With these cautions, however, we may venture to apply our general considerations to some of the practical problems that lie immediately before us. Especially, we may make some attempt to indicate what seem to be the main lines along which progress may fairly be anticipated.

3. *Main Lines of Progress.*—Progress, to be secure, must not be over-hasty. We must, as Bacon insisted,[1] stand on the old ways, and look forward to the new. A living thing grows almost imperceptibly. It is only occasionally that it can be pruned or grafted without injury to its life. On the other hand, it is vain to try to revivify what is already dead; or, according to another metaphor, to put new wine into flasks that are outworn. Between these two opposite dangers, we have to do our best to steer our way. What we have chiefly to aim at throughout is the control of what is lower in our nature and surroundings by what is higher. There would seem to be three main aspects of the kind of control that it is important to secure: (1) The control of natural forces by human agency; (2) the control of individuals by the communal spirit; (3) self-control. On each of these a summary statement may be useful.

(1) *Conquest of Nature.*—It is hardly necessary to emphasize the importance of gaining control over the forces of nature. The whole of our Western civilization has been absorbed in this, more than in almost anything

[1] *Essays,* xxiv.

else, during the last century; and the East has at least begun to follow our example. But the work has been conducted in a somewhat chaotic fashion, from lack of clearness of vision. We have tended to become enslaved by our own instruments. In the famous words of Emerson,

> 'Tis the day of the chattel,
> Web to weave and corn to grind;
> Things are in the saddle,
> And ride mankind.

Much of our energy in recent times has been devoted to the perfecting of instruments of destruction; and a good deal of the rest has gone to the production of futile and often pernicious luxuries.[1] What is wanted is a better understanding of human needs, and a better direction of human enterprise to the discovery of the best means of satisfying those needs. Many people, even in those countries that reckon themselves most highly civilized, have difficulty in getting a sufficient supply of wholesome food and drink, clothing that is adequately protective, and houseroom that makes possible a decent mode of life. We are not pure spirits. The external conditions of existence claim our attention. Hegel's inversion of a well-known saying is not without its point: "Seek first food and clothing, and the kingdom of heaven will be added unto you." In the warmer parts of the earth, which were apparently the first habitations of the human race, such needs are perhaps less insistent; and many of the counsels of perfection that were uttered by the prophets in such regions—such as "take no thought for the morrow"[2] —are not quite applicable in regions of a different type. In some respects we have taken our ideals of life too slavishly from the East, with the result that there is often

---

[1] On this subject reference may be made to the essay on "Luxury and Refinement" in Bosanquet's *Civilisation of Christendom*.

[2] In a more general sense, of course, such sayings have still a great deal of value for us. It is only the letter that kills.

a sad gulf between our ideals and our practice. Even Milton complained that the "cold climate" of Great Britain hampered him in his imaginative work; and there are certainly many who suffer more from the cold than he did. The fact that many people are inclined to attach too much importance to the comforts and luxuries of life must not blind us to the necessity of satisfactory material conditions for the development of our higher powers. What is chiefly essential is that these conditions should be recognized as a common good, rather than as a merely individual one. Certainly the physical conditions of the majority of people in our country leave much to be desired, and yet they are undoubtedly better than in a good many others. Our cities are overcrowded and ugly. Ruskin, though perhaps rather too petulant and impatient, was surely not wrong in urging that the greater part of some of them should be ruthlessly swept away. Country life, on the other hand, is isolated and ill-organized, and seriously hampered by bad conditions of land tenure. Town and country will have to be more fully assimilated,[1] large holdings probably to some extent broken up, and better houses provided. The industrial world will also have to be better organized, so that the important needs of life may be more readily supplied, without wasteful competition. But this leads us to notice the second mode of control.

(2) *Social Control.*—The importance of social organization also hardly calls for much further emphasis at this point. We have seen its significance in connection with education, industry, the State, and international relations. The particular directions in which such organizations may be profitably extended cannot be with any definiteness forecast. It may be said, with confidence, however, that in our own country at present education is in an extremely chaotic condition; and nothing could well be more fatal to national efficiency. It must be conceded that it is difficult to combine thoroughness of

[1] This is well brought out in the book by Professor Geddes on *ities in Evolution*.

organization with elasticity in adaptation to individual needs and capabilities. But certainly we might hope, at the higher end of the educational ladder, to see a more adequate provision for research; and, at the lower end, less overcrowding and a more definite effort to develop thought and individuality of character. In industrial life, wasteful competition might be more carefully checked; the prime necessities of life might be made more universally accessible; and scientific methods might be more fully applied. In the life of the State, an attempt might be made to guard against the opposite dangers of a self-satisfied and self-interested plutocracy, on the one hand, and the chaotic working of democratic forces on the other. The one kind of government sees too clearly what is for its own apparent good; the other does not see clearly enough what is for the good of the whole. Neither has, in general, much of an eye for the future. Second Chambers are rather at a discount at present; but a genuine advisory Senate would probably be a real help. It would be difficult to find the best constitution for it; but it would be better to face that difficulty than to face anarchy and national ruin. In national life generally, the encouragement of art is an obvious desideratum. It should not be treated as a luxury, but as one of the essentials of life for every one. It is shocking to think that we have not even secured a national theatre. On the development of international relations, it is perhaps not necessary to add anything to what has been already stated.

(3) *Self-Control.*—The discipline of self brings us back to education. We have to remind ourselves that a genuine education is both the preparation for life and its highest end. We have to rid ourselves of the conception of it as the pouring of instruction into an empty vessel, and to think of it rather as the securing of Aladdin's magic lamp, that is to open for us all the treasures of wisdom and enable us to build the enchanted palace of an ideal society. We have to think of it as the strengthening of character, the subordination of the lower needs, the control of the animal impulses, and the wise direction of the higher desires. It

is vain to seek to crush out the lower elements in our composite nature. *Expellas furca tamen usque recurrent.* But we may turn them into a fresh channel by the expulsive power of a new affection ; and so make them the servants, rather than the masters, of our higher selves. It may be possible, for instance, to find a " moral equivalent for war" in wholesome play, in creative art, in scientific adventure, and in strenuous devotion to human progress. The only real value of war has lain in the fact—on the whole, undeniable—that it is, so far, the only kind of enterprise in which it has been found possible to unite a whole people in a work in which they can almost entirely forget their own peculiar interests, and in which even the humblest individual can learn to devote himself to the common good in such a spirit of heroic self-sacrifice as to be enabled to " dread the grave as little as his bed." So long as it is only in war that such a spirit is evoked, it can hardly be doubted that the nations that cultivate warlike arts will continue to be the most vigorous and dominant.[1] It ought to be possible to cultivate such a spirit in the service of love, as well as in that of strife ; in the work of the reconstruction of civilized life, as well as in that which threatens its ruin. There may certainly, in this sense, be a substitute for war ; and perhaps for the other devastating passions of humanity ; but only by merging them in something higher and more absorbing. Unfortunately, men are more readily united by the fear of a common danger than by the hope of a common happiness. Even herds of animals are generally brought together by danger and scattered by security. " Sympathy " means community in suffering.[2] Community in the pursuit of a positive good is probably more difficult to develop strongly on an extensive scale. It would seem that this is only possible by the cultivation of a spirit that is, in its essence, religious. Hence, in seeking for substitutes, we can hardly go so far as some Germans

[1] Kant, perhaps the sanest of all the great advocates of an enduring peace, was thoroughly aware of this.
[2] The German *Mitleid* makes this more apparent.

have sought to do. E. Dühring, in particular, wrote a book of some interest on a substitute for religion (*Ersatz der Religion*). Even in our own country, Darwin seems to have thought that a substitute might be found in science and the domestic affections. But, if we understand by religion what in a previous chapter it has been described as being, it seems clear that there cannot be any substitute for it. Nothing can take the place of devotion to truth, beauty, and goodness. The only substitute for a defective religion is a better one; and religion, in the fullest sense of the word, is and has always been the only possible substitute for what is illusory in human ambition and disappointing in human endeavour.

Here, however, it must be confessed, we come upon a real difficulty. If religion is to serve such a purpose as this, it must be a religion that can make its appeal to human nature without reserve. It must be purged clean from every stain of idolatry and superstition, and must be in harmony with all that we know about ourselves and the world in which we live. The currency of the " musical banks " (to use Samuel Butler's imagery [1]) must be of a kind that is acceptable in the market-place. This, it is to be feared, is a condition that we cannot hope for at once; and some patience is called for in those who most deeply feel the want of it. As religion is the highest of human goods, it is least easy to tolerate its imperfections; and yet it is probable that there will always be imperfections in any public forms that it may take. There are times, however, when these imperfections become specially prominent. Creeds outworn sometimes become so contemptible that even their priests, like the Roman augurs, can hardly meet without laughing; and then the impatient reformer is tempted to set out as Voltaire did, *écraser l'infâme*. But the opponent of particular religions, as well as the supporter of them, has to learn toleration. Different religions, it is now pretty generally allowed, are suitable for different stages of human development; and to deprive any one of his religion, till a better one

[1] *Erewhon*, chap. xv.

can be provided, may be simply to take the heart out of his life. The attitude of Nietzsche is certainly not an encouraging one—that way madness lies. It is probably a mistake, in general, to suppose that worn-out religions are kept alive by the artifices of priests. It is rather the needs of the people—especially the needs of the imperfectly educated—that tend to prevent them from dying even when the brains are out. It has always to be remembered that the care of the feeble-minded is one of the essential functions of a church. On the other hand, that feebleness is largely due to the defects of early education; and churches might be able to do something to remedy this. It can hardly be denied that, in our own country, the retardation of educational progress has been largely caused by the quarrels of those who might have been expected to be the most eager to secure its fullest development. It has to be admitted that we cannot hope for universal agreement; nor perhaps can we hope that in any large popular organization it can ever be possible to proclaim quite clearly all that is known of truth. Symbolism and parables and dim religious light may always be necessary. All that can be fairly asked for is toleration and sincerity. On the latter, I should suppose, the words of Sidgwick[1] might be taken as final. "The Preacher has said that 'there is a time to speak and a time to keep silence,' and this ancient wisdom is not yet antiquated. But he has not said that there is a time to speak truly and a time to speak falsely; and I think that, in religious matters, the common sense of Christendom will reject this addition to the familiar proverb." When the forms of religion become so corrupt as to represent nothing that can be sincerely believed, we may be pretty sure that some

> Two-handed engine at the door
> Stands ready to smite once and smite no more.

The corruption of what is highest cannot be long endured.

Reflection on all this, however, may lead us to realize

[1] *Practical Ethics*, pp. 176-7.

that the struggle upwards in human life is not an altogether easy one; and it may be well to attempt at this point to sum up what appear to be the chief difficulties in the way of human progress.

4. *Chief Dangers.*—There is certainly no royal road to the establishment of an ideal world, or of an ideal state, or of that order and beauty which Blake described as the building of Jerusalem.[1] After Aladdin had built his palace, it was whisked off by a wicked magician to a far country; and even after he had recovered it again, he was persuaded to hang up the roc's egg in it, which had nearly proved his ruin. Such wicked magicians and such baleful roc's eggs are always with us; or, in more theological languages, we have always to reckon with the Devil. The Devil takes many forms, and we cannot hope to follow him through all his transformations. But the chief dangers that we have to take account of are pretty directly connected with the conditions of progress that have been already indicated. The downward path is the opposite of the upward one, and it is often difficult to know on which of them we are actually moving. The following brief statements may, however, serve as a sufficient summary of the chief tendencies that threaten to drag us down:

(1) *The Dominance of Vegetative Needs.* Of all our needs the economic ones are the most universally and permanently insistent, and there is a constant danger that they may override the others. Many people can do little else than struggle for bare existence; and, though the struggle for wealth is, in general, a struggle for comfort and power—sometimes even for freedom and beauty and the higher goods of life—rather than for existence, yet it is primarily concerned with material goods; and the power that is sought depends largely on the possession or control of these. The influence of this factor in human life is so great that almost every form of government

---

[1] I will not cease from mental fight,
Nor shall the sword sleep in my hand,
Till we have built Jerusalem
In England's green and pleasant land.

tends to be in some degree plutocratic. It is difficult to devise any system by which this can be wholly prevented; yet there is nothing that is more fatally opposed to the recognition of a common good. Though it is not wholly true that all conflicts are economic, it does appear to be true that economic motives are nearly always mixed up with them.

(2) *The Insistence of Animal Impulses.*—The chief animal impulses are those of love and strife, and they are both very deeply rooted in human nature. Love, by itself, tends, of course, to promote unity; but it is generally a limited unity to which it leads. One mode of unity is apt to oppose itself to another, and so become the basis for a more intense strife. Love between persons becomes a basis for jealousy and envy; the unity of peoples provokes the antagonism of others; even the sense of human brotherhood may be perverted into a source of indignation and intolerance. Hatred, as Carlyle said, is a kind of " inverted love ": " They are Adam's children—alas yes, I well remember that, and never shall forget it; hence this rage and sorrow." [1] It is difficult to eliminate strife from human nature without destroying its vital energy. We may seek a moral equivalent for war in more innocent forms of rivalry; but play has a fatal facility for turning into earnest. Men can hardly entertain themselves with military manœuvres without the dawning of the wish " If only it were the real thing ! " Strife can only be checked by the kindling of a fresh enthusiasm, which it is not easy to arouse: and even a new enthusiasm may bring " not peace, but a sword."

(3) *The Mastery of Mechanism.*—Even the attempt to apply thought to the control of the lower nature may lead to disastrous modes of organization. Life is essentially a growth, and it may easily be crushed under the weight of machinery—even of that which is most perfectly devised. Thought itself has sometimes been almost killed by scholastic pedantry, which is apt to become the ally of extinct dogmatism. Industrial machinery, which is apt to be controlled by a hard plutocracy, may be so

[1] *Latterday Pamphlets,* II.

used as to create more evil than benefit. The free development of national life may, in like manner, be destroyed by a soulless bureaucracy, the last support of faded despotisms. Germany and Japan are the most striking instances in recent times of the rapid development of large modes of organization;[1] and in both cases there seems to be some loss of the more spontaneous features of national life. In our own country that particular danger is probably less than it once was. Heine said that in England the machines are almost like living beings, and the living beings are almost like machines; but it would seem that it is rather to Germany now that we have to look for that kind of mechanical perfection.

(4) *Anarchism.*—Yet it would be futile to suppose that we can guard against the dangers of organization by a return to anarchy. Professor Bergson, who has emphasized the unsatisfactoriness of purely mechanical modes of order, has probably given too much encouragement to the blind working of the vital force. The vital force is not a unity, but rather contains within itself a number of conflicting tendencies, that have to be controlled by the power of thought. Nor can we hope for salvation from the exercise of merely individual thought. I think that Professor Small is right in maintaining[2] that " the law of *individualization by virtue of socialization*, rather than the fantasy of individualization by resisting socialization, is the peculiar lesson that our generation needs." The coarser forms of individualism have perhaps been sufficiently discredited. Even in our own country, I suppose it would be an exaggeration now to characterize the general attitude of the people, as Matthew Arnold did[3] (probably with some exaggeration even then), as upholding " the Englishman's right to do what he likes, to march where he likes, meet where he likes, enter where

---

[1] This is forcibly brought out in the recently published work by Benjamin Kidd on *The Science of Power*, pp. 107-9. But see also M. Bergson's essay on the *Meaning of the War*, where some of the defects of such organization are emphasized.

[2] *General Sociology*, p. 478.   [3] *Culture and Anarchy*.

he likes, hoot as he likes, threaten as he likes, smash as he likes"; but there is still sometimes a tendency for the finer individuals in particular societies to withdraw from the struggle and endeavour to find peace in the culture of their own personalities. No doubt, this has been much more common in the East than in the West. The Indian mystics or the hermits of the Middle Ages are somewhat remote from the life with which we are familiar;[1] but even now there are not wanting artists and dreamers who seek for themselves a not altogether dissimilar refuge. It is often an excellent thing to seek as a temporary expedient, when they are able afterwards to return to the common life enriched with the fruits of their quest. Otherwise, they tend to have what Hegel described[2] as "the guilt of innocence." They evade the problem of human life, instead of solving it. Yet it must at least be allowed that there is no form in which the devil appears more radiantly as an angel of light than in such concentration on individual self-development.

(5) *Conservatism.*—Even when a civilization has been built up in which the dangers that have now been referred to are, to a large extent, avoided, it cannot hope long to preserve itself without a constant renewal of its upward efforts. The danger of an established civilization is, in general, that it relies too much upon its past. It can hardly be doubted that this is a tendency to which the older civilizations in Europe are specially prone. We are apt to be too self-satisfied with our institutions and modes of life. In our own country it shows itself perhaps chiefly in a rather thoughtless contentment with the state of individual freedom, subject only to the control of certain conventions that have become almost instinctive and certain modes of conducting public affairs—certain modes of "playing the game"—that have become traditional. In France the form it takes seems to be rather more definitely that of satisfaction with an existing social

[1] It is perhaps true, however, that there are some signs at present of a tendency to revive even those types of life.

[2] See Caird's *Hegel*, pp. 29–31.

order by which the individual is guided in the observance of what is regarded as correct or *comme il faut*. What is valued in such societies is generally more or less good; but it is apt to be the kind of good that is the enemy of the better. They are conservative in appearance, but often they carry within them the canker of decay, because they lack any clear vision of a higher development. I suppose it was partly a similar self-satisfaction, a similar contentment with what was only half-good, a similar absence of fresh ideals, that led to the destruction of the Roman Empire. Societies do not necessarily decline and fall, as individuals do; but to be content with past achievements is, nearly always, to be on the road that leads to death.[1]

Such appear to be the chief dangers in the way of social advancement. There are times when such dangers are brought home to men's minds by a violent shock. The time of the French Revolution and the years that immediately followed were such a period; and it would seem that we have now entered upon another. Goethe's description of the time of the French Revolution might almost be applied to the present—

Alles regt sich, als wollte die Welt, die gestaltete, rückwarts
Lösen in Chaos und Nacht sich auf;[2]

and one almost hesitates to add " und neu sich gestalten." Yet there is certainly some soul of goodness in such evils. They compel us to think, and to seek about for some means of reconstructing a better world. Have we any grounds for believing that such a reconstruction is possible? A few words on this must suffice.[3]

---

[1] China might be thought to be an instance against this. But it seems to be a mistake to suppose that there has been no progress in China. The secret of its persistence may be found in the slow and cautious manner in which its advancement has been won. But it is not a good example of strenuous liberty.

[2] All is in tumult as if the ordered world sought to resolve itself back into Chaos and Night and order itself anew.

[3] On the problems of reconstruction at the present time a great deal has now been written; and on the value of much of it I am not qualified to pronounce an opinion. *The Principles of Social*

5. *Chief Grounds for Hope.*—Having thus tried to deal faithfully with these somewhat doleful prognostications, we may now turn to the brighter side of the outlook. Even at the present time of trouble, as at the time of the French Revolution, there is a great hope in the world that a new and better mode of life may come into being ; and, though hopes may be dupes, fears may also be liars. The French Revolution did, to some extent, purify the world ; and there are always grounds for hoping that fine ideals, supported by strenuous efforts, will not prove wholly fruitless. The thoughts at least that they awaken can hardly die, even if the working of them out in practice may be long delayed. Progress is essentially natural in human life, though it is often impeded and set back. The loss of the civilizations of Greece and Rome, and perhaps of some others still earlier than these, was undoubtedly a terrible calamity ; but the modern world has saved a good deal even from those disasters. Much of their poetry and art still speaks to us, and helps to fashion our spiritual life. We can still find intellectual inspiration from the courageous dialectic of Socrates, the imaginative insight of Plato, and the comprehensive and matured sanity of Aristotle ; and the laws of the Romans continue to yield us a standard of justice and order. We still have the religious aspirations of the Jews, and some older religions have become more intelligible to us. It may seem, no doubt, but a poor comfort to think that future generations may, in like manner, extract something of a

Reconstruction, by Mr. Russell, may certainly be recommended for its vigour and lucidity ; but its psychological basis seems to me very questionable, and its conclusions somewhat anarchical. *Labour and the New Social Order*, the programme of the Labour Party, is a carefully thought-out document, whatever may be our views with regard to the practicability of its proposals. Mr. W. H. Dawson has edited a number of papers on special problems by writers of recognized competence for the treatment of the questions with which they deal (*After War Problems*) ; and Professor Chapman has more recently brought out a somewhat similar volume on *Labour and Capital after the War*, which includes the very valuable First Report of the Whitley Committee.

permanent worth from the ruins of our modern civilization. But we may venture to hope for something better than that. The whole world has become more of a unity than it was in the past ; and we may fairly expect that the cohesion of the whole will suffice to rescue the parts from destruction. That at least appears to me to be the chief ground that we have for hopefulness at present. The forces that make for order are probably stronger than those that make for disruption. Right is not necessarily might, but it has some tendency to gather might around it. The ways of transgressors are not always hard, but they are generally divided. Men are not easily welded together by any other conception than that of a common good,[1] or at least the removal of some common evil. We have already seen how this conception may be applied, not merely in the ordering of a state, but in the building up of an international organization. It is for the practical statesman and the social reformer to work out the details of such reconstruction ; and it would be vain to pretend that it can be an easy task. We are not entitled to believe, as Herbert Spencer tended to do, that the forces of evolution are bound to carry us to an ultimate perfection. We have learned that evolution is somewhat slow and precarious. The fittest to survive, whether individuals or societies, are not always the most worth preserving. It is only by conscious choice and effort that we can hope either to produce or to preserve what is best. But unless we are incurably foolish, we can hardly fail to profit both from the errors, the follies, and the crimes of the past, and also from its great achievements. Fortified by these considerations, we may still venture to believe, in spite of all the dangers that beset us, that it will be

[1] On the way in which the forces that make for good tend to be more powerful than those that make for evil, some instructive statements will be found in Dr. Ward's *Realm of Ends*, pp. 130–7. He urges that, even on a pluralistic view of the world, the reality of such a tendency can be established. The grounds for its support are, of course, still stronger if we are entitled to believe that the world is a Cosmos, or part of a Cosmos. But this is a question that we cannot here discuss.

possible, in the not very remote future, to build up a finer and more stable order of society, against which the " Gates of Hell" shall not prevail. What is specially clear, I think, is that that better order must not be supposed to be the peculiar privilege of any one people. It must be, in the fullest sense, a common good. Different peoples will probably always have different tongues, different manners, different laws, different modes of thought and action; and we may rightly value what is most familiar to us and what we can best appreciate. But it is pretty certain that the time is past when it would be fitting for any people to think of " Deutschland über Alles," or of Britannia ruling the waves, or of fair France as the sole mistress of civilization or of Rome or Athens or Mecca or any other sacred seat, as an exclusive object of devotion.[1] The earth is our country, and all its inhabitants are our fellow-citizens; and it is only the recognition of this that entitles us to look for any lasting security. And perhaps at a time when the military domination of Prussia is supposed (I think rightly) to be the chief disturbing influence in this common world, we may find inspiration from a voice out of the older and better Germany—the voice of one who did more than almost any to break down the spirit of national exclusiveness in Europe—

> Die Zukunft decket
> Schmerzen und Glücke;
> Schrittweis dem Blicke,
> Doch ungeschrecket,
> Dringen wir Vorwärts.[2]

---

[1] It may be well to note that this is in no way opposed to such a nationalism as that of Wordsworth or Mazzini. The claim that such writers make for their own nationality is one that they make equally for every other.

[2] In Carlyle's translation :—

> The future hides in it
> Gladness and sorrow;
> We press still thorow,
> Naught that abides in it
> Daunting us, onward,

Certainly, it is only by the constant struggle for what is better that we can hope to preserve what is good. Granting that essential condition, "we could have confidence in the future," as Dr. Bosanquet has well said,[1] "not because we could predict the detail of what must come, but because whatever comes, under the influence of such inspiration, and to a people so prepared to suffer and be strong, could not be other than good." But such confidence depends on the general diffusion of a thoroughly sound civic and moral education. It is on that fundamental condition that all our hopes must rest. The presuppositions of human progress lie mainly within ourselves, rather than in any external circumstances; but they imply the co-operation of many in a common aim.

[1] *Social and International Ideals*, p. 188. Goethe's general attitude, to which reference has been made on the previous page, is well brought out by Mr. J. M. Robertson in his book on *The Germans*, pp. 203–6, where justice is done both to its strength and to its limitation.

APPENDIX A

SOME NOTES ON PLATO'S *REPUBLIC*

1. *Introductory.*—Plato's *Republic* has a special value for us, as being the earliest attempt to deal systematically with social philosophy. It is still, in many respects, the most profound and stimulating work on the subject; partly because Socrates and Plato were probably the men of greatest genius (either jointly or severally) who ever devoted themselves to philosophical studies, and partly because the simpler conditions of life in the small City States of Greece made it easier than it is in the more complex conditions of modern times to take a comprehensive survey of the life of the citizen. Hence I have thought it desirable to give frequent references to the dialogue throughout the foregoing sketch; and I assume that any one who seeks to make a thorough study of the topics with which we have been concerned will in some degree familiarize himself with Plato's treatment of them. Plato's statements are, in general, singularly clear and illustrated with extraordinary vividness; yet there are some points at which they are liable to be misunderstood; and, to guard against such misunderstanding, it may be well to add some notes on his general line of argument, as I interpret it.[1]

The chief misunderstanding to which the *Republic* is liable is due to its dialectical character. Readers are apt to assume that the statements put into the mouth of Socrates at various points of the dialogue are to be taken as final expressions of

[1] For further light upon it, reference should be made to the Commentaries by Nettleship and Bosanquet and to Mr. Ernest Barker's book on *The Political Thought of Plato and Aristotle*. On the educational part Mr. K. J. Freeman's *Schools of Hellas* may be consulted. The articles on "The Plot of Plato's *Republic*," by Professor P. S. Burrell, in *Mind* (1916), may also be referred to with advantage.

Plato's own views. It is pretty certain that one of Plato's chief reasons for adopting the dialogue form was to obviate such an interpretation. He has taken care to indicate at various points that he does not regard the method of treatment that is adopted as finally satisfactory. Some may regard this as a serious defect in such a work; but, to my mind at least, it is one of its highest merits. It would be exceedingly foolish for any one, however great his knowledge and ability might be, to suppose that he could say the last word on such a theme; and Socrates, who professed that the only thing he knew was that he knew nothing, was of all men the least likely to fall into such a mistake. Plato may have had rather more confidence in his own insight—perhaps with reason; but, on the whole, he followed his master pretty closely in this respect. Hence his dialogue is not to be accepted as setting forth a dogmatic system, but rather as a discussion of difficulties, with some suggestions of possible solutions. It is only as we approach the end that we can see at all clearly what his attitude is; and even then his latest utterance is in the form of a parable. It would be a gross misconception to think of him as an ancient Ruskin (though Ruskin had caught a good deal of his spirit).

Hence, in particular, the work, though containing a sketch of an ideal state, is not to be thought of as altogether on a par with the various Utopias that have been constructed in more modern times—sometimes at least with Plato's treatment as their model. Plato has made it quite clear that he did not intend his sketch to be taken as a practicable plan for the constitution of a perfect state. It is rather a study of the City States with which he was familiar, bringing out the significance of their leading features, indicating the chief dangers to which they were liable, and suggesting possible remedies. We, with the larger knowledge of different types of community that is now available, ought certainly not to suppose that he has discussed everything that is important, either in the way of interpretation or of possible improvement. But modern conditions are so complicated that it is a great help to us to study a simpler plan.

Such cautions are, of course, necessary not only with regard to the dialogue as a whole, but to the various special points in Plato's treatment, such as his discussion of education, of the place of art, of the position of women, and of the conception of immortality. He had strong and earnest convictions on these subjects, and most of his suggestions are of great value; but, if we were to take what he states at any particular point quite literally, we might be very seriously misled. In a good many places he has been at pains to indicate quite definitely that they are not to be taken literally; but I believe it must be admitted also that there are some places at which he gives evidence of the influence of certain prejudices, which most of his modern readers are not likely to share. Plato was undoubtedly one of the wisest of men, and he was able to avail himself of the wisdom of Socrates, as well as his own. In the special gift of what may be called imaginative thought, he is, I suppose, without an equal among the writers of the world; but, of course, the thought and experience of subsequent generations are not a negligible quantity.

In what follows I intend to call attention only to those passages that seem specially liable to misconstruction.

2. *Argument of Book I.*—The first Book deals with the general conception of Justice (δικαιοσύνη), understood rather in the sense of personal righteousness than in that of the right ordering of a community. This ambiguity of the Greek term causes some degree of confusion throughout. It was pretty fully cleared up by Aristotle.[1] The various views that are set forth in the first Book are skilfully arranged so as to lead up from the attitude of ordinary common sense, through poetic interpretations, to sophistic theories. The arguments brought forward against these views are themselves, in some degree, sophistical. Sometimes they can only be defended on the principle of answering a fool according to his folly.[2] But they suffice to show that the definitions that are dealt with are confused and unsatisfactory, and to prepare the way for the more thorough treatment in the following Books.

The first Book is the only one in which the discussions are conducted according to the familiar Socratic method. Even here it is difficult to believe that any actual discussion, arising in the somewhat casual way that is described, could have fallen into quite so perfect an artistic form; but probably it repre-

[1] *Ethics*, Book V.
[2] I believe Plato was quite aware of the unsatisfactoriness of this method of argument. The somewhat similar discussion in the *Gorgias*, though less elaborate, is on the whole more direct and convincing.

sents pretty accurately the general opinions and methods of Socrates. It is certainly much more doubtful whether so much can be said for what is contained in the following Books. It is unlikely that anything is ascribed to Socrates even in them that would have been actually contrary to his way of thinking and speaking. His character is undoubtedly well sustained. But we are hardly entitled to assume that what he is represented as saying is always an exact expression either of his own views or of those of Plato. I take it rather to be what Socrates *might* have said, and what Plato thinks would have been worth saying; and, as in the first Book, it has been artistically arranged, so as to carry the argument forward from point to point.

3. *Argument of Books II–IV.*—In the second Book the method of discussion adopted in the preceding Book is subjected to adverse criticism, and a more subtle method is adopted. The theory of a Social Contract is suggested, in a form that pretty definitely anticipates that which was afterwards put forward by Hobbes. The introduction of this view changes the main problem from that of individual righteousness to that of social justice, and necessitates the consideration of the general structure of society. Socrates, having now ceased to be critical and become constructive, urges that the existence of a community depends on the fact that an individual is not self-sufficient; and goes on to maintain that its fundamental principles are those of co-operation and division of labour. A simple society in which these are the only important aspects, is then briefly and charmingly sketched. But such a community is condemned as inhuman; and, at any rate, as not throwing much light on the life of an organized state. In order to deal with this, the element of luxury has to be introduced. Luxurious tastes involve intercourse with other communities, and eventually lead to the demand for expansion. This produces war, and gives rise to the existence of a dominant military class.

It is easy to misinterpret Plato at this point. His suggestion may be understood in two opposite ways, both of which are probably erroneous. On the one hand, it may be said that he describes the simple community as the healthy one, and the more complex as diseased; and that he represents war and the distinction of classes as arising from this diseased condition. Thus it would seem that the simple community is the ideal one. On the other hand, it may be urged that it is the complex community that he expounds as the ideal state; and that he assumes throughout that it will be in a constant condition of war, or of preparation for it. Which is the true view of Plato's meaning? The true view, I believe, is that he is not, in reality, trying to construct an absolute ideal at all, but rather to understand the nature of human society. In order to do this, we have to take account of all the complex elements of human nature, even if they do tend to be sources of disease.[1] Another way of putting it might be to say that, in describing an ideal society, he does not assume that it will be composed of ideal human beings. Rather he assumes that all the members of his community will be in need of a somewhat stern discipline, leading eventually to an attitude of self-control; and that the majority of the members will be quite incapable of attaining to such an attitude. Hence even his ideal community will not be a perfectly healthy and ideal one in all its parts. Its health will consist in the fact that its dominant part is healthy, and is able to prevent the latent disease in the other parts from seriously affecting the life of the whole. Thus the important consideration comes to be that of the kind of life that is to be lived by the governing class. What is primarily necessary is that they should be carefully selected and thoroughly educated, with a view to the double function of guarding and governing. It hardly seems to occur to Socrates that these two functions might be regarded as quite distinct, and properly belonging to different types of people; just as, at a later point, he does not appear adequately to recognize the difference between purely theoretical studies and the practical application of theoretical principles. In these respects, it may be urged that the

[1] If he had been anxious to represent his State as an absolutely ideal one, he might have urged that the need for War and Government arose from the luxury and consequent need of expansion in *surrounding* communities, rather than from internal disease. The readiness with which he admits internal disease shows that he is describing a *typical* state rather than an absolutely ideal one. It is of some interest to contrast Plato's simple community with the one that is eulogized in Montaigne's *Essays* (I. xxx), in which there is no government, and hardly any division of labour, but certainly no lack of fighting.

principle of division of labour is not carried out with sufficient thoroughness. Aristotle did something to correct this.

Plato goes on to urge that those who are to be prepared to guard and govern the State must be segregated from those of a baser nature, and must be trained to devote themselves exclusively to the interests of the whole. This involves the abolition of private property and of the life of the family. The significance of this has been sufficiently considered in the body of the present work; and so have the general discussions with regard to the nature of justice in the State and to the divisions of the individual soul. Justice in the individual is not explained with equal clearness. It is somewhat difficult, in Plato's account, to distinguish it from temperance. This is mainly due to the fact that an individual does not contain parts that can be regarded as corresponding to the separate members within the State. But this we need not here discuss.

Some readers are apt to be repelled by Plato's suggestion that, in order to keep people in their proper places, it is necessary to make use of medicinal falsehoods; but, of course, this is what has been done by the churches in all ages, especially when they have been under the control of the State. This was what Gibbon meant by saying that all religions are useful to the magistrate. Probably no one is more eager than the German Emperor to promote piety among his people. The chief value of Plato's statement lies in his distinction between the merely verbal lie and the lie in the soul. Religious fictions are no worse than legal fictions, if what they are intended to emphasize is substantially correct. It may be untrue, for instance, that wicked people will be punished in Hades, but it is true enough that their evil actions have consequences that are incalculably disastrous both to themselves and others. Large questions affecting human life can seldom be adequately explained and answered in language that is strictly accurate; and imaginative fiction is often the best way of bringing home their significance. Certainly Plato's suggestions are not more extravagant than many of those that have been current among ourselves.

With regard to the education that is to be provided for the ruling class,[1] it should be noted that the adverse criticisms on Homer are not to be taken too seriously. It has to be remem-

---

[1] Some general criticisms on Plato's educational scheme will be found in Professor Dewey's *Democracy and Education*, pp. 102-6.

bered that, in Plato's time, Homer was not only the Shakespeare of Greece, but also its Bible and its fairy tales. Plato had no objection to Homer as a poet; but he thought him unsatisfactory as a Bible and as a purveyor of tales for children. The modern world is pretty well provided with the latter; but perhaps some of Plato's remarks are still worth considering by those who write such tales. As for sacred books, it is unfortunately not very easy to alter them; but they can be criticized and explained—or explained away. Plato was playing the part that is played in modern times by expositors and commentators.

The criticisms of dramatic art are more serious. They are due to Plato's anxiety that the rulers of the State should be single-minded in their devotion. Many-sidedness would be fatal to the proper discharge of their functions. Plato was forced, evidently with some reluctance (being himself something of a dramatist), to adopt this attitude. Goethe, curiously enough, followed him in this, with a still more definite expression of reluctance.[1] The point of view is intelligible. If we are to have a class of rulers, they must have a certain rigidity. They must be more like Cromwell or Frederick than like the Charleses. Certainly Plato, in urging that the members of the ruling class will have no time to be sick, carries the hardening process pretty far. There was a strong element of asceticism both in Socrates and Plato;[2] though, in the former at least, it was qualified by a considerable degree of bonhomie, and by an almost rollicking humour, which he did not hesitate to turn against himself.[3]

---

[1] *Wilhelm Meister's Travels*, chap. xiv. The value of dramatic performances in early education is well brought out by Mr. H. Caldwell Cook in his book on *The Play Way*.

[2] The *Phædo* may be specially referred to for further illustration of this. It was probably most characteristic of Socrates, in whom it was associated with an extraordinary power of physical endurance. It would seem that he could stand almost any amount of heat or cold—or wine.

[3] Good illustrations of this are to be found in the *Theaetetus* and the *Symposium*. It is said that, when Aristophanes's caricature of him was exhibited, Socrates stood up among the audience so that they might have an opportunity of comparing the original with the copy. One can hardly imagine Plato doing this. The general character and influence of Socrates has been excellently

4. *Argument of Books IV-VII*.—The abolition of the Family in the ruling class is more definitely insisted on in the fifth Book, and the position of women is considered. Plato is sometimes regarded as a pioneer in the enfranchisement of women. It is doubtful whether he really deserves much credit for this. His attitude is due almost entirely to his determination to get rid of the Family ; and his conception of the place of women is dependent on his views that they are simply inferior men. This comes out more definitely in the *Timæus* (42 B). On this subject he seems, rather strangely and perversely, to ignore a pretty obvious distinction of function. He takes no account of the special fitness of women for the care and education of young children, and for the management of a household. Even Homer might have taught him something about this.[1]

The idea of a philosopher-king should not mislead us. Plato is not really thinking of any one like Frederick the Great. I suppose Burke or President Wilson would serve as a better illustration of what he meant—one who had both made a profound study of the nature of the State and also had considerable experience in its administration. It may be noted that our use of the term " expert " is apt to be somewhat misleading, on account of these two aspects of experience. We tend sometimes to mean by an expert simply one who has had a long practice in some kind of work. In this sense of the word, an " old parliamentary hand " would be an expert in politics. On the other hand, we may mean by an expert one who has devoted a great deal of study to the principles involved in some particular work. In this sense, Aristotle would be the expert, rather than Pericles. A good illustration of this distinction is supplied by Professor Dicey's recent work on *The Statesmanship of Wordsworth*. Wordsworth was certainly not an expert, in the former sense of the word ; but he had thought a great deal about political problems, and observed the political movements of his time ; and Professor Dicey urges, with much force, that, in many important respects, he

described, in a manner that is at once scholarly and popular (though perhaps somewhat overloaded with modern illustrations), by Mr. R. Nicol Cross, *Socrates, the Man and his Mission*.

[1] Chiefly in the *Odyssey*, however, which, according to Samuel Butler, was written by a woman.

showed more real insight than was shown by the practical politicians of the day. Of course, the best expert is usually one who is an expert in both senses. Burke, as I have already said, might be taken as an instance; but Professor Dicey quotes an interesting statement from Burke himself, which goes some way to show that practical experience may sometimes be almost a disqualification. "It may be truly said," Burke affirms,[1] "that men too much conversant in office are rarely minds of remarkable enlargement. Their habits of office are apt to give them a turn to think the substance of business not to be much more important than the forms in which it is conducted. These forms are adapted to ordinary occasions; and therefore persons who are nurtured in office do admirably well as long as things go on in their common order; but when the high roads are broken up, and the waters out, when a new and troubled scene is opened, and the file affords no precedent, then it is that a greater knowledge of mankind, and a far more extensive comprehension of things is requisite than ever office gave, or than office can ever give." It is just this "knowledge of mankind" and "extensive comprehension of things" that Plato is anxious to secure in his ruling class. What he has in mind is a thoroughly educated aristocracy; and he proceeds to deal with the kind of education that they will require. This involves a considerable modification of his previous treatment of education. The cultivation of scientific thought is specially emphasized—more particularly through mathematics and metaphysics. The modern mind will naturally miss any account of the value of the more observational and experimental sciences and of the study of human history; but Plato can hardly be blamed for such omissions. The more comprehensive mind of Aristotle did something to supply the gap. On the other hand, it is well to notice that Plato anticipates here the modern view that the early study of mathematics should be playful.

5. *Argument of Books VIII and IX.*—That Plato's object is to understand the State, rather than merely to set an ideal before us, is evident from the care with which he depicts those forms of constitution that he regards as defective. He represents the defective forms as arising from the deterioration of the best; just as irregular curves might be represented as deviations from the circle. This way of looking at them is

[1] Quoted in *The Statesmanship of Wordsworth*, pp. 63-4.

natural to one who was specially devoted to mathematics, as Plato was. It strikes most modern minds as an inversion of the natural order. The doctrine of evolution leads us to think of states as gradually approximating to an ideal form, rather than as falling away from it. But even modern science teaches that organisms tend to deteriorate, if they are not kept up and advanced by some form either of natural or of artificial selection. There is a downward tendency, as well as an upward one.[1] Plato hoped to counteract the downward tendency by his system of selection and education; and probably he was essentially right in thinking that it is only by such means that it can be counteracted. Assuredly he did not disbelieve in the upward path; but he was convinced that the struggle upwards is a hard one, requiring the exercise of constant thought and vigilance.

His suggestion that the decay of the ideal state would probably be due to some neglect of the principles of eugenics is at least sufficiently modern. Both here and in the discussion of degrees of happiness in Book IX he gives some mathematical formulæ for the calculation of the conditions. I believe that these are not intended to be taken seriously. They are partly to be interpreted as Plato's way of saying that the conditions would be extremely difficult to calculate, and partly, I suspect, as a somewhat ironical reference to certain Pythagorean applications of mathematics.

In the account of the imperfect constitutions, he probably had in mind some historical changes with which he was familiar; and it is pretty obvious that he is specially anxious to criticize the type of democracy that was before his eyes. It has to be remembered that this type was very unlike the modes of representative government that are what we generally understand by democracy in modern times.[2] Also, we have to bear in mind

[1] Huxley's *Evolution and Ethics* may be referred to in connection with this.

[2] Bryce, in his *American Commonwealth*, gives a very different picture of democracy from that given by Plato. He represents it (especially in chap. cxx) as tending to suffer from too much uniformity, instead of the excessive variety described by Plato. What we mean by democracy in the modern sense could hardly have been possible before the invention of printing. Even now, it is greatly hampered in its working by the fact that a large number of people cannot read with any real profit.

that, in an ancient democracy, the whole population did not have a share in the government. Those who would correspond most nearly to our labouring men were to a considerable extent in a condition of slavery. Hence what Plato calls democracy would be, on the whole, what most people now would describe as the rule of the *bourgeoisie*. But a good deal of modern democracy is also of that type.[1]

It would be easy, however, to illustrate many of Plato's points from later history. The feudal system, with the Catholic Church as spiritual guide, bears some resemblance to Plato's ideal constitution, though on a greatly extended scale; and it would be interesting to trace the way in which this gave place to more purely military states, and afterwards to plutocracy and certain forms of democracy. The rise of Napoleon might be taken as illustrating the way in which a democracy tends to pass into a tyranny; and perhaps we might also find some illustrations in Russia at the present time. There is little doubt that Plato shows a great deal of insight in the account that he gives of such tendencies. But we cannot pursue this subject here.

The suggestion that, in estimating the happiness of different types of life, we have to accept the judgment of those who have had experience of all kinds of happiness[2] is one that was afterwards adopted by J. S. Mill. Plato, however, could use it more consistently than Mill, as he did not conceive pleasure as such to be the sole test of value. But the consideration of this also would carry us somewhat beyond our province.

---

[1] It is sometimes said—notably by Professor A. K. Rogers (*Student's History of Philosophy*, p. 71)—that Socrates was more democratic in his sympathies than Plato. There appears to be very little foundation for such a view. I suppose he had a simpler nature and a more open humanity; but, in the *political* sense, there is probably no ground for any such distinction. On the evidence of the *Republic*, the *Statesman*, and the *Laws*, I should be inclined to think that Plato was rather more favourable to democracy than Socrates was. I suppose it is obvious that Aristotle was more democratic than either of them. But the attitude of all of them—so far as it is really possible to compare ancient views with modern ones—was more like that of Carlyle and Ruskin than like that of Mill and Spencer.

[2] But the writer of *Ecclesiastes*, who apparently had tried most, does not seem to have thought much of any.

At the end of the ninth Book, Plato gives a pretty definite indication that he does not regard his ideal State as actually realizable; as, indeed, he had told us before. It is only a conception by which the good citizen may guide himself in trying to reform the particular state in which he happens to live; and it is even hinted that the good citizen will probably not, in general, be very much of a politician. He will only concern himself with politics when he sees a definite chance of introducing valuable reforms. Thus, after all, it is in the individual life, rather than in the life of the State, that the ideal is primarily to be achieved—not, of course, in the isolated individual, but in the socialized individual, the individual who has the Kingdom of Heaven in his heart. This is further emphasized in the following Book.

The suggestion that the pattern of the ideal state is laid up in heaven is apt to seem unsatisfactory to the modern reader. It is, of course, somewhat metaphorical; but it is perhaps essentially truer than the statement of Green,[1] that it " has its being solely in consciousness." What I take Plato to mean is that it is involved in the nature of things, and may be gradually discovered and partially realized.

6. *Argument of Book X.*—The tenth Book is the most difficult to interpret; and I believe it has nearly always been misunderstood. It is apt to seem at first as if it were an Appendix—and an Appendix dealing with two disconnected subjects—rather than an essential part of the treatise; and this would be strange in a work that is otherwise so artistically planned. But I think it will be found, on consideration, that it supplies the natural close to the discussion; and that it is no less artistic than the rest. What chiefly tends to prevent us from seeing this is partly the failure to realize the dialectical character of the whole treatise, partly the obsession with the idea that Plato's main object is that of describing a perfect state, and perhaps most of all, inability to appreciate the part that is played by humour in the method of Plato—or, it might be truer to say, in the method of Socrates. Plato, especially when he is writing in the name of Socrates, mixes a vein of playfulness with his treatment of serious subjects in a way

---

[1] *Principles of Political Obligation*, § 136. Dr. Bosanquet's distinction between true and false ideals may be referred to in this connection—*Social and International Ideals*, chap. v.

that is often not a little perplexing; but those who are familiar with his method in this respect can generally be pretty certain that, when he is specially rich in humour, he has a rather particularly serious purpose; or that, when he has a particularly serious purpose, he may be expected to lead up to it in a humorous way. Now, at the end of the tenth Book, we are introduced to the doctrine of immortality, to which we know, from his other writings, that Plato attached the greatest importance. It may seem strange that he should introduce this doctrine in a work that is concerned mainly with the constitution of states. But is it concerned mainly with the constitution of states? I think Plato would have said that it is concerned mainly with the value of righteousness in human life; and that, though that value is partly—and perhaps most obviously—seen in the life of states, it is only fully apparent in the development of souls.

But, it may be asked, what has dramatic or imitative art to do with this? For us perhaps not much, but certainly for Plato a good deal. The whole of the previous account of the State was set forth in a largely pictorial and dramatic fashion; we were presented with images at every turn—not least in the ninth Book; and Plato is now anxious to call attention to the unsatisfactoriness of such a mode of treatment. In order to do this, he seeks to insist that art has an essential function, but that its function is that of suggestion, rather than that of literal exposition. He had already brought this out in his account of the place of art in education; but he now emphasizes it afresh, and endeavours to drive it home by an attack on the various forms of realistic art. His purpose here has, I think, been generally very much misunderstood. It is, no doubt, a little puzzling (especially if we forget that it is Socrates who is supposed to be speaking) that, instead of recalling the more positive view of the suggestive function of art, he recalls rather the negative criticism on the more purely imitative forms of artistic production. Moreover, he seems now to out-Herod Herod in his attacks upon them, including in his denunciation not only the more realistic dramatists, who were fair game, but also Homer and all other artists, so far as they were merely or mainly imitative. Every reader feels that there is a great deal of extravagance in this. But surely the surprising thing is, not so much that Plato should have written this, but rather that it should ever have been supposed that what is obvious to every reader was not obvious to Plato himself, and that he did not intend it to be obvious to his readers. It was not Plato's habit to tell us plainly " this is a joke," or " this is a myth," or even " this is a fallacy "; but I think we are entitled to believe that he could see a joke or a fallacy as well as the majority of those who read his works —even when they are German commentators. And surely he has not concealed his humorous intent at this particular point. Rather, he has taken very special pains to make it apparent. Not only does he heap absurdity on absurdity; not only does he suggest that the poets would probably be able to make a good defence; but he actually combines his travesty of Homer with a travesty of his own ideal theory. He represents it as meaning that there is only one real Bed, which was made by God. If Plato ever understood it to mean anything even approximating to this (which I venture to doubt), it was at least surely not at the time when he wrote the *Republic*. I take him to mean simply that such an interpretation of the ideal theory would be on a par with the interpretation of Homer that he is considering. He is pouring scorn on every kind of literal misconstruction. The whole passage seems to me to be quite obviously a piece of rather uproarious fun—delightful foolery, however, which is quite in the manner of Socrates, and which has a serious purpose. Socrates lived at a time of extravagant comedy, which had been turned against himself; and he probably wanted to show that he was quite capable of retorting it. Indeed, he tells us that this is his object. Plato (or Socrates) had no real quarrel with Homer, though perhaps he would have preferred a poet rather more like Dante or Goethe. His quarrel is only with a misguided realism in art (of which we have plenty of specimens in our own time), and probably still more with a falsely realistic interpretation of what is really good in art. He seeks to bring out the absurdity of supposing that real poetry, or real art in general, is purely or mainly imitative. Not that he did not believe (as I suppose every one must) that even the best art has in it an element of imitation; but he believed it, I think, only in the same sense in which Shakespeare believed it, and which he expressed (almost in the language of Plato) through the mouth of Hamlet—" the purpose of playing, whose end, both at the first and now, was and is, to hold, as 'twere, the mirror up to nature; to show virtue her own feature, scorn her own image, and the very age and body of the time his form and pressure."

Plutarch tells us [1] of a Spartan who, on being informed that he might hear a performer who could sing like a nightingale, answered: " I have heard the nightingale herself." A similar reply might well be made to all the claims of art, if its aim were merely to imitate things that can be seen or heard ; and the delightful satire of Plato on Homer, or rather on some of Homer's interpreters (who seem to have been as obtuse and pedantic as any of the moderns), is surely intended to make this clear. It is true that the *Ode to the Nightingale* by Keats, or Shelley's *Skylark*, does contain some imitation of the song of a bird ; but what the poet essentially gives us is not the sound of the song, but the thoughts and feelings that the song suggests. I understand Plato's meaning to be that this is the true function of poetry. It gives a local habitation and a name, not indeed to airy nothing, but to things that cannot be seen or heard, and that cannot be stated or proved in a purely logical fashion. He seeks to show, as he has done elsewhere, how poetry may be brought into the service of philosophy, or philosophy into that of poetry, and surely it may be said that modern poets at least have not been slow to learn his lesson. Are not Dante and Goethe, are not Spenser and Wordsworth and Shelley and Tennyson (to name no others), all, in some degree, his disciples ?

Having thus indicated what he believes to be the true function of poetry and of other forms of art, he proceeds to illustrate it by a mythical representation of the eternity of the soul—a representation that anticipates in a slighter, but in some respects a more profound and suggestive form, the treatment of the same subject in Dante's *Divine Comedy*. This mythical mode of dealing with great problems was very freely used by Plato ; and its significance is now pretty fully recognized—perhaps chiefly since the publication of the excellent book on the subject by Professor J. A. Stewart. We cannot here enter into any detailed consideration of this particular instance ; but its general purport seems clear enough. His point is that, in the existing world, or in any world that is ever likely to exist, the just man will not, in general, be able to take any very direct part in political affairs, or to shape the life of society much more nearly to his heart's desire. At least

[1] *Life of Lycurgus.*

he will have to think of himself as a citizen of the Kingdom of Heaven, rather than of the particular state within which he lives; and it is only as a member of that kingdom that we can hope to show, in any way that is finally convincing, that his life is essentially happy and victorious. We have to think of him, not as a member of the State, but as a member of the Cosmos. Plato's contention is that, as such a member, his happiness lies in the fact that he is on the Upward Path, and in harmony with the ultimate meaning of the universe. He sets this forth in a mythical fashion, because he has no precise doctrine on the subject, though he has a firm conviction that the life of the individual soul is an essential part of a process that is eternal. With the statement of this conviction he rounds off, with perfect subtlety and grace, this remarkable combination of art, humour, statesmanship, religion, and philosophy—the most wonderful combination of them that the world has ever seen.

APPENDIX B

A NOTE ON SOCRATES AND PLATO

AT several points in the foregoing statement I have referred to the difficulty that there is in knowing how much of what is set forth in the *Republic* is properly to be ascribed to Socrates and how much to Plato. It is a subject that has been a good deal discussed; and it can hardly be said that any final conclusion has been reached. One is sometimes tempted to refer to the speaker as Platocrates,[1] to indicate that he is probably not quite either the one or the other. The view to which I incline, as I have already indicated, is that we are not entitled to assume that any of the actual statements were ever made by Socrates; but that in the first Book he is represented as speaking very much in the way in which he actually did speak, and that throughout the rest of the dialogue his general character is more or less preserved, but with an increasing infusion of ways of thinking and speaking that belong rather to Plato himself. I am led to this view largely on grounds of style. In the *Symposium*, Alcibiades is represented as describing the style of Socrates in the following terms: " His words are ridiculous when you first hear them; he clothes himself in language that is as the skin of the wanton satyr—for his talk

[1] There would be no great profanation in this. Plato (meaning Broad) was not much more than a nickname. I suppose Glaucon (Blue) was also a sort of nickname. It is pleasant to think of that character in the dialogue as an eager young man with prominent blue eyes. Glaucon and Adeimantus, it should be remembered, were Plato's brothers. It would seem that all the characters in the dialogue were real persons. Plato's actual name was Aristocles. There is a curious appropriateness in some of these Greek names—Socrates (reserve power), Aristocles (the best prophetic voice), Aristoteles (the best ending). One might even add Aristophanes (the best show).

is of pack-asses and smiths and cobblers and curriers, and he is always repeating the same things in the same words, so that an ignorant man who did not know him might feel disposed to laugh at him; but he who pierces the mask and sees what is within will find that they are the only words which have a meaning in them, and also the most divine, abounding in fair examples of virtue, and of the largest discourse, extending to the whole duty of a good and honourable man."[1] I think we may assume that this is a fairly correct account of the Socratic manner of speaking. It corresponds well enough to the records of it that are given by Xenophon, and throughout a large part of Plato's more purely Socratic dialogues, including the first Book of the *Republic*; but surely there is a great deal in the later Books, and in other dialogues, to which such a description is wholly inapplicable. I suppose that the more elevated style in these dialogues is the style of Plato himself; and I suppose this because he seems to make his other leading characters speak in the same style, whenever they become impassioned; just as Shakespeare gives his own style to all his characters in similar circumstances. I have thought it well to add this explanation, but, beyond the general impression that I have thus formed from the style, supported by what I seem to perceive in the way of change of method and opinion, I have no right to pronounce a judgment on this very vexed question. The writings of Professors Burnet and A. E. Taylor[2] may be referred to upon it.

---

[1] This is Jowett's translation. I feel doubtful whether it is a very good one, but have not ventured to alter it.

[2] *Varia Socratica* and *Plato's Biography of Socrates*. The view that Professor Taylor takes seems to me somewhat extreme. Mr. G. C. Field's *Socrates and Plato* contains some criticisms of it. So does the book by Mr. Nicol Cross previously referred to. The statements in Professor Burnet's *Greek Philosophy* give an excellent and well-balanced summary of all that appears to be really known on the subject.

INDEX

Amateurs, 231
Anarchism, 120
Anaxagoras, on human superiority, 31
Angell, on economic influences, 198
Animals, 32-3
Aristocracy, 171-2, 181-4
Aristotle—
  his treatment of politics, 22-3, 41-3
  on social unity, 35
  on forms of government, 140
  on justice, 160-2
  on growth, 170
  on friendship, 175, 181
  on slavery, 178, 206
  on poetry, 237
Arnold, M.—
  on barbarians, 67
  on the State, 147, 152
  on religion, 211
  on culture, 230
  on anarchy, 252
  T., on force, 136
Art, 40, 97-8, 233-5
Associated homes, 88
Austin, on democracy, 172

Bacon—
  on wisdom for a man's self, 183
  on standing in old ways, 243
Bagehot, on human nature, 30
Barbarians, 67
Beauty, 98, 234
Bergson, his philosophy, 151, 252
Blake, on building Jerusalem, 250
Bluntschli, on the State, 145
Bosanquet, B.—
  on the General Will, 52
  on Individualism and Socialism, 120

his view of the State, 149
  on religion, 209
  on grounds of hope, 258
Bosanquet, Mrs., on the Family, 93
Brook, Clutton, on amateurs, 231
Browning—
  on elevating the race, 184
  on love, 240
Bryce, on democracy, 268
Burke—
  on social contract, 48-9
  on private reason, 242-3
  on political experts, 267
Burnet, on education, 102-3
  on science, 232
  on Socrates and Plato, 276
Burns, R., on equality, 178
Butler, Bishop—
  on social unity, 44-5
  on force and authority, 139
  Samuel, on tools, 31
  on churches, 248

Capital, 30, 114-7
Carlyle—
  on friendship, 125
  on conventions, 131
  on force, 136, 150, 202
  on aristocracy, 172, 178, 183
  on captains of industry, 205
  on religion, 209
  on hatred, 251
China, 254
Christianity, 178
Church, 24, 217-9, 248-9
Cities, 71-2, 245
City States, 22, 143, 187, 222, 259
Civilization, 71-2, 193

INDEX

Cobden, his hopes for peace, 197-8
Common Good, 51-2, 55, 57, 99
Communism, 58, 121
Compensation, 160-1
Competition, 119
Comte—
  his sociology, 15, 24
  on leadership, 183
Contract, 46, 143, 160
Convention, 20-1, 45, 78, 131, 225
Co-operation, 53, 114, 258
Culture, 70, 227-40

Dante, his view on Church and State, 219
Darwin—
  his view of evolution, 37
  on substitutes for religion, 248
Democracy, 140, 142, 172-4, 268-9
Dewey, on education, 95
Dicey, on statesmanship, 266-7
Dickinson—
  on East and West, 126
  on League of Nations, 206
  on influence of religion, 209-10
Duelling, 200
Dühring, on substitutes for religion, 248

Economics, 17-18, 66-7, 87-8
Education, 16, 84-6, 94-5, 137-9, 213-18, 228-9, 240, 258, 264-5
Emerson—
  on prophetic limitations, 203
  on materialism, 244
Epicureans, 23
Equity, 166
Ethics, 15, 22-3, 155
Eugenics, 82-3, 268
Evolution, 15-16, 37, 256, 268
Exchange, 161
Experts, 231, 246, 266

Familia, 79
Family, 75-93, 266
Fichte, his view of the State, 148
Force, 133, 135-6, 152, 192, 208

Galton, on eugenics, 92
Germany, 101, 127, 133, 148-9, 199, 207, 252

Gibbon, on religious toleration, 219, 264
Giddings—
  his treatment of sociology, 13-15
  on likeness of kind, 61
Goethe—
  on education, 104-5
  on religion, 226
  his alleged egoism, 228, 258
  on French Revolution, 254
  on hope, 257
  on dramatic art, 265
Government, 17, 69-70, 141
Greek philosophy, 19, 255
Green—
  on Common Good, 55, 57
  on education, 107, 229
  his view of the State, 153

Harrison, on leadership, 183
Hegel—
  his view of the State, 147-9, 153
  on the Kingdom of Heaven, 244
  on guilt of innocence, 253
Heine, on machinery, 252
Heraclitus, on strife, 36
Hill, on government, 141
History, 18
Hobbes—
  his view of contract, 46, 262
  on rights, 167-8
Hobson, on power, 136
Homer—
  on strife, 36
  on aristocracy, 171, 183
  his place in Greek education, 265
Hugo, on substitutes for literature, 252

Individualism, 58, 120, 252-3
Institutions, 62-3
International law, 143, 195-7
  morality, 190-2
  trade, 197-9
  religion, 222-3

James, on moral equivalent of war, 205
Japan, 81, 84, 101-2, 252
Johnson—
  on poverty, 157
  on toleration, 180

INDEX

Jones, on Hegel's view of the State, 153
Justice, 154-6

Kant—
  on liberty, 179
  his view of the State, 192
  his view on peace, 247
Kultur, 71-2, 191, 229

Labour, 109-112
  division of, 112-14
Land, 114-5
Language, 30, 37, 63-6, 98, 197
Law, 97, 135, 177
League of Nations, 206-8
Leisure, 41, 104-7, 123
Likemindedness, 61, 65-6
Lincoln, on democracy, 142, 173
Love, 36, 68-9, 81, 231, 240
Luxury, 244

Machinery, 30-1, 115, 117, 244, 252
Maine, on status and contract, 143
Maitra, H., on religion, 223-5
Marshall, on economic and religious influences, 198
Marx, his economic interpretation of history, 198
Mazzini, his nationalism, 229, 257
Mill, on liberty, 181
Milton, on influence of climate, 245
Montaigne—
  his influence, 203
  on pedantry, 231
  his picture of a simple community, 263
Moral equivalent for war, 203, 205, 247
Morality, 211

Nature, 20, 21, 23, 44, 77, 97, 131
Nietzsche—
  on master and slave, 178
  on war, 203
  his general maxims, 206
Non-resistance, 151

Obligations, 168-9
Organism, 49-50, 59

Patriotism, 127

Pedantry, 230-1
People, 125, 173-4
Philosopher-king, 40-1, 266-7
Philosophy, 13-15, 236-7
Plato—
  his *Republic*, 21, 38-43, 49, 89-90, 154, 185, 187, 259-274
  on art, 97, 104, 271-3
  on division of labour, 113
  on wealth and poverty, 118
  on force, 133
  on the Family, 137, 266
  on forms of government, 140
  his view of justice, 156-9, 168, 171
  on classes, 178, 182
  on the individual life, 227-8
  on scientific study, 233
Pope, on government, 141
Property, 116-17
Prussian view of the State, 136, 148, 192
Psychology, 16
Punishment, 163-5

Race, 127
Religion, 119, 179, 209-226, 248-9
Reward, 163-5
Rights, 167-9
Roman Law, 23, 193, 255
Ross, on social control, 132
Rousseau—
  his view of contract, 26, 47
  his theory of General Will, 51-2, 55-6
Ruskin—
  on war, 203
  on cheap literature, 236
  on cities, 245
Russell—
  on the Family, 93
  his philosophy, 152
  on reconstruction, 254-5

Science, 14, 231-3
Senate, 246
Shakespeare—
  on social order, 47-8, 132
  illustration of co-operative will, 53
  on England, 127
  on dramatic art, 272-3
Sidgwick, on sincerity, 249
Slavery, 79, 269

INDEX

Small—
  his view of sociology, 15
  on individualization, 252
Smith, on division of labour, 113
Socialism, 58, 121–2
Sociology, 13–5
Socrates, 265–6, 269, 275–6
Sophists, 20, 25
Sorel, on violence, 151, 205
Sovereignty, 80, 129–30, 200–2, 206–7
Spencer—
  his conception of evolution, 15, 37, 256
  his view of liberty, 26, 179, 181
  on punishment, 165
  on equity, 177
  on industrialism, 198–9
Spinoza, on Common Good, 51–2, 57, 182, 199
State, 17, 24, 69, 90, 107–8, 117, 129, 157–9, 217–19
Stoics, 23, 42
Strife, 36, 68–9, 119
Strikes, 205
Struggle for existence, 133, 204–5
Sweetness and light, 136, 230
Swift, on marriage, 86–7
Sympathy, 247
Syndicalism, 122

Tagore, on art, 106, 239
Tennyson—
  on a people, 125
  on culture, 229
Toleration, 180, 220–2
Tolstoy, on art, 236, 239
Tools, 30–1, 115
Treitschke, his view of the State, 133, 148–150, 192, 201–2

Universities, 100–3
Utopias, 185

Veblen, on leisure, 106
Violence, 151, 193, 205
Voltaire, his attitude to the Church, 248

War, 200–5, 247, 262–3
Ward, on power of Good, 256
Whitman—
  on animal life, 33
  on America, 127
  on law, 135
  on equivalence, 167
Wordsworth—
  on Rob Roy, 154
  on national unity, 197
  on hope, 241
  his nationalism, 257
  as statesman, 266